Lennart Svensson & Barbro Nilsson (eds.)

Partnership

– As a Strategy for Social Innovation
and Sustainable Change

Santérus
Academic Press
Sweden

www.santerus.se

All rights reserved. No part of this publication may be reproduced, stored in a retrieval system, or transmitted, in any form or by any means, electronic, mechanical, photocopying, recording, or otherwise, without the prior written permission of the publisher, except in the case of brief quotations embodied in critical articles and reviews.

© 2008 the Authors and Santérus Academic Press Sweden
ISBN 978-91-7335-011-2
Layout: Harnäs Text
Cover illustration: Lipaxir (1956) © Olle Bærtling/BUS 2008
Cover profile: Sven Bylander
Santérus Academic Press is an imprint of
Santérus Förlag, Stockholm, Sweden
academicpress@santerus.se
Printed by BOD, Germany

Content

PREFACE	VII
LIST OF ILLUSTRATIONS	IX
1. INTRODUCTION AND BACKGROUND by Lennart Svensson & Barbro Nilsson	1
2. PARTNERSHIPS IN AN ORGANISATIONAL AND SOCIETAL PERSPECTIVE by Lennart Svensson & Barbro Nilsson	9
3. DEFINING OUR TERMS AND CLARIFYING OUR LANGUAGE by Ken Caplan and Leda Stott	23
4. ARE PARTNERSHIPS INNOVATIVE? by Erik Lindhult	37
5. PARTNERSHIP FOR SUSTAINABLE WORK ENVIRONMENT DEVELOPMENT by Ingela Målqvist and Marianne Parmsund	55
6. ADVISORY PARTNERSHIPS IN A GOVERNMENTAL MANDATED NETWORK by Barbro Nilsson	81
7. YOU'RE WELCOME TO PARTICIPATE – BUT ON WHOSE TERMS? – ON EMPOWERMENT AND STRUCTURAL IMPACT by Ann-Christine Larsson	101

8. WITH THE TARGET GROUPS AS PARTNERS 121
   by Maria Bogren

9. BIRDS OF A FEATHER FLOCK TOGETHER – ON REPRESENTATION
   AND EQUAL RELATIONSHIPS IN PARTNERSHIPS 139
   by Sofia Wistus

10. INCLUSION OF IMMIGRANTS – EFFECTS OF DIFFERENT KINDS OF
    PARTNERSHIPS 159
    by Ragnar Andersson

11. WHO IS ALLOWED TO CONTRIBUTE TO SUSTAINABLE
    DEVELOPMENT BY PARTICIPATING IN PARTNERSHIPS? 173
    by Hanna Westberg

12. PARTNERSHIPS FOR SUSTAINABLE CHANGE: THE AUSTRIAN
    PACTS AND THEIR CONTRIBUTION TO SUSTAINABLE CHANGE
    EXEMPLIFIED BY THE 'GREEN PAPER FOR THE ELDERLY' 191
    by Anette Scoppetta

13. PARTNERSHIP, GENDER AND DEMOCRACY 209
    by Gun Hedlund

14. SOME PRACTICAL AND THEORETICAL CONCLUSIONS 233
    by Lennart Svensson & Barbro Nilsson

THE AUTHORS 257

Preface

This book is different. It is based on the participants' experience of using partnership as a way to promote social innovation and change. As a researcher we have analysed these experiences together with the participants. We have used an interactive research approach, that is, we have tried to make research *with* – not *on* – the people involved. A R&D centre (see www.apel-fou.se) has provided research support to different partnerships. This work has been funded from the Swedish EQUAL-programme.

The book is intended to act as source of ideas and inspiration for anyone who is interested in, and works actively with organising innovation and change. It does not, however, provide quick and easy solutions or simple advice. We aim instead to present the experience we have gained, discuss the problems we have encountered and provide a certain amount of guidance on how this experience can be used in other contexts. The authors are mainly researchers in the field and most of them come from Sweden.

The main ambition with the book is to analyse if partnership can be seen as a strategy for sustainable change. Most of the chapters in the book are based on empirical studies, but the theoretical framework provides a context and a critical perspective on the various options and the limitations with the partnership organisation.

The participants in the R&D project have been most helpful in the analysis of the data presented and the model developed. The following people have taken part in a lot of analytical seminars in the project: Ulf Brangenfeldt, Folke Brolin, Arion Chryssafis, Solveig Jansson, Sven-Olof Larsson, Erik Lindhult, Solgun Lundgren, Inger Paris, Kicki Risander, Lena Rogeland, Gisela Spak, Torsten Thunberg and Annika Öhgren.

The research group at APeL have been involved in the empirical work.

This group consist of the following people: Mats Andersson, Mattias Dyrvik, Andreas Eriksson, Karin Isaksson-Iliev, Patrik Jonsson, Barbro Nilsson, Lennart Svensson and Sofia Wistus.

Many thanks to you all!

Linköping and Lindesberg
October 2007

Barbro Nilsson *Lennart Svensson*

List of illustrations

Tables

Distinctions between PPPs and MSPs. Source: BPD Water and Sanitation,   p. 25
Partnership resource inputs,   p. 30
General levels of partnership participation,   p. 31
Changed resources, activities and results,   p. 110
Example of TEPs, their emphases and areas of action, as well as their main partners in 2006,   p. 193
The structure of the 'Strategy for the Elderly' published in the Green Paper,   p. 201–202

Figures

Spectrum of engagement. Source: BPD Water and Sanitation,   p. 26
Social innovation and the partnership model,   p. 51
Organisation chart for the work environment organisation in the brewery sector (Phase 2),   p. 65
Complexity in organisation of the partnership,   p. 105
An illustration of an interactive research process with different roles and interests (Larsson 2006, p. 245),   p. 108
The context within and outside the partnership,   p. 133
Representation of different organisations in partnerships,   p. 147
Process of establishing the White Paper,   p. 199
Scope of opportunities,   p. 206
Three functions in an analytical model used to analyze sustainable change,   p. 242

1. Introduction and background

In this introductory chapter some necessary information will be given about the growing interest in partnership and about the research issues in this book. A short presentation will follow of the Swedish research project on partnership as a way of organising change and innovation. The contents of the different chapters are briefly presented.

1.1 A growing interest in partnership

Change and innovation are put forward as the determining characters of the new information society (Castells 1996). But the traditional forms of organising change and innovation are not seen as efficient any more. A new way of organising a *sustainable* change is demanded. Networks, the Triple Helix, clusters, the innovation system etc. are put forward as strategies for solving complex problems in a holistic and long-term perspective. These strategies can be seen as representing a *system* perspective on change. 'To change a system, a system is needed', is the idea behind these 'new' strategies.

Partnership can be seen as an example of such a strategy on a system level, that is on an organisational, a regional, national or transnational level. The interest in partnership is growing quickly partly because of the directives in different EU programmes, like the EQUAL programme.[1] The OECD LEED Forum on Partnership and Local Governance includes 2 600

---

[1] EQUAL was a large EU programme (in all costing more than 4 billion Euros) working against discrimination and exclusion on the labour market.

partnerships (see chapter 13). Another reason for the growing interest in the partnership organisation is the ambition to develop the more informal cooperation in the network organisation into a more structured collaboration between different stakeholders who have a more action-oriented focus (Andersson et al. 2006).

The idea behind the book is to acquire new data and make a careful analysis of the partnership *organisation* both in theory and practice. We will analyse whether the partnership organisation is effective in implementing changes and innovation with long-term effects rather than short-term results. Can the use of partnership as an organisational principle be a way of overcoming the limitations of the project organisation and its focus on short-term outcomes? Or is the interest in the partnership organisation only an expression of a trend or a fashion in the growing market for organisational development in complex situations?

Partnership will thus be addressed as an *organisational* issue put in a societal context. We will analyse if the partnership organisation represents a new kind of strategy, which may overcome the limitations of earlier strategies (Svensson & von Otter 2001).[2] The traditional 'top-down' strategy is not effective for a lot of reasons. It will not motivate the participants; it is not flexible; it does not include reflection and learning about new – and unforeseen – events in the change process. The alternative – a 'bottom-up' strategy based on activation of the participants – is, on the other hand, not useful in creating long-term effects. It is difficult to organise such a mobilisation process for a long time; the changes will easily be encapsulated in the existing structure and be difficult to disseminate; management will often be hesitant about changes 'from below' because they are considered to be difficult to control and direct.

The partnership organisation can be seen as representing a 'double strategy' for change, which includes both a strong representation 'from the top' (a system approach to change) and a participation 'from below' (an activation strategy). Whether this vision of an all-encompassing strategy for change is possible or realistic is the topic of the book. This question cannot easily be answered, but empirical data and analysis can give us some hints on how to continue the search for a better answer to a strategy for sustainable change.

---

2 Strategy is seen as the pattern or plan that integrates 'goals, policies and action sequences into a cohesive whole' (Quinn 1996, p. 3). A strategy should provide direction for developmental work but is often overridden by short-term objectives (Jacobs 2000, p. 36).

1.2 The research project

The idea of writing a book about partnership was developed in a research and development project. This project *Developmental Partnership* is financed by the EQUAL-programme in Sweden. It is a project, which has been running for five years (between 2002-2007). One outcome of the first part of the project was the book *How to Develop Partnership* (see www.apel-fou.se). The book is based on eight case studies of developmental partnerships in the Swedish EQUAL programme. The focus is on the development *process* in the partnerships – the initiation, the change process and the dissemination phase. The target group for this book is practitioners working with the partnerships organisation.

The continuation of this R&D project (2005-2007) has focused on different kinds of partnership in the Social Fund in Sweden, both of a more action-oriented and a representative character. We have studied the partnerships in the EQUAL programme (25 all together), but also regional partnerships working to promote the training of employees and organisational development. We have used different research methods – surveys, interviews, group discussions, seminars etc.

One final outcome of this R&D project will be this book which is directed both at the research community and at reflective practitioners working in this field. We will present the outcome of our research, but we also want to include results from other researchers in the field. In the last chapter, we present two models for analysing the partnership organisation. Most of the chapters are written by Swedish researchers.

Different disciplines are represented – sociology, pedagogy, political science, gender studies, economics, psychology etc. – and in this way the partnership issue can be addressed in a way that will lead to a richer outcome.

The book has been written as an anthology with contributions from different researchers. The ambition is to unite and direct the different contributions by – as far as possible – using the same concepts and getting the authors to relate to the research issues presented below.

1.3 The research issues

The ambition is to address practical dilemmas and problems in the partnership organisation by using different theoretical perspectives – theories about organisational learning, strategies for change, power and empowerment, gender analysis, governance and participation etc. The analysis made will be given practical relevance by presenting different perspectives and by pointing to different possibilities for action. By focusing on urgent problems in developmental work we think that the analysis will also be more interesting from a theoretical perspective. Four such problems or dilemmas are presented below. We have tried to select authors that all find these questions challenging for their theoretical work and compatible with their research data.

The first dilemma is that between a *system* perspective on the one hand and an *individual* perspective on the other. Will the system approach in the partnership strategy exclude an individual perspective? Will the partnership organisation be so complicated – bureaucratic and professionalised – that the individuals (the target group/beneficiaries) will be excluded from participation and decision-making? Are the procedures and activities in a partnership formalistic and professionalised instead of demand-based, informal and voluntary?

The second dilemma is that between a *holistic* and an all-embracing *approach* on the one hand and a focus on a *specific* objective or *outcome* on the other hand. Will the ambition to include 'everything' in a large partnership lead to a wide focus where nothing is accomplished? The partnership intends to work on many levels and with different objectives at the same time. Will this multi-level ambition lead to a superficial approach with a lack of focus? Will the *talking* component dominate over the *action* ingredient because of a lack of focus and a 'distant' approach to the immediate interests of the participants? Such a critique is directed towards innovation systems (Miettinen 2002), but will it also hold for the partnership organisation?

The third problem or dilemma concerns the role of partnerships in relation to democracy? Will the partnership organisations take over some of the responsibilities that traditionally belonged to the democratic system? Will the partnership vitalize the democratic process or will the recruitment process to the partnerships imply a strengthening of already strong actors and organisations in the decision-making processes? Who has the right to participate in a partnership organisation? Will the recruitment to the partnership organisations exclude certain groups from participation? It is important to analyse the issue of representation by formal organisations in a partnership versus the democratic principle of individuals with equal rights in a democracy. What will happen to the interest groups that are not organised in society – the unemployed, youth, immigrants etc. – if more developmental work is carried out by partnership organisations? Will they participate as equal partners or will they be addressed as 'objects' for social engineers in the new partnerships? Women in the Scandinavian countries are rather well represented in the democratic system. Will they lose some of their influence if the partnership organisations get stronger at the expense of the democratic system?

The fourth dilemma has to do with the critical potential of the partnership organisation. Can a consensus-driven organisation[3] really change a system that it is a part of? If the members in a partnership represent the existing power structure, will they not have a strong interest in the preservation of these unequal relationships? We will see if issues of power, conflicts and differences in interests are put aside in the partnership organisations.

These four dilemmas will be addressed in the different chapters of the book. In the last chapter we will try to summarise the results of the research presented. We do not expect to get any definite answers to the questions presented above. A sustainable change cannot be organised by finding simple solutions to complicated problems. Instead, we think that the research presented can be valuable in getting a deeper understanding of the pros and cons of the partnership organisation. When can it be useful? What kind of problems can be addressed? What are the necessary conditions to be met if the partnership model should be used?

This is the practical outcome of the book. There is, hopefully, also a theoretical value of the book. We will discuss classical research issues that focus on the relationship between a system and an individual perspective, between a holistic and a contextual paradigm, between cooperation in new forms in relation to democracy, between a consensus and a conflict orientation. Perhaps we will not be able to develop new concepts and theories in this book, but we hope to formulate some new research issues and hypotheses which will be brought up in new research projects. We will use a theoretical model, which has been developed in earlier research projects, and use it to analyse the findings presented in this book. We will also try to refine this model for analysing the partnership organisation.

1.4   The perspective and idea behind the book

The first part of the book is an introduction, which includes two chapters. These two chapters are written by the editors in order to give an orientation and a theoretical 'umbrella' for the rest of the chapters. This first chapter gives a background and an introduction to the book. In a theoretical chapter (No. 2) some research on partnership will be presented, and some

---

3   In the EQUAL programme, consensus is required on important issues, e.g. on documents that are delivered to the European Social Fund. One partner can block an initiative by using a veto.

essential concepts will be defined. Chapter 3 presents different definitions of partnership and relevant concepts.

The second part of the book will include nine empirical chapters. Each of these chapters addresses a practical problem or a dilemma (see above) by using an analytic framework that is briefly presented in chapter 2.

The third part contains two chapters. Chapter 13 analyses partnership from a gender and democratic perspective. The last chapter draws some conclusions and makes some suggestions both of a practical and theoretical nature.

1.5 Content of the book

Chapter 2 presents the partnership organisation in an organisational and societal perspective. A comparison is made with the network organisation and project work. The developmental partnership is given special attention. The gender issue is introduced in chapter 2. The ambition is to make the gender issue central and explicit in all the chapters.

In chapter 3, *Ken Caplan* and *Leda Stott* define some terms and clarify the language used to discuss partnership. The overall aim of the chapter is to call for greater clarity and rigour in our use of partnership definitions and terms in order to promote more coherent cross-sectoral understanding. The authors hope that such a contribution will assist in ensuring that partnerships are made more effective at both the individual and organisational levels and thus gain greater potential to promote sustainable change and innovation.

The *second* part of the book will be more encompassing and include empirical research on the partnership organisation.

Erik Lindhult (chapter 4) deals with social innovation in a partnership organisation. An object-oriented versus an interactively-oriented perspective on innovation is clarified and two models are presented to illustrate these different perspectives. Both theoretical and empirical arguments are used to clarify the differences between these perspectives. Lindhult argues that the partnership organisation is more useful in promoting social innovation.

A risk with large partnerships that use an all-embracing approach is that there will be a lack of focus and few concrete actions and practical outcomes. A case study, which is presented in chapter 5, challenges this idea by pointing to a very successful outcome. This partnership approach included employers, trade unions, researchers and state officials. The co-operation had a clear focus on dealing with the work environment of drivers in different breweries. Chapter 5 is written by *Ingela Målqvist* and *Marianne Parmsund* who were responsible for the field work.

In chapter 6, *Barbro Nilsson* focuses on the partnerships in the Objective 3 programme. Based on an empirical study of four partnerships, she analyses the conditions for the partnerships to work as a base for regional change and collaboration. She also discusses the role of advisory partnerships within a government-mandated network structure.

The conflict between the empowerment ambition on the one hand and the focus on structural change on the other hand in the EQUAL programme is analysed in chapter 7. *Ann-Christine Larsson* presents a case-study based on interactive research on a group of women who were on a long-term sick leave. She analyses whether the involvement of the women in the local project activities had any effect on the decision making in the partnership organisation.

Maria Bogren has a similar focus in her chapter (No. 8). She has conducted research on an unusual partnership in an EQUAL programme in which the target group was represented. Different forms for securing the influence for the target group are experimented with in this partnership.

Sofia Wistus discusses (in chapter 9) whether the partnerships are democratic – from an external idea of representation and/or from an internal consideration of equal relationships. Her study is based on extensive surveys and different case studies of the Swedish partnerships in the EQUAL programme.

Ragnar Andersson has studied 21 regional partnerships in the Growth Programme (chapter 10). They all had an ambition to include immigrants in their partnerships. But, in fact, the opposite happened at all levels in the partnership organisations. The immigrants were excluded for different reasons – power relations, lack of resources, organisational logics, different networks, etc. A comparison with the EQUAL programme points to similar mechanisms of exclusion.

Hanna Westberg focuses (in chapter 11) on to what extent the partnership organisations (with examples from the Regional Growth Agreements and the Regional Growth Programmes in Sweden) include women in their work and in the decision-making activities. One case study of the building of a strategic platform for gender work in one large region is presented in which the researchers had a supportive role. The chapter tries to shed light on the different conditions for women and men in the local and regional community, which will have important consequences for recruitment to the partnerships, the formulation of the objectives, the work forms, the outcome etc. The author argues that the participation of both sexes is needed to achieve sustainable growth and an innovative climate.

An example of how the partnership organisation can be supported and promoted at the regional level in Austria is presented in chapter 12. This chapter is written by *Anette Scoppetta* who herself plays an important role in supporting and disseminating the partnership organisation in Europe.

The *fourth* part of the book includes two chapters of a more general character. *Gun Hedlund* presents a critical analysis of the partnership organisation from a gender perspective (chapter 13). In Sweden, women are rather well represented in political life and in the publicly-organised welfare system. What will happen to gender representation if different partnerships take over responsibilities and authorities from political organisations? Issues of power, control and consensus are discussed from a gender perspective. Theories of governance are presented and used in the analysis.

In the last chapter some practical and theoretical conclusions are drawn and proposals for further research are made. Two analytical models are presented. Some central research findings are presented in relation to our findings. This chapter is written by the editors based on a dialogue with all the authors.

References

Andersson, M, Svensson, L, Wistus, S, Åberg, C (2006) (eds.) *On the Art of Developing Partnerships*. Stockholm: Arbetslivsinstitutet

Castells, M (1996) *The informational age: Economy, Society and Culture. The Rise of the Network Society*. Oxford: Blackwell

Jacobs, B (2000) *Strategy and Partnership in Cities and Regions*. London: MacMillan Press

Miettinen, R (2002) *National innovation system: scientific concept or political rhetoric*. Helsinki: Edita

Quinn, B J (1996) Strategies for change. In Minzberg, H & Quinn, B J (eds.) *The Strategy Process: Concepts, Contexts, Cases*. New Jersey: Prentice Hall

Svensson, L & von Otter, C (2001) *Projektarbete. Teori och praktik*. Stockholm: Santérus

2. Partnerships in an organisational and societal perspective

The first chapter was an introduction to the book. This chapter intends to present the partnership organisation in different contexts.

Instead of presenting a closed definition of a partnership organisation we would now like to present a number of other terms and concepts that are used for organising developmental work. Describing partnership as an *organisational* form and relating it to other concepts – such as projects, networks, clusters, innovation systems and the Triple Helix – is not simple and could indeed fill a book of this size. It is not possible to explain or define these terms simply or explicitly, and in everyday speech they are often used carelessly without really thinking about their specific meaning (see Chapter 3). Our point of departure here is that the terms stand for or are believed to represent different *strategies,* which are used to stimulate and implement innovation and sustainable change. A strategy is something more than a method for change. A certain strategy – like the planning strategy – can be seen as a perspective on or a framework for change, which includes different methods.

2.1 What is a partnership?

Significantly, there does not seem to be any clear and unanimous definition of partnership either nationally or internationally (SOU 2003:123). All definitions refer, however, to a more or less formal *co-operation* between actors in the private and public sectors – such as state authorities and agencies, municipalities, county councils, autonomous regional bodies and bodies for municipal co-operation, actors in the field of industrial policy at the local and regional levels, business and industry and commercial and industrial organisations, trade unions and other organisations and a great number of other actors with an interest in growth and development issues, e.g. local development groups and community associations. Actors at the national, regional, municipal and local levels are often united in one and the same partnership.

A partnership represents an organisational form for co-operation. What then *is* partnership in comparison with other forms of co-operation? Is partnership yet another new term for a traditional way of working? Is there a risk that partnership will become a new in-word that will be used for all conceivable forms of co-operation in the same way as the term network? EU-officials believe that the term partnership, in its real sense, designates a different way of working compared to traditional network co-operation.

Partnership is thus a form of work used in social planning and development in which actors with complementary and sometimes overlapping interests and areas of responsibility are involved in a common planning, decision-making and implementation process (see below). The aim is to promote participation in order to mobilise and co-ordinate resources and thus improve the efficiency of the work. What differentiates partnerships from, for example, networks is that they have been given a *nominal status*. On the other hand, partnerships have no formal decision-making powers, nor are they regulated by law.

Working in a partnership entails awareness and commitment on the part of those involved in a more explicit way than co-operating in a network does. While networks are based on voluntary participation, partnerships are often established to perform a task or solve a complicated problem. The partners should 'own' the task together. A partnership should, in contrast to a network, be composed of the actors that will make it possible to perform the task concerned. With the 'wrong' partners in a partnership, the desired changes will not be achieved, which is similar to what the advocates of the Triple Helix say. The difference between partnership and the Triple Helix, however, is that the adopted task governs the selection of partners in a partnership, while the Triple Helix always presupposes co-operation between society's three basic 'pillars' (the private and public sectors and research). As a partner in a partnership it is not enough to willingly contribute to an external change, awareness that the external change may also require an internal change, i.e. within one's own organisation, is also required. More is thus demanded than a willingness to 'make decisions by consensus' or 'meet each other half way', as in traditional forms of co-operation between different parties.

In contrast to networks and project organisations, in which individual actors can take part for the sake of their own development, a partnership entails a real *commitment* on the part of those actors that become partners. As a partner, an actor is one of several that together will take concerted action to solve a (social) problem or achieve (structural) changes. Networks, clusters, innovation systems and the Triple Helix can therefore be described as forms of organisation that are more unconditionally composed than partnerships.

As the partners are part of the solution of the partnership's common problem, partnerships require integration with the regular operations of those involved in a more explicit way than the forms of organisation mentioned above. A comparison with the traditional project organisation illustrates this difference. The activities of a project usually take place outside or alongside the regular operations of the actors concerned, and in the *best* case successful project results are integrated with the regular operations following the completion of the project. During the course of the project, however, the activities and organisation of the project lie outside the regular operations.

The link between regular operations and the work of a partnership is clearer. In order to be successful, the work of a partnership requires support and understanding, willingness to change and commitment on the part of the organisations that form the partnership. The activities of the partnership cannot therefore lie outside the regular operations. The partnership is thus simultaneously *within* the structures and the existing operations and *outside* – in the form of an organisation for collaboration that may temporarily be funded by means of external support. Partnerships handle financial resources and make decisions. In many cases, they also run activities that involve participants from, for example, the employment agency or the social insurance office

The role of partnerships – to be outside the regular operations and structures but at the same time to work within them – risks giving them an unclear status. The need for transparency, the possibility to call people to account and a clear division of roles are therefore of central importance. The fact that partnerships make decisions and run operations that have a real effect on both individuals, i.e. those the partnership is trying to help, and public authorities, means that it is important to discuss the issue of democracy in partnerships. What representation is there in the partnerships? Who can influence the decisions of the partnerships and how? Is there a risk that important social decisions will be made by public officials rather than by politicians?

The potential that partnerships offer, and which we would particularly like to underline, is encompassed by the drive, energy and ability to take action that stems from the explicit commitment of each of the partners, although the unclear status of partnerships gives rise to a number of difficulties that it is important to consider.

The description of a partnership organisation above is of an ideal-typical and normative character, which is often used by EU officials and regional representatives. In this book, we will try to determine whether this description is realistic or not. We cannot say whether partnerships are a better way of achieving innovation and change. We would like to point out that working in a partnership should be seen as a learning process in which there is not *one* best solution that applies in all situations; the solution is tied to the local context.

To summarise this section, we have not adopted an exact definition of partnership, but our starting point is that a partnership can be seen as a collection of actors/organisations who join together to address a common issue, where all the partners (using their competence, experience and resources) can contribute to a joint development.

In the following sections we will try do get a better understanding of the partnership organisation by comparing it with project work and a network organisation.

2.2 Partnership in comparison with project work and a network organisation

A partnership represents a different way of working compared, for example, to a network. In a partnership, the partners own the issue or task at hand jointly, which requires a commitment from the participants in a way that networks do not. In the EQUAL Programme, the aim is also to have a structural impact, and some of the partners in each partnership thus constitute a part of the structure that the partnership is trying to influence or change. This means that a willingness and desire to critically examine one's own activities and operations is an important precondition for the work.

> The difference between a development partnership and a project is that you don't just want to change the world around you, in a development partnership you also have to be prepared to change yourself. (A co-ordinator in the Swedish EQUAL Programme)

The quotation above indicates the importance of the entire organisation, not just a number of individuals, becoming a committed partner.

Partnerships are considered to be suitable for more extensive and complex operations, whereas projects are more appropriate for limited assignments where both the means and the objectives are predetermined. The work of a partnership is open in nature in that the formulation of objectives and the testing of methods is a process that must be open as it aims to provide innovative solutions. Another clear difference is the joint responsibility in a partnership, which comprises everything from operation to development (e.g. financial aspects, formulation of objectives, influence, new thinking, dissemination and impact). In a project organisation, however, there is a steering group or project manager with responsibility for ensuring that the assignment is conducted according to plan and in line with the predetermined objectives.

Projects and partnerships also differ in terms of their composition. Partnerships represent organisations that are affected by a shared problem, which means that the organisations themselves are responsible for ensuring that changes occur. Responsibility for the changes cannot be shouldered by a single individual but must be assumed by the organisation as a whole. A partnership is thus made up of organisations rather than individuals. In projects, on the other hand, responsibility for completing a certain assignment may often lie with an individual and not necessarily require real responsibility on the part of the entire organisation. Projects can thus include organisations as well as individuals.

It is important to stress that the presentation above is based on a theoretical approach that describes the extremes of the two forms of organisation. There are of course projects that are very like partnerships as an organisational form and vice versa. The distinction made above nevertheless presents important factors that are unique to partnerships and that are necessary for partnerships to function as such.

An evaluation of the Swedish EQUAL programme (*Ledningskonsulterna* 2004) has shown that many partnerships have in fact been run more like traditional projects than partnerships. The co-ordinators have acted more or less as project managers and have assumed – or been allocated – a strong role, while the partners in the partnership have been passive. This clearly illustrates how important it is to establish from the start, and to clarify to yourself, the organisation you represent and the other partners, exactly what working in a partnership entails.

2.3 What is a developmental partnership?

The developmental partnership (DP) is fundamental to the EQUAL programme. In the R&D project we will try to understand how this kind of partnership is related to other similar arrangements – i.e. the partnerships in the Leader Programme and also the Swedish tradition of co-operation between the partners on the labour market.

A DP works with a certain theme or with a specific objective by bringing together different partners for joint development. Such broad DPs can consist of local and regional authorities, organisations, companies, associations, unions etc. The DPs can be organised in different ways – geographically (in a municipality or a region) or based on a certain sector or branch.

The DPs should consist of involved actors who are working for a joint goal. The work is based on equal worth and the decisions are taken by consensus. The ambition is to promote innovative solutions with a focus on preventing discrimination and exclusion in working life. The co-operation should be based on a common strategy, a detailed programme, clear responsibilities for each partner, a high degree of participation and innovative methods for change and dissemination (EQUAL 2000, p. 5).

The transnational co-operation is a necessary component in a successful strategy for change – it is a way to bring in new perspectives, to give inspiration, to support learning in networks, and to disseminate information.

The general objective of the EQUAL programme is to promote innovative and creative thinking by experimentation in which new solutions are developed, tried and validated. The experimentation will concern new methods, changes in attitudes, innovative practices, new developmental processes etc. The outputs will be tools such as good practice, descriptions, models, recommendations etc.

2.4 Creating a partnership that offers gender equality and inclusion

We have previously admitted that we do not know if or to what extent partnership is a better form of organisation than others for conducting development work. There is criticism of partnership in this respect. For example, one can discuss to what extent partnership is an organisational form that determines whether development work will be successful or not. Perhaps we put too much faith in new forms of organisation as a solution to problems relating to co-operation?

Another criticism levelled at partnerships is that they entail the transfer of economic resources and decisions from democratically elected representative bodies to partnerships in which the representatives have not been democratically elected. There is a risk of considerable resources and power being accumulated by organisations that are not transparent or publicly accountable, and that also exclude many actors.

With this in mind, it is important to reflect on to what extent partnerships include or exclude. We have therefore chosen to underline the importance of an inclusive perspective in the work of a partnership in terms of representation, forms of work and concrete operations. One way of addressing the question of exclusion may be to consider who is included in the partnership, who makes the decisions and how, who does the talking and who is listened to. We should also consider the fundamental ideas on which the partnership bases its operations. Transparency, participation and a non-hierarchical organisation are some of the most important factors in preventing partnership from becoming an organisational form only for actors/organisations with an abundance of resources.

There is not much research on partnership as an organisational model and gender equality, but the Emma Resource Centre[1] has conducted research on clusters. This research reveals that the gender perspective is conspicuous by its absence in most regional development work. Definitions of innovation, regional development and clusters are based on the male point of view, which leads to women being excluded from regional development work (Petterson & Saarinen 2004). Whether these results may also be relevant to partnerships and gender equality is discussed in Chapter 13.

The labour market in Sweden is gender segregated and many organisations have a patriarchal structure in which men in general have more power than women. How can we prevent partnerships from recreating this unequal structure? Working in a partnership touches on several aspects of gender equality as well as equality in a wider sense. We will focus here on gender equality within partnerships, but also on equality in the relations between a partnership and the group that it is working to include on the labour market. Gender equality is a term that is often associated with demands and documents (e.g. gender equality plans). As a result of the demands for gender equality and the application of a gender perspective, the concepts are well established at a rhetorical level: We often say that we are for gender equality. But what is the situation in reality, in terms of concrete action? When we are asked to specify in what ways we have

---

1 The Emma Resource Centre is a competence development centre for regional development from a gender equality perspective. For more information on the Emma Resource Centre see www.emma.se.

promoted gender equality or taken the gender perspective into account we often find it difficult to do so: What have we actually done? This shows that there is a gap between rhetoric and action with regard to gender equality. What is it that makes it so difficult to actually specify concrete measures even though so many people are for gender equality?

Gender equality is not just about statistics, i.e. about the number of women and men in a partnership. A partnership may include an equal number of women and men, but still have a hierarchy that favours men and disfavours women, or vice versa (see Chapters 7 and 9). Gender equality and the gender perspective are above all about power relations. This means that it is important not only to strive for an even gender distribution, but also to reflect on and identify the power relations that exist in the partnership (see Chapter 13). This will highlight the fact that gender equality is not simply a women's issue but fundamentally an issue concerning the power relations between women and men. Certain groups (men) benefit from the fact that other groups (women) do not have power. This also enables us to understand why this type of analysis, which challenges the prevailing power relations, arouses a certain amount of resistance. Who wants to lose their position of power?

Co-operation is based on mutual social relations, even in partnerships, and it is therefore important to address the aspect of power in these relations. The point of departure for analysing power relations is to study, which individuals have or do not have access to resources, networks, mandates and information. The Emma Resource Centre has identified a number of important factors for analysing power relations within a cluster. These are homosociality (the fact that men often choose men in an organisational structure), power, harassment, marginalisation, status and the ability to express yourself so that others listen to what you have to say. We believe that these factors may also apply to working in partnerships.

Ensuring gender equality requires analysing the work of a partnership at several levels. The following questions can act as a guide when reflecting on gender equality:[2]

Are women and men represented in the partnership? At what levels and in what functions? What is the situation regarding representation in formal and informal contexts? Does the information required reach everyone? What consequences do representation and resource distribution have for the participation of women and men in the partnership? How are the partnership's common problems, aims and objectives defined? What values and norms govern the partnership's work?

---

2 The questions are based on Åström's (1999) 3R method; representation, resources, realia.

An example from one of the partnerships in the EQUAL Programme that has worked with gender equality demonstrates the resistance that can arise, especially if the aim is to influence the situation in a partner's own organisation. It is important to think about how to deal with such resistance and how to support people who are at risk because they raise issues that may put them in an uncomfortable situation – for example by being exposed to the silent treatment, denigrating comments or even personal attacks.

Gender equality is particularly important with regard to relations between the partnership and those groups who are supposed to benefit from the partnership's work. Experience has shown, for example, that notions about what work is suitable for women and immigrants govern the support that these women or immigrants receive when they apply for jobs that do not fit the norm for the kind of work that they are expected to want to do. Are people encouraged to step outside the norms on a labour market that is segregated in terms of gender and ethnicity, or does encouragement and support fade away in such situations?

Other matters that it is important to consider with regard to gender equality are what information is provided and what decisions are made at the formal and informal levels. In an inclusive partnership, an alternative may be to ensure that no issues that should be dealt with formally are taken up in informal contexts unless everyone concerned is involved. At the informal level, it is a question of ensuring that responsibility for the work is assumed in such a way that everyone is comfortable with it. At both the formal and informal levels, for example, language can have an excluding effect.

The subject of gender equality is not expressly dealt with in all the chapters, but several of the questions raised can be analysed from a gender perspective. Participation and the attempt to find forms of work that suit everyone are examples of subjects that can create an inclusive partnership. It is not easy to identify and change power relations. On the contrary, it is often difficult to define power, and few people will admit that they have a position of power. People that others perceive as being powerful may themselves feel that they are powerless. Handling issues like this sometimes requires support and expertise from outside, e.g. a process manager who is not included in the partnership but who can identify power relations and initiate discussions about them. There are of course many more questions to be raised and to reflect on, but this is a gateway to a partnership that offers gender equality and inclusion.

Innovation and sustainable change are central concepts in the book. We will discuss what these concepts mean in the final sections of this chapter.

2.5 Innovation

What is an *innovation*? An innovation is something that exceeds its own assumptions and creates something new, i.e. that changes an existing practice (Andersen 1997). The content of an innovation may, however, vary. It may relate to technology, products, services, organisations, processes, markets and so on (Janszen 2000). Traditionally, the term innovation has often been used in connection with the development of new technology, but today it has acquired a much wider use.

An innovation can arise in many different ways and take many different forms. The new aspect may consist of elements that are already known but that are combined in a different way to form a whole with a new function. The development may be driven by an individual innovator, but innovations can also be created by unexpected meetings between various actors and systems. It is here that partnership becomes interesting as a form for organising innovation, especially in a regional perspective. Networks are not adequate to create a sufficiently sustainable and strong structure that can combine different interests and radically influence other structures and traditions. The main challenge is to ensure that the strength of the formal and strategic co-operation in a partnership is not established at the expense of creativity and innovativeness (Andersson et al. 2006).

'Innovation system' is now a central theoretical concept and a strategy for regional and national development. What does it mean that an innovation takes place in a *system*? Seeing innovations as part of a system appears to be contradictory. We associate the term 'system' with something stable, fixed and sluggish. A system can take different forms, but a common feature is that the term designates a whole that operates cohesively. The whole comprises different parts that mutually condition and limit each other (cf. Edquist 2000, p. 39). Lundvall (1992) who coined the term innovation system refers to 'all the parts of the economy that influence learning and discovery'. We are therefore not talking about a mechanical system with linear connections, but about *processes* that generate feedback, interaction and learning. This interplay comprises manufacturing, technology, research, customer demand, political decisions and so on (Edquist 2000).

An innovation system is based on a holistic view and long-term thinking and thus entails a critique of short-term, limited project thinking. Projects are compared to 'building cathedrals in the desert' (Cooke et al. 2000, p. 149). An innovation is not seen as a single event performed by isolated individuals, but as a combination of activities in a complex situation involving a large number of actors.

The context is thus important in a system perspective. It is not possible to simply transfer a 'best solution' or a finished model 'from above' or 'from outside', which is a common ambition in development contexts. Instead, detailed knowledge on the local situation and the system of which it forms a part is required. If innovations are to be sustainable they must be developed in a natural way and based on the forces that exist in a certain environment, but they must also strive to change this environment.[3] The comparison with the Trojan horse has been made in this connection. A change is 'snuck in' but subsequently has radical consequences for the system.

2.6 Sustainable change

The term *sustainable development* is central in the book. We wish to investigate whether partnership as a form of organisation makes development work more sustainable compared to other – top-down and bottom-up governed – change strategies.

Internationally, sustainable development has become a political objective for social change. Originally, the term related to the environment and environmental policy, but it has gradually been dramatically extended (SOU 2003:123). A number of companies in the private sector have also taken the concept of sustainability on board, although this is usually expressed in terms of the companies' Corporate Social Responsibility. The term sustainability is not exact. Sustainability is usually defined as meeting current demands without endangering future resources.

In working life, it could be said that sustainability is about ensuring that operations and processes create and recreate human resources rather than consuming them. Sustainability entails adopting a resource perspective, i.e. making sure that demands in the long term are in balance with the available resources, or that resources develop in balance with higher demands. Sustainability thus has a content aspect – what sustainability concerns – but also a form aspect, i.e. different forms for organising development so that it becomes sustainable.

The literature on the form aspect of sustainable development work (sustainable change) highlights the following preconditions (cf. Docherty et al. 2002, Svensson et al. 2007):

- Strong support 'from above' (from managers, owners/politicians);
- A high degree of participation on the part of those concerned in the entire implementation process;

---

[3] It is a question of both assimilation and accommodation, to use Piaget's terms on learning (Cooke et al. 2002).

- A clear link between development and operational issues
- An integration of efficiency, work environment, quality, and gender equality issues;
- That the required resources are allocated to the development work;
- Elements of learning and reflection that allow corrections to be made on the basis of the experience gained;
- A competent project management and an efficient project organisation.

Olsén et al. (2003 pp. 11–12) highlights the importance of creating context on the basis of a democratic sustainability perspective. According to the authors, this means basing development on the context of peoples' lives. Social development can therefore not be founded on either political, top-down governed processes or solutions governed by experts. It is instead the concrete activities of people themselves in their interplay with social institutions that lie at the centre of sustainable, democratic development. Social imagination is a form of knowledge and a social orientation that makes it possible for the participants to see context and to switch perspectives in order to perceive a link between local phenomena and social conditions (ibid. p. 14).

In the case of public enquiries, it seems that the sustainability concept has been concretised to only a very limited extent in the form of ideas about the role of working life in sustainable development. The sustainable development of working life has not yet acquired the clarity required to be able to trace and test more stringent hypotheses on the basis of the concept. Sustainability as a key and collective term is also problematic from the point of view of research because the subject of the research often relates to activities that are conducted within a relatively limited period of time. Research often lacks the stamina required to follow a phenomenon over a long period of time, which means that we must to a great extent rely on assumptions concerning the links between measures and effects. This leads to a higher degree of uncertainty in our conclusions than would be the case if follow-up took place over an extended period (Svensson et al. 2007).

References

Andersen, E (1997) 'Innovation Systems: Evolutionary Perspectives'. In Edquist C (ed.) *Systems of Innovation. Technologies, Institutions and Organizations*. London: Pinter.

Andersson, M. Svensson, L, Wistus, S & Åberg, C (2006) (eds.) *On the Art of Developing Partnerships*. Stockholm: Arbetslivsinstitutet

Cooke, P, Boekholt, P & Tödtling, F (2000) *The Governance of Innovation in Europe*. London: Pinter

Docherty, P, Forslin, J & Shani, A B (2002) 'Emerging work systems: from intensive to sustainable'. In Docherty P, Forslin J & Shani A B (eds) *Creating sustainable work systems*. London: Routledge

Edquist, C & McKelvey, M (2000) (eds.) *Systems of Innovation: Growth, competitiveness and employment*. Cheltenham: Elgar

EQUAL (2000) *Gemenskapsinitiativprogram för EQUAL 2000-2006 SVERIGE*. Stockholm: Svenska ESF-rådet

Janszen, F (2000) *The Age of Innovation: making business creativity a competence, not a coincidence*. London: Financial Times Prentice Hall

Ledningskonsulterna i Stockholm AB (2004). *Halvtidsutvärdering II EQUAL. Interimsrapport. Styrning och ledning*. Stockholm: Svenska ESF-rådet

Lundvall, B-Å (1992) (ed.) *National Systems of Innovations. Towards a Theory of Innovative and Interactive Learning*. London: Pinter

Olsén, P, Steen Nielsen, B & Aagaard Nielsen, K (2003) *Demokrati og bæredygtighed. Social fantasi og samfundsmæssig rigdomsproduktion*. Roskilde: Roskilde Universitetsforlag

Pettersson, K & Saarinen, Y (2004) *Kluster som ett regionalpolitiskt redskap i ett könsperspektiv. Män som hjältar i manliga kluster* Emma Resurscentrum (www.emma.se)

SOU 2003:123 *Utvecklingskraft för hållbar välfärd*. Delbetänkande av Ansvarskommittén. Stockholm: Fritzes offentliga publikationer

Svensson, L, Aronsson, G, Randle, H & Eklund, J (2007) *Hållbart arbetsliv – projekt som gästspel eller strategi i långsiktig utveckling*. Malmö: Gleerups

Åström, G (1999) *Jämställdhetsverkstan. Om jämtegrering och 3R-metoden i svenska kommuner*. Svenska kommunförbundet

3. Defining our terms and clarifying our language

This chapter explores both the concept of partnership and the terminology that is being used in connection with it. Through such an examination we hope to promote a clearer understanding of what a partnership is as well as draw attention to some of the issues and challenges that are embedded in the use of much 'partnering language'. Our premise is that greater clarity and rigour in the use of partnership definitions and terms is important in order to ensure that these forms of collaboration are made more effective at both individual and organisational levels and thus have greater potential to promote sustainable change and innovation.

3.1 What is a 'partnership'?

The term partnership elicits much confusion. It is often used to describe widely different constructs ranging from loose networks and alliances to more institutionalised joint ventures. Their branding as 'partnerships' appears to be based upon the fact that they involve some form of combined activity that is mutually beneficial to those involved, often with reference to such characteristics as the voluntary nature of their collaboration, the pooling of resources, the sharing of risks and benefits and capitalising on synergies. Some examples include:

> Partnerships are of a voluntary, 'self-organizing' nature; they are based on mutual respect and shared responsibility of the partners involved ... (UN Dept of Economic and Social Affairs 2006)

> Partnership involves an agreement to work together to fulfil an obligation or undertake a specific task by committing resources and sharing the risks as well as the benefits. (DFID, p. 2)
>
> Partnership is a cross sector collaboration in which organisations work together in a transparent, equitable and mutually beneficial way. The partners agree to commit resources, share the risks as well as the benefits to work together towards a sustainable development goal. (IBLF 2006)
>
> People and organisations from some combination of public, business and civil constituencies who engage in voluntary, mutually beneficial, innovative relationships to address common societal aims through combining their resources and competencies. (Nelson & Zadek 2000, p. 14)

It is our contention that these commonly used definitions are too simplistic. They tend to mask the various obligations to participate, the **overemphasis placed on** financial contributions above other kinds of resource contributions, and the distinct differences between organisations that make partnership processes so challenging. Clearly partnerships involve some form of horizontal decision-making processes (i.e. shared power), valued contribution of different kinds of resources (beyond financing), and flexibility to adapt the objectives and activities as circumstances dictate. We must be somewhat careful, however, in that in many countries, the term partnership refers to a legal, contractual construct.

The following definition serves as a useful starting point in assisting us to gain a clearer understanding of what a partnership is.

> Partnerships involve two or more organisations that enter into a collaborative arrangement based on:
> 1) synergistic goals and opportunities that address particular issues or deliver specified tasks that single organisations cannot accomplish on their own as effectively, and
> 2) whose individual organisations *cannot* purchase the appropriate resources or competencies *purely* through a market transaction.[1]

Within this description, partnership may have a wide variety of objectives along a spectrum from a specific task-orientation (the installation of 500 water connections, the building of a hospital or clinic or the provision of training opportunities to targeted groups) to more systemic objectives that are aimed at changing rules (the development of new regulatory standards, guidelines or legal instruments) or behaviours (a national education or health promotion programme or awareness-raising on issues of social

---

1 This definition is used by the organisation Building Partnerships for Development in Water and Sanitation (BPD) www.bpdws.org and is based upon one developed by the London based organisation AccountAbility www.accountability.org.uk

concern). The first part of the definition is fairly common. The second part offers a more interesting element as it raises issues around power and mutual need, donor/funder and recipient relationships, and the value of the variety of resources that are brought to the table.

3.2 Public-Private Partnerships and Multi-Stakeholder Partnerships

Encompassed by the partnership definition above we are likely to find a range of multi-stakeholder relationships,[2] including what are commonly called Public-Private Partnership arrangements. Multi Stakeholder Partnerships (MSPs), however, are different from Public-Private Partnerships (PPPs) in a few key ways (see Table 1). PPPs tend to involve a legally binding contract with evident vertical accountability structures based on a relationship generally between two signatories. MSPs involve less transactions-based relationships with more of an emphasis on horizontal accountability. Targets, deliverables and timeframes are generally more clearly defined in PPPs whereas MSPs usually have similar, and sometimes additionally ambitious, but more flexible goals in these areas. PPPs operate under a clear legal and/or regulatory construct while, though the partners themselves may be regulated, MSPs themselves are not regulated and more often than not have no legal identity. It is this last set of factors that makes accountability more difficult to pin down.

Table 1. Distinctions between PPPs and MSPs. Source: BPD Water and Sanitation

Public-Private Partnerships (PPPs)	Multi-Stakeholder Partnerships (MSPs)
Contracts or transactions-based arrangement (with clear vertical accountability structures)	Less emphasis on transactions with significantly more emphasis on horizontal accountability among the partner institutions[3]
Specific performance targets / deliverables and timeframes	Greater flexibility around targets, deliverables and timeframes as they are expected to emerge or evolve organically based on processes with stakeholders
Operate within legal / regulatory constructs	Partners operate within legal / regulatory construct but partnership is unregulated
Limited stakeholder consultation – clearly proscribed in the agreement	Extensive stakeholder 'engagement' considered a critical success factor

2 These include partnerships described as: cross-sector, inter-sectoral, multi-sector, multi-partite and tri-sector.

3 The one caveat is that often the funder or financier has the hierarchical edge and may use this power in the partnership to their advantage.

3.3 The nature of the relationship

We see partnerships somewhere along a continuum between networks and joint ventures.

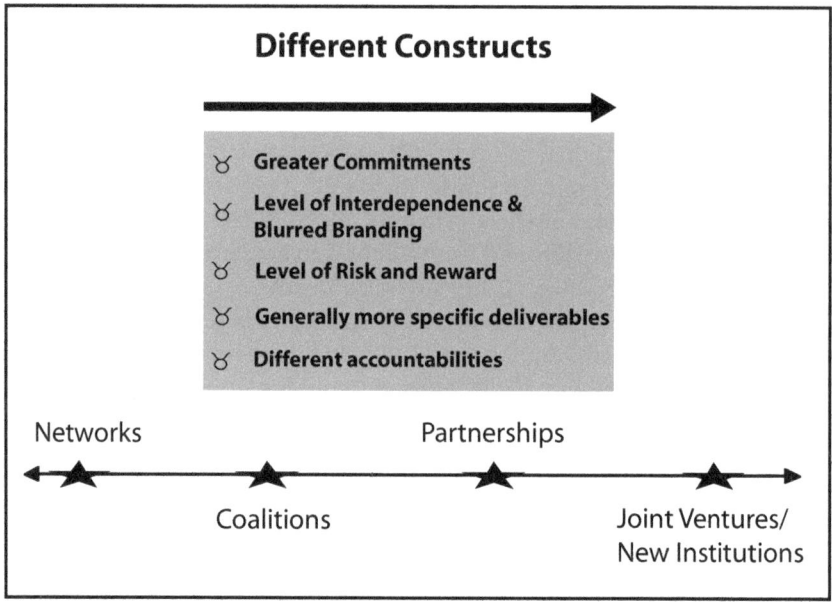

Figure 1. *Spectrum of engagement. Source: BPD Water and Sanitation*

As Figure 1 shows, networks are generally less rigid arrangements with presumably less risk, looser aims, and lower commitment levels, and with accountabilities between the participating organisations at a minimum. Joint ventures are where participating organisations' identities are largely subsumed under a new institution, accountabilities are high, both between partners and externally, and generally oriented around contractual relationships with clients and customers. Partnerships, as defined above, involve a mix of these characteristics. It is also important to note that partnerships, in this sense, are not designed to exist permanently but instead serve as transitional mechanisms until practices become more institutionalised or transactions-based.

3.4 The language of partnerships

As well as clarification around what partnerships are, we also need to address the issue of the language that we use in relation to them. The word 'partnership' itself evokes 'a certain simplicity and harmony' (Caplan 2006, p. 11) and glosses over the many challenges that creating and developing partnerships involves. At the same time partnership literature is peppered with 'participatory language' (Harrison 2002, p. 593) urging engagement, empowerment and inclusion and the development of partnering relationships that are trust-based, transparent and equitable. The generalised and positive tone of this terminology creates false expectations. It 'conceptualises collaborative processes as inherently nonconfrontational' (Poncelet 2001, p. 22) and runs the risk of enabling their easy dismissal by sceptics of partnerships as 'fuzzy' at best and, at worst, 'delegitimising' more adversarial methods for achieving radical and innovative change. Thus, as Poncelet warns, '... partnerships are ultimately constrained by the very discourses and practices that they tend to privilege' (ibid, p. 23).

The view that partnership language is shaped by, and promotes, particular worldviews and cultural perspectives is important as it masks deep-seated issues of power and control. An underlying assumption is that the terminology used is understood by all involved in the building of a partnership (Vargas 2002, p. 1549, Rein et al. 2005, pp. 10–11). The concepts implied by 'partnership participation', however, may be interpreted in different ways in different contexts and by different audiences. As a result, '... the blanket use of participatory language may hide the complex interaction of history and individual positioning that make the meaning of participation so variable' (Harrison 2002, p. 593).

Partnerships require the commitment and consensus of a wide range of players. In order to bind them together, calls for 'inclusivity' with the full and equal 'participation' of partners and the active 'engagement' of stakeholders are understandable. However, within both these groups there are likely to be differing levels of commitment to, and interest in, a partnership's work. These will relate to the wider context in which the partnership is situated, the nature and scope of the partnership and the importance the partnership plays in delivering different partner and stakeholder goals. In addition, the degree of participation of different interest groups will be conditioned by factors such as time, resources and convenience.

3.5 Voluntary participation?

The premise that partnerships involve the coming together of different partners on a voluntary basis, without any statutory or legal requirement to do so, is widely promulgated. As Caplan observes (2003, pp. 33–34), the use of the expression 'voluntary' implies either a 'willingness' or an 'option' to partner (or not) and thus skims over the fact that partnership-building necessitates hard work and commitment. The term 'voluntary' belies the fact that partners must need each other to ensure meaningful collaboration. Whether there is a choice to partner or not, and with whom, needs to be better understood. In many cases, the issue of choice is masked by a sense of obligation on the part of a partner to at least *have to be seen* to be at the table or not to want to relinquish decision-making on issues that affect them without their participation. In addition the different reasons for partners to work together and the risks and rewards for them in doing so also need to be analysed. Different partners, it is to be assumed, are likely to be valued quite differently by both partners and external stakeholders.

3.6 Partners and stakeholders

Notions of partnership 'participation' and 'engagement' are complicated by the distinction between partners and stakeholders, especially because this is often based upon different perceptions of a particular organisation's role in relation to a partnership. *Partners* make substantive contributions to a partnership and have usually signed up to a partnering relationship. In this sense contributing financial resources, as a donor for example, does not automatically qualify an organisation as a partner unless other critical resources (convening power and leverage, technical skills, etc.) are also put into the partnership. Partnerships are established in part to share risks. Whilst there might be some risks to a donor in providing financial support to a partnership, this generally, though not always, bears very little resemblance to the nature of risk for the implementing partners. Similarly, receiving a benefit from the partnership may not automatically qualify an organisation as a partner. This does not relate to the bearing of risk, as discussed below, but rather to how integrated they are in the design and implementation of the partnership. It is important to note that this involvement may change over time as, through the process of partnering, organisations may become more active in the partnership.

The term *partner* also needs to be understood at two levels: that of the individual representing a partner organisation and that of the organisations themselves. Although presumably overlapping, the interests of the individuals and those of their organisations may be somewhat different. However, while it would appear that the notion of 'individual interest' runs counter to the essence of a partnership, individual interests and concerns are a critical aspect of partnerships. Partnership efforts are initiated and fundamentally driven by the interests of individual members and their parent organisations or constituencies. Indeed, for a partnership to emerge in the first place participants must believe that working together will serve their own interests. Recognition of individual interests, and attention to understanding these, is therefore important when unpacking participation issues.

Stakeholders are also widely mentioned in relation to partnership participation. Failure to incorporate key stakeholders into partnership decision-making and communication processes is often highlighted as a key barrier to partnership development (see for example Yakovleva & Alabasterb 2003). The term *stakeholder* is not easy to define and is generally unhelpful as it is used to refer to groups who may be affected, influenced by, or concerned with the work of the partnership.[4] In this regard, it is important to make clearer distinctions between those stakeholders that may exert an *influence upon* the partnership (for example, the media, government authorities, regulators, academics, etc.) and those that are *influenced by* it. Needless to say, these two groups are not equal. The former bears very little risk if the partnership fails but the latter may ultimately bear a great deal of risk. Different terminology that more accurately reflects their relationship to the partnership would be helpful. This might distinguish between *'interested observers'* (those that exert an influence upon the partnership) and *'risk bearers'* (those that are influenced by the partnership). The critical aspect of these distinctions is to determine whose risks matter most and whose opinion carries more weight. Given also that few players could genuinely be described as neutral, we need to understand the politics that drive interested observers to seek to influence a partnership. We also need to be aware that risk bearers who do *not* contribute to the partnership will not have the same incentives to want to see the partnership succeed.

Both resources and/or clarifying both resource input and/or degree of participation is a useful way of exploring definitions of partners and stakeholders. Ultimately different voices should be considered but their opinions should be understood in the context in which they are offered. It is also important to remember that relationships may change over the

---

4   The term 'Boundary Partners' has also been used to describe 'those individuals, groups and organisations with whom the program interacts directly and with whom the program anticipates opportunities for influence' (Earl et al. 2001).

lifetime of a partnership. Conflicting and changing loyalties and demands, and the contextual issues that cut across these, can thus influence both the manner and depth of participation.

3.7 Resource inputs

Financial resources are usually prioritised within a partnership and often carry the most 'weight', giving those that contribute them a particularly powerful partnering role, whether or not this is openly acknowledged. However, a range of other important non-cash resources are also vital to a partnership's effectiveness. Table 2 outlines some of these resource contributions in more detail.

Table 2. Partnership resource inputs

People	Qualified and experienced personnel with appropriate knowledge bases for partnership activities
Skills/expertise	Technical and 'soft' skills – communication, advocacy, mediation and capacity-building abilities
Relationships	Contacts with policy makers, wider networks, media, stakeholder groups etc.
Knowledge	Contextual information, trends, market analysis
Equipment	Computers, furniture, stationary, transport
Physical space	For partnership office, meetings, events etc.
Products	Project-related items/commodities produced by partner organisations
Reputation	Convening power and leverage
Finance	Funds, grants

Examining different partner inputs and assessing their value can assist in determining partner status as well as identify whether a stakeholder is an 'interested observer' or 'risk bearer' as outlined above.

3.8 Degree of participation

Participation and engagement can encompass a range of options for partners and stakeholders. These range from a limited or passive connection with the partnership, in which they might receive information or be involved in discussions, to a more active connection where they might initiate or take the lead in a decision or course of action.

Table 3. General levels of partnership participation

4	CONTROL	Initiates or leads particular steps or activities
3	INFLUENCE	Participates directly in decision-making, has a vote
2	CONSULTED	Involved in discussion, able to express opinions & give feedback
1	INFORMED	Receives information

Drawing on work by Stott and Keatman (2005), Table 3 offers a limited dissection of possible participation levels. The categories outlined in the table obviously contain many variances within them which warrant further unpacking. Our aim, however, is simply to emphasise that 'participation' involves a range of different options which require examining in relation to different partnership interest groups. By exploring how particular partners or stakeholders are involved in a partnership we can more clearly understand their relationship to it.

3.9 Empowerment

Assessing resource inputs and the degree to which individuals and organisations are informed /consulted or how far they influence/control, enables deeper analysis of power relations in specific partnership contexts, processes and strategies. It can also show us whether different partners or stakeholders have been 'empowered' by taking on more active roles, growing in confidence and more strongly asserting themselves through their contribution or involvement in the partnership. 'Empowerment' is frequently outlined as a desirable partnership requirement as it promotes the voice and presence of those who may otherwise be marginalised or excluded. In the generalised labelling of such target groups, however, we often ignore the divisions and differences that they may comprise. So, for example, when calls are made for the empowerment of small partner organisations or women stakeholders, analysis of exactly *which* particular organisations or groups of women we are talking about, when and why, is necessary.

In order to more deeply address the issue of empowerment, the visibility, and invisibility, of both individuals and organisations connected to the partnership need to be understood. This may involve regularly checking the assumptions of partner representatives as well as examining which particular individuals in partner and stakeholder groups appear to dominate in decision-making processes, which do not, and why. Power relationships within a partnership are often a reflection of wider socio-economic and contextual divisions as well as cross-cutting issues such as gender, ethnicity, educational or political background, race, age or religion. In all cases it is therefore worth investigating why a particular attitude may be adopted; what this stance might suggest in relation to questions of power, and how it might best be addressed.

Both the positive and negative effects of empowerment also need to be considered. Positive effects may include the growth of an organisation's capacity, reach and skills or the increase in confidence and voice of a hitherto marginalised stakeholder group. On the negative side, the notion of 'participation as empowerment' can, as Kapoor (2002, 2004) makes clear, quite easily slide into 'participation as power'. Viewed in this way, an emphasis on empowerment may stifle plurality, conform to bureaucratic and/or organisational needs and, ultimately allow vested interest groups, be they internal or external, to control a partnership and become its prime beneficiaries (ibid. and see also Rein et al. 2005, p. 10).

3.10 Transparency

In order to ensure equitable relationships, partnership transparency is often called for. Power dynamics, however, can limit the effectiveness of this. In certain contexts or situations, for example, partners may feel threatened by what they are expected to share and how 'honest' they are required to be in relation to their motivations for engaging in the partnership and their expectations of it. They may also be concerned about divulging details of their own internal organisational processes to other partners. While partners may agree that sharing information about activities related to the partnership is desirable, in reality there will probably always be 'hidden agendas'.

'Hidden agendas' often centre around unstated or unresolved competition between partners. Although partnership language centres on the contribution of each partner's core competencies to the partnership, which then complement those of others, competition often exists over ideas, ownership, constituencies or other issues. Calls for transparency and clear divisions of labour mask competition among the individuals and institutions who enter into partnership relationships.

It is also important to acknowledge that while the overarching mission of the partnership will probably revolve around a common goal agreed to by all partners, it is highly unlikely that partners will share a common vision of how to get there. Each might have different perceptions about what would best meet, say, the needs of a community or target group with whom they are working. Whilst every partner will be in favour of ensuring that the goal is reached, views around choices for achieving it are likely to be different. These different interpretations can make transparency less than straightforward.

3.11 Trust

Linked to transparency is the issue of trust which is regularly highlighted as a key ingredient for partnership success. A distinction needs to be made here between trust between individuals and trust between institutions. Individuals may come to trust each other but partner organisations that come from different sectors and have different interests, are unlikely to have trust-based connections. It is more realistic to expect, and aim for, partners to respect different contributions, with confidence in the processes of the partnership and an understanding that their interests, concerns and grievances will be heard within it. It is also worth pointing out that where there is an option to choose a partner, the opportunity to emphasise trust is greater. Where choices are limited, however, this is more difficult. In the latter case a focus on ensuring that there is an understanding for what partner organisations can deliver, or delivering what they said they would deliver, may be more important.

3.12 Partnership drivers

The rationale for partnership is to bring together diverse types of organisation, with different skills and resources, to address a particular issue or task. Different organisational dynamics and *raisons d'être* are thus central to partnership and if partners fail to understand each other in these terms, they are likely to misinterpret each other's motivations and actions. Each partner, be they an individual or organisational representative, will enter a partnership and adopt a particular stance because of:

- Incentives: that motivate engagement for the furthering of partnership processes or objectives
- Sanctions: negative consequences or penalties for failure to participate in the partnership
- Obligations: commitments to provide certain inputs and outputs and participate in certain partnering processes

These 'pushes' and 'pulls', which are driven and conditioned by particular operational contexts, are at the heart of comprehending partnerships. The unique and complex interrelationship between a partnership and its specific setting is further complicated by the changing nature of organisational and individual behaviours, biases and interests.

Partnerships are rarely as simple as the language suggests. They bring together individuals and organisations whose perspectives and positions are often in conflict. In addition, partnership governance and accountabilities, as well as commitments and deliverables, are not static. To ensure that partnerships work effectively *and* produce results, a clear understanding of changing contextual issues and partnership drivers is required. Recognition that the process of partnership-building faces many challenges and requires time, energy and commitment is also vital. Franker appraisals of what partnerships are, how they work and our expectations of them will help to ensure that the possibilities they offer for sustainable change and innovation are taken seriously. A more careful and studied use of partnership terminology is central to this.

References

Caplan, K (2006) 'Creating Space for Innovation: Understanding enablers for multi-sector partnerships'. In *Partnership Matters, Current Issues in Cross-Sector Collaboration*, 4, London: IBLF

— (2003) 'The Purist's Partnership: Debunking the Terminology of Partnerships'. In *Partnership Matters 1*, Copenhagen: The Copenhagen Centre

Caplan, K, Gomme, J, Mugabi, J & Stott, L (2007) *Assessing Partnerships: Understanding the Drivers for Success*, London: BPD Water and Sanitation

DFID (undated) Department for International Development, UK, *Partnerships with Business*. London: Business Partnership Unit

Earl, S, Carden, F & Smutylo, T (2001) *Outcome mapping: building learning and reflection into development programs.* Ottawa: International Development Research Council (IDRC)

Harrison, E (2002) 'The Problem with the Locals' Partnership and Participation in Ethiopia. *Development and Change* Vol. 33, No. 4, pp. 587–610

IBLF (2006) International Business Leaders Forum, *Partnerships.* http://www.iblf.org/activities/Partnerships.jsp (accessed December 4, 2006)

Kapoor, I (2004) 'The Power of Participation, Participatory Development: A Promise Revisited'. *Current Issues in Comparative Education* [Online],Volume 6, Number 2, May 10, http://www.tc.columbia.edu/cice/

— (2002) 'The devil's in the theory: A critical assessment of Robert Chamber's work on participatory development'. *Third World Quarterly*, Vol. 23, No. 1, pp. 101–117

Nelson, J & Zadek, S (2000) *Partnership Alchemy.* Copenhagen: The Copenhagen Centre

Poncelet, E C (2001) 'A Kiss Here and a Kiss There: Conflict and Collaboration in Environmental Partnerships'. *Environmental Management* Vol. 27, No. 1, pp. 13–25

Rein, M, Stott, L, Yambayamba, K, Hardman, S & Reid, S (2005) *Working Together, A Critical Analysis of Cross-Sector Partnerships in Southern Africa.* Cambridge: CPI

Stott, L & Keatman, T (2005) 'Tools for Measuring Community Engagement in Partnerships'. *BPD Practitioner Note*, London: BPD Water and Sanitation

UN Dept of Economic and Social Affairs (2006) *Bali Guiding Principles.* Partnerships for Sustainable Development, Division for Sustainable Development. http://www.un.org/esa/sustdev/partnerships/bali_guiding_principles.htm (accessed Nov 26, 2006)

Vargas, C M (2002) 'Women in Sustainable Development: Empowerment through Partnerships for Healthy Living'. *World Development*, Vol. 30, No. 9, pp. 1539–1560

Yakovleva, N & Alabasterb, T (2003) 'Tri-sector partnership for community development in mining: a case study of the SAPI Foundation and Target Fund in the Republic of Sakha (Yakutia)'. *Resources Policy* Vol. 29, pp. 83–98

4. Are Partnerships Innovative?

4.1 Introduction – purpose and background

An important aspect of partnership organization in dealing with social problems and social improvement is its potential and capacity for innovation. Both in the structural funds and the social programmes of the EU, innovation is emphasised in partnership work.

At the same time, the empirical evidence of the innovativeness of partnership organisation is at best unclear. Also theoretically, the link between the partnership organisation and innovation has not been clarified. The focus in this chapter will be on the question: In what respects can partnership organization further innovation? I will particularly focus on social innovation, that is, new social methods and praxis. The focus is on theoretical clarification, but also on innovation processes in the context of partnerships work.

My experiential point of departure is the EU funded EQUAL partnership *Dropin* (see http://www.vkl.se/dropin/) which focuses on study and career options for young people that drop out of school and/or have incomplete study results from college. How can these young people on the edge of becoming dropouts, with the risks, social costs and health problems that this implies, find ways to 'drop into' working life or school? Dropin focuses on discrimination-related ill-health at the personal and institutional levels. The purpose of Dropin is to improve conditions for the transfer from school to work for young people. In order to contribute to improved learning, personal development and health among young people, different methods and forms of collaboration are developed and tested. The vision of the project is to function as an experimental workshop in order to identify and test new practices and to change discriminating structures in working life. Three municipalities in central Sweden, with the focus on the work on three colleges, are experimenting with new practices and methods. Dropin is a broad partnership, which consists of many organizations in the region working with unhealthy and risky behaviour among young people without college exams.

A point of departure for this chapter is the confusing lack of clarity about the concept innovation not only in Dropin, but in EQUAL partnerships and European Social Fund discussion in general. The concept that is used is vague and uncertain. The respondents give very vague answers when asked about innovation. Nor is it a central concept in the partnership organisations.

These findings indicate that the area of innovation calls for clarification both conceptually and empirically. This also raises more fundamental questions like: What is the character of social innovation? How recognize something as an innovation? Often the theme of innovation is focused on technical and economic issues, not on social innovation (see Rogers 1995). Rogers says that 'we often use the words 'innovation' and 'technology' as synonyms' (ibid. p. 12). I have an interest in innovation from my engineering background, from my earlier research on organizational development and from taking part in setting up and running an interdisciplinary innovation program.

The theme of innovation also has important links with the issues discussed in this book. Innovation is one important way of linking local change processes to broader structural changes. By being innovative, partnerships can develop new ideas and practices that can be disseminated more generally in society. Without innovation, the development work risks leading to something that is already available or is only useful in the local context. Innovative work can also be presumed to challenge established systems and discriminating structures that hinder people from finding livelihoods and self-employment and gaining access to the labour market.

4.2 Social innovation and partnership

What has the partnership organisation to do with innovation? How can partnerships contribute to innovation? I will start by identifying some positive connections between innovation and the partnership organisation.

Partnerships can be conducive to innovation in different ways. One immediate connection to innovation in a social perspective is that partnerships create and recreate social relations between actors and organizations perceived as partners. Interaction and dialogue among different parties is one important dimension in processes of creating something new. Mumford even sees it as a core element in the definition of social innovation: 'the generation and implementation of new ideas about how people should organize interpersonal activities, or social interactions, to meet one or more common goals' (Mumford 2002, p. 253). New ideas and practices in social areas are often interactive and depend on new relations between people. One example of this form of innovation in Dropin is the experimentation with more constructive discussions between professionals and young people. An important point in partnership organization is that the interactions and linkages should be horizontal, not hierarchical. Research has shown that such lateral linkages are conducive to innovation, e.g. by furthering interactive learning processes and innovation-oriented collaboration.

Another important innovation role for the partnership organisation is to create arenas and to mobilize resources for experimentation. In the case of Dropin, this has been formulated as the overall vision. In this case there has also been an input of new ideas, practices and methods. A communicative space has been established to support creative discussion and brainstorming. Many people already have ideas that have not been given space for growth and experimentation or economic resources. In Dropin, a core feature of the experimental workshops in the three municipalities has been the idea to find solutions to existing problems and improve established praxis concerning young people at risk. The inflow of external ideas and experiences has complemented and helped to specify the local ideas.

Partnerships can also help to integrate new ideas and practices into established organizations and activities. Dropin has developed organizational commitments for new ideas and practice in the participating organizations, particularly in the three colleges involved where much of the experimental work was done. Dropin has also funded competence development in order for professionals to learn new social methods – such as ART (Aggression Replacement Training), MI (Motivational Interviewing) and network management. These methods have been implemented in the operative work with the young people.

Partnerships can also help to create an arena for the presentation and dissemination of innovations, something, which is part of the general goals of the EQUAL programme. This is done in Dropin through a number of publications, meetings and conferences.

Moulaert et al. (2005) stress that social innovation has normative-political dimensions. It could be seen as a creative response to the social needs and problems in society. Their way of conceptualizing social innovation is quite conducive to the EQUAL ideology. They see social innovation as a way of listening to and recognising the alienated needs of discriminated groups. It is a way of empowering these actors and of achieving social inclusion.

Partnerships can further innovation in different ways, but they can also circumscribe, restrict and even block innovation, e.g. by restricting what can be developed and disseminated. Some partnerships may be formed in order to hinder certain types of innovation. Even innovative partnerships strive to move in certain directions, and will resist other orientations. In the case of Dropin, the focus is on innovation relating to young people.

In this chapter, I will concentrate on the positive relation between innovation and the partnership organisation. I will start with a conceptual clarification of innovation, particularly social innovation, which is the focus in the EQUAL context.

4.3 From technological to social innovation – a critique and framing of the concept

The initial clarification provides a promising picture that there are a number of ways that partnerships can be important in supporting innovation. But the problem I have experienced is that when we 'scratch the surface' and start to look more closely at what is really innovative, the images become more vague, ambiguous and blurred. This is particularly obvious when we focus on social innovation which is less tangible compared to technical innovation.

There are many types of definition of innovation. Often innovation is seen from a technical, business or economic perspective, e.g. how innovation can create advantages and contribute to growth in the economy. But the concept is used more or less actively in many social and technological sciences. The innovation literature predominantly focuses on technical-economic matters. When reviewing the research literature on social innovation, the results are surprisingly meagre. In what way do socially-oriented innovations differ from technical innovation?

I will use an overview of the literature by Moulaert et al. (2005). I will argue that common assumptions concerning innovation are in need of problematisation, particularly when we are studying social innovation.

Innovation can be both seen as an object/product and as a process. Seeing innovation as an object is the dominant perspective. Rogers (1995, p. 11) understands innovation as an object, and defines it as 'an idea, practice, or object that is perceived as new by an individual or other unit of adoption'. Also the common distinction between product innovation and process innovation still focuses on innovation as an object, although the later has a focus on how to do things.

Today, innovation management is more in focus. In recent studies it is often understood in a more process-oriented way – innovation as *innovating*. An example of a leading text is Tidd et al. (2001). These researchers see innovation as a core process in or between organizations, which can and should be managed. When they talk about innovation, 'essentially they mean change'. Innovation and change are often used without clarification of how they are distinct or overlapping. Change is commonly understood as a movement from a state A to another state. Innovation is not only a matter of change in this sense. Both Rogers (1995) and Tidd et al. (2001) emphasize that innovation also conceptually is connected to something new. Innovation means that change is made through a development process, which leads to the introduction of something new that is valuable and useful.

What is 'the new' that is the result of innovation? What is the point of such a strong focus on novelty? I think that this is the core issue in innovation theory. The difficulty with the question is that it seems to be a self-evident concept. It is difficult to pinpoint and measure what is new. For whom is it new? From what perspective is it new? What is new must be related to the particularity of circumstances or the personal knowledge of the individuals concerned. How interesting is something that is new? Maybe it is just an uninteresting oddity? The perceived 'novelty' of something in a change process is also partly dependent on how it is framed. Tidd et al. (2001) start by defining novelty technically as well as by the amount of changes it produces ('radicality' of innovation). Then, suddenly they take a perceptual turn – in line with Rogers (1995) – stating that 'we should remember that it is the *perceived* degree of novelty which matters; novelty is very much in the eye of the beholder' (ibid. p. 8). Their illustration, like Rogers, focuses on the perception of the adopter as crucial.

According to Schumpeter (1947), news must be defined in relation to the market. This Schumpeterian view is evident in Tidd et al. (2001, p. 5) understanding of product and process innovation: 'Being able to make something no one else can, or to do so in ways which are better than anyone else is a powerful source of advantage'. To be 'new' it needs to be valuable in a general sense. In Schumpeter's theory, innovation becomes the source of profit by creating a temporary monopoly and by being ahead in the competition. This is also the main significance of 'radical' or 'breakthrough' innovation. Such 'grander' innovation is something that promises a bigger leap ahead and by implication higher profits. But it is also recognized to imply a greater risk of failure than incremental innovation. One aspect of the market perspective on innovation is the risk of disregarding the human and social factors of innovation.

To summarize: innovation must produce something 'new' which has a value and is useful. It should be of a general character and be transferable to other contexts and practices that can exploit its value. Thus innovation implies a striving to objectify a change process and transform it into an exchange value.

I would like to start from what the late Schumpeter calls 'creative response' to conditions. In contrast to adaptive responses as 'expansion within its existing practice', creative responses mean 'doing something else, something that is outside of the range of existing practice' (Schumpeter 1947). The issue of innovativeness seen in this light underlines a central issue in studying live innovation: what is it that makes actors tend to deviate, and to be able to deviate, from established ways of thinking and doing in a way that leads to innovations? Can the partnership organisation play a role in expanding the space for, and creating arenas for, 'doing something else'?

According to Moulaert et al. (2005) there is a broader social view of innovation in Schumpeter. I believe Schumpeter's idea of creative response points to a broader definition of innovation, which includes the development, introduction and institutionalization of new social praxis, where technological processes are one of many possible dimensions of novelty. Novelty is thus something that is moulded in the process of innovation as well as framed in different ways by various actors.

From this point of view, the social character of innovation is obvious. Technical innovation requires simultaneous social innovation processes in order to be workable and attain full efficiency. For example, a new computer technology requires a different social praxis for its production, delivery and use. As Schumpeter recognized, innovation requires the breaking of social habits and customs by entrepreneurs, and at the same time the replacement and sometimes destruction of established praxis. What Schumpeter did not fully appreciate is the amount of social innovation that is part of these processes of change. Often the social innovation has to be made by the users themselves. Already in the 1920s, the sociologist William Ogburn in his studies of innovation recognized that the technical culture changed faster than the social culture, causing cultural lags, disruptions and exclusion. Because the social innovation dimension often cannot be given a market value, it is often not made visible.

There is a lot of innovation, which is predominantly social, e.g. innovation in caring or other social services, in management and organisation, as well as in everyday human practices. The social aspect is the focus of Dropin. One innovative aspect is to organise discussions between professionals and young people in a new way. Another important area of social innovation is to improve the cooperation between local actors working with youths who run the risk of being drop-outs.

In comparison to technological innovation, social innovation can be seen to have relatively more of the following characteristics: (see also Moulaert et al. 2005)

- There is *less information* on its degree of novelty.

- It is more *process-oriented* in the sense of not producing material products, but instead new social praxis.

- It is more *contextual*. It is dependent on how it is enacted in each situation by its performers.

- It is more *actor specific*, and dependent on the experience, skills, interests, values and understanding of the actors.

- It is more *'plastic'* because it can be moulded in different ways. For example a new approach to discussion between a professional and a young person can momentarily be turned in many different ways.

- It is more *enacted* in the sense that is produced and reproduced by skilled actors in an interaction between them.

- It is more *hybridic* in the sense that the new can merge or be moulded together with the old in many ways.

- It is more *normative*, and more explicitly normative, in the sense that it directly involves values and interests, and how to take into account other people. It is also more normative in the sense that it is often governed by social norms of behaviour that may be a constitutive part of the innovation itself.

- It is more *relational*, that is, involves the ways that people interact and relate to each other (see Mumford 2002).

I would also like to add that there is *no inherent goodness* in social innovation. Social innovation can be used for manipulation, exclusion and exploitation as well as for inclusion, liberation and democratization.[1]

The characterization of social innovation presented above has important implications for research and management focused on social innovation.

4.4 Is it innovative – what is the point of the question and how to answer it?

Earlier I presented a quite promising initial overview of how partnerships can contribute to innovation in several respects. But on the other hand, when I interviewed the participants they gave vague answers to questions about innovation and partnership. I think we must start with the fundamental question: What do we mean by innovation? What is our concern? What are we trying to achieve? For whom is the innovation intended?

Besides my own personal interest, a basic point was the aim of the EQUAL-programme, that is to produce something valuable for discriminated groups on the labour market and to get transferable results. Can the conceptual discussion above help us to clarify and explain the uncertainty about social innovation?

First, a main reason for the vague answers in the study is the lack of information about social innovation. Without such information, it is quite difficult to have an opinion about what social innovation is. A consultant to the Swedish Social Fund proposed that novelty reviews should be conducted of the different projects and programmes. The activities in the EU-programmes include instead making study visits to 'interesting' workplaces, consulting experts, taking part in professional networks, and retrieving synthesizing reports on similar work in other contexts. This is often not sufficient to understand what is new in a social innovation. What is new and old in social praxis is difficult to sort out. One example from Dropin is the use of MI, motivational interviewing, which is used in discussions between professionals and young people. How it is used is related to the situation.

The question of novelty is also ambiguous. New in what sense? New in relation to what? New to whom? Without clarification, the question is difficult to answer. Rogers (1995) defines new as a matter of the perception of the adopter. But who is the adopter?

---

1   Moulaert et al. (2005) implicitly assumes that the word social stands for something good.

The issue of the degree of novelty is not only ambiguous, but even meaningless, in the sense that novelty is in the eye of the beholder and something that is developed in the innovation process. The starting point of innovation is, as Schumpeter says, a creative response to conditions by doing something else, something different, compared to established social praxis. At an early stage, the understanding of the character, significance and use of different ideas or practices may be limited. What is new can be recognized in hindsight, from the perspective of a diffusion researcher or historian. But in the actual process, the understanding and distinctiveness of what is new is successively developed in the course of the innovation work. And precisely as with a piece of art, the consumer and user of it has an important, maybe the most important, say on the issue.

Furthermore, the issue of innovation and novelty is largely irrelevant to the people developing something for their own use in a local context. The relevant issue is whether the solution can solve problems and can lead to improvements in their praxis. It is the usefulness and problem-solving capacity that is relevant, not the degree of novelty.

What is seen as something new is often based on how it is presented. In business and on the market, it is common to present something as completely new and much better, often accompanied with simplistic solutions and presented in a pompous language. The novelty of an idea is an important sales argument. But often it turns out to be a case of 'the emperor's new clothes'. On the other hand, newness may be felt as too big a claim for everyday innovations. To claim that something is new has the ring of bragging, so sometimes in the conversation with colleagues, it is felt appropriate to avoid this claim through a side sentence 'this is of course nothing new'.

To be a social innovation, it is not sufficient that the participants see the event or activity as something new. This was clear to the respondents in my study. To be really innovative, it seems that the novelty must be broader than that. On the other hand, the participants in my study had expertise in the area through their earlier experience and co-operation with professionals. So if the changes are new to them, this is an indicator of novelty in a more general sense. But the answer 'this is new to us, and this is enough for us' cannot eliminate the possibility that it is just a local thing, something odd that will not be understood and acknowledged by others.

The answer about novelty can only be 'solved' through a dialogue with other actors, their reception of the idea as well as their use of it. Partnership activity can help to come to terms with the issue of novelty in different ways by providing a forum for a dialogue where the issue of novelty can be assessed, better understood and further developed. It is also important that there are opportunities for interacting with professionals, experts, adopters, and other stakeholders in the process of innovation.

4.5 Innovation processes in Dropin

What is innovative in Dropin? What kind of innovation processes are going on? What kind of innovations are emerging?

What is new is unclear, but it is successively understood and clarified in the process of innovation. Dropin is now in its final phase and the picture is getting clearer. We are now beginning to understand what it has been all about. In my judgment, the main innovation path of Dropin is the emphasis on the development of *social learning for young people*, with a focus on learning capabilities in the participating colleges. In the concept *social learning*, I include learning that give insights and competencies as part of the development and growth of the young people in a wide sense – including employability, interest in further studies and their everyday life situation. Successful social learning requires that the young people themselves learn, but it also requires learning and competence development among the professionals working with the young people. It may also involve the learning and competence development of the social network of the young people, e.g. their parents and friends.

Although the social learning of young people is included in the official goals of the schools, in practice it tends to be awarded secondary status with limited resources. For most young people, social learning takes place 'naturally' in the context of life as part of socialization processes or by trial and error. For some young people, such 'natural' learning processes are insufficient or even a hinder to their social learning. Insufficient social learning is often invisible, until the young people concerned begin to cause problems when they fail to live up to social norms and rules. From the perspective of the young people it is rather a matter of an existential problem that affects their life chances. Another problem is when the young people cannot live up to the achievement standards set in school, or in other social contexts ('academic underachievement'). Often these problems are strongly related and they tend to lead to a third type of problem – unemployment problems.

Social learning among and about young people can take place in many situations, both inside and outside of school. Those young people that run the risk of becoming 'drop outs', often meet a number of local agencies and actors that try to influence and support – and sometimes obstruct – their social learning. I will give some examples of different types of ongoing innovation processes in this partnership.

The focus of innovation is *relational*. The ambition is to improve the relations between professionals and the young people, and between different professional agencies that work with youth issues. In some areas, the innovation work has the character of incremental operational change, as in the development of tight collaboration between local agencies. In others instances, different experiments have been tried, such as student coaching at one of the participating colleges. In one smaller college, a unit focused on young people with special needs has been established. The focus of the innovative work in this unit is on the development of an integrated concept and practice – from the introduction to the point where the young people leave the school. At another college, the innovation focuses on the development of a discussion tool for productive discussions between professionals and young people. Dropin supports the introduction of different social methods – like ART (Agression Replacement Training), MI (Motivational Interviewing), network leadership, and salutogenic health work – through competence development and the application of these methods in the local settings.

Youth coaching is conducted in different forms in all three municipality workshops. At two of the workshops, the basis of the experimentation is giving time – as well as consultation, support, and competence development – for some professionals to have more frequent contacts and communication with a group of Dropin youths. In one case, this entails a method for student coaching at the school. In the other case, the young people being coached have intensified contacts with the social services office. In this case, the ambition is to increase the chances that the young people can mange without support from the social services.

These coaching-oriented projects are both open-ended experiments where the people involved have additional time to search for and to try out new ideas and practices. This open-endedness and experimental freedom may be seen as an aspect of its innovativeness with regard to organising change. What will emerge as 'new' and valuable for improving praxis in the social coaching of young people is not given beforehand, but it will become clear in the course of reflection and evaluation at the end of the project.

Another experimental focus is on the development of an integrated model at a smaller college unit for young people with special needs. The vision is to build supportive environments for the development, growth and learning of the students. This school is receiving young people with more problems than before, implying a need to develop a competence and organization to support these young people. The school organises networks with different supportive environments and organisations. In this way it can expand the opportunities for the students for learning and development. It can also create better opportunities for life after school in relation to finding a place in society and the labour market.

The focus on social development and learning is crucial for this group of young people. This process can involve identity development – a way to 'find themselves', to develop social insights and competencies, to try out different possibilities on the labour market, to grow and hopefully find their preferred and workable roads in life. In the project, an integrated model of working has been developed, including different partial models and tools. An integrated, coordinated and explicit way of working with the young people is seen as a way of achieving quality control.

An advantage in this case is that the school is small with 40 students and 9 professionals, where all teachers are part of the Dropin project. The work is based on a combination of practice and theory. The young people spend three days a week at different workplaces. The ambition is to combine practical experience with more general knowledge. The pedagogical model has been developed step-by-step through discussions and experimentation. It is based on the participants' own ideas as well as methods from external sources. Some ideas were just embryos, but these ideas were supported by the Dropin partnership – like the tripartite dialogue, ART, and Forum play. Through these innovation processes, developed in a partnership context, the model has successively been more clear and specific.

Another area of innovation is new forms of collaboration between local agencies and organizations. The focus here is on solving problems and at the same time developing new forms of co-operation between the organisations involved. The work is not based on a fixed plan, but on finding practical solutions to urgent problems. The organisations are committed to change, but they do not know where to go. The road is invented in the course of the journey, and based on the joint experience gained. In this sense it is an example of embedded innovation that is innovation based on real-life changes in practice. Is this way of organising changes really something new? It is new to the people involved. The value to them is that young people at risk of dropping out is detected early and supportive measure can be undertaken in a co-ordinated way. Is this method new to others? At the moment this is an open question. To answer that question we need to conceptualize what they are doing in a theoretical model to analyse the policy at the local and institutional levels.

Another example of innovation is the tool for discussion between professionals and the young people. Often these young people have to answer the same questions again and again in their meetings with different adults and professionals. Sometimes they want to avoid the discussion altogether by answering 'I don't know'. This is a defence strategy for avoiding negative and blaming discussions. The tool is a simple and flexible computer-based questionnaire. Answers can be given to questions 'in private'. More 'objective' feedback can be given where a young person can compare himself or herself with others. It is possible to focus on what is good, what is working, and also to set targets for their own development. Thus, the discussion tool opens up a less defensive and more productive discussion between professionals and the young people. The tool is at the moment being tested by the school nurses, the young people and some teachers at the school. Is it a new tool? It is highly unlikely that similar practices have not been used in other places. Does this matter? At the moment, the most important thing is to implement the method in the professional-young person discussion in an effective way. The computer software that has been developed is general. Basically, it provides a simple way of presenting the answers individually and for a certain group. Because of the generality of the software it soon occurred to the school nurse that it could be used in other areas, which can lead to a new innovation process.

What is the role of the partnership in the innovation activities? The innovation processes in Dropin are relational. The partners need to change their relations in order to develop something new together. Such changes have occurred between different public organizations. Building new relations with private employers has proved to be more difficult (see Chapter 8). More specific, limited and flexible partnership relations with private companies seem to be more appropriate compared to a joint partnership approach.

In Dropin it is appropriate to distinguish between the regional and local levels of the partnership organizations taking part. At the regional level, the partnership co-operation is focused on managing the whole project and creating links and exchanges with external actors (like the transnational partners). It is a way of acquiring new ideas and experience and of connecting to national organisations, other regions, and other partnerships. In the final stage, an important task is the dissemination of experience and innovations, and to influence political and legal structures.

At the local level, the partnership relations involve three municipalities, which are conducting the practical experiments. The partnership organisation is useful in developing personal bonds, producing mutual knowledge and combining different resources in an innovative way to create new solutions. The main objective at the local level is better integration and collaboration between the different organizations. There are indications that fewer young people are now coming to the social services office to get financial support, which can be an effect of improved social learning at the schools and better co-operation between different organisations at the local level.

4.6 Modelling social innovation and partnership

The data from Dropin provides a point of departure for clarifying social innovation in a partnership context. Innovation is all about change as Tidd et al. (2001) say, but it is not only about change. It is also about novelty. To intentionally produce change by introducing something new is the specific feature of innovation. A core point for the growing interest in innovation is that what is invented can be transferred to and used in other contexts. Innovation – in comparison to change – is more focused on developing and disseminating something new. Innovation must include a learning component. In this way, what is new can be extracted and generalized from the individual cases, which is a necessity for a dissemination process.

Figure 1 tries to conceptualize the character of social innovation processes and indicate its relation to partnership organization. On the basis of my earlier work on organizational development and innovation in the Scandinavian tradition (Lindhult 2005), I synthesized the first upper-left circle of innovation, specifying basic activities and dimensions of innovation processes – tension, interaction, experimentation, and integration. This is based on an *interactive view* of innovation where the new is something that is locally constructed in each organizational setting based on both internal and external interaction and communication. Imitation in the sense of applying general organizational models in local praxis seldom works. Instead, innovation is seen as a matter of the development and reconstruction of the local theory of each organizational setting, where general elements – ideas, methods, rules – can be important combined with local knowledge. An interactive view is more praxis oriented in the sense of starting from ongoing activities and existing resources that can be mobilized and improved through experimentation and interaction.

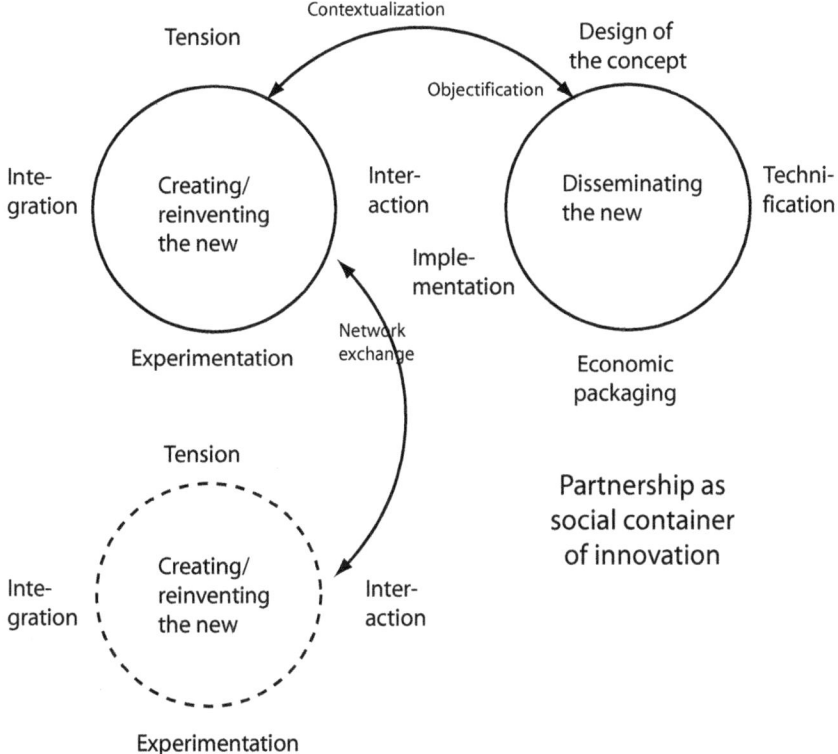

Figure 1. Social innovation and the partnership model.

The upper-right circle is more appropriate for an *objectified view* of innovations. Object-oriented views on innovation start from the assumption that innovations can be objectified, decontextualized, generalized and disseminated. This second circle tries to capture the innovation activities when the new is objectified and disseminated in a broader context. A first step is the *design* of the concept in order to articulate, visualize, formulate and synthesize the core aspects of the new element. Another activity is specifying the *how* issue, that is, a *technification* of the new element. It is important to specify the practice in terms of methods, procedures and routines. Without specified practices synthesized from the working knowledge of practitioners, it cannot be disconnected from skilled individuals and their tacit knowledge.

A third activity is *packaging*, particularly economic packaging. This can be done using handbooks, training programmes, the specification of roles and responsibilities or market offerings of products and services. Reproducing the new in other contexts requires resources as well as the clarification of interests and agents that can carry on the innovation processes. Often, consultants are the carriers of innovations in a market context.

There is also a phase of *implementation* when the new element is assimilated in a new context, which often implies adaptation and reinvention. An important aspect of innovation in Dropin has been the support from experts in the implementation of different social methodologies (e.g. ART, motivational techniques, network leadership, tri-party dialogue, COPE). An adaptive capacity and local-reconstruction capability are important in this phase. The Dropin partnership has been a vehicle for such dissemination-oriented innovation processes.

The different circles interact when the innovation processes are objectified and decontextualized. A more generalized object can be more broadly disseminated, but in the implementation phase it needs to be recontextualized and often reinvented in the local setting. Reinvention is a process where the new element is changed or modified by the user in the process of adoption and implementation (Rogers 1995, p. 174). The active role of the user in the implementation (von Hippel 2005) also makes the user a producer of innovation.

Social innovations can also be objectified, like ART or MI, and then both be technified and 'economisised'. But social innovations are more difficult to objectify. Instead, a more interactive logic of innovation must be used because the new is difficult to decontextualize and integrate in a specific context. Then the dissemination of the innovation more takes the character of network exchange between innovating units, e.g. through study visits. The objectification of the local innovations in Dropin is as yet unclear, but would make dissemination easier.

How is partnership organization related to social innovation? There are several ways that a partnership can support social innovation. I do not think that this support can be condensed into one comprehensive model. Instead, I will use the complexity concept from Dal Fiore (2007) that I believe is fruitful and can capture some important features of Dropin. Dal Fiore distinguishes and compares communities and networks as 'social containers of innovation'. 'The container' may be a somewhat too restrictive physical metaphor. 'Organizing context' may be preferable, although I will here use Dal Fiore's concept. He conceptualizes communities and networks as two extremes on a continuum of social containers for innovation. Communities, at one end, are based on common obligations and a collective identity where communication is a centripetal force. Networks, at the other end of the continuum, are more open ended and can be exploited by actors for individualistic purposes. In networks, communication is more divergent and centrifugal 'and ends up bridging different universes of meaning to generate new paths of meaning' (ibid. p. 860). Partnerships can be seen as a form of organisation closer to the community end.

What is the connection to innovation in this model? Del Fiore sees networks as places for boundary-crossing learning and thus for radical and breakthrough innovations, whereas communities further more specialization-based and linear innovation. In the adoption phase, on the other hand, incremental innovation needs networks (horizontal communication) to be propagated, while 'combinatorial' innovation needs a community (vertical communication) to become a socially rooted practice. So both these types of social containers for innovation are needed.

An interesting finding is that the regional dimension of the Dropin partnership has functioned like a network for boundary-crossing learning. The locally-based dimension of the Dropin partnership has worked in a more community-like way as a space for belongingness, and has been used for more specialized and incremental innovations. The understanding of innovation as 'radical' and 'breakthrough' may be difficult to pinpoint at this stage in Dropin, and may be a more problematic category in the social area. There are some indications of combinatorial innovation in Dropin. Also here, combinatorial innovation may have a different character in the social area.

4.7 Concluding remarks

Innovativeness is important in partnerships that want to be of broader significance. Producing innovation is one way for partnerships to have societal relevance in the sense of offering something new and valuable that others can adopt. But the understanding of social innovation, as well as its connection to partnerships, is unclear. Based on a critical conceptual discussion of the social dimension of innovation, and experience from the EQUAL partnership Dropin, this chapter has made an effort to clarify these issues.

An object-oriented versus an interactively-oriented perspective on innovation has been applied and two models have been presented to clarify these different perspectives. I hope that the models can provide a point of departure for further research both on social innovation and on the innovative potentials of the partnership organisation. It can be assumed that partnerships are more crucial in cases of innovation that are more social in nature, more relational, more systemic and more structural in the sense of requiring structural change. Both more theoretical and empirical research is needed to further clarify these issues.

References

Dal Fiore, F (2007) 'Communities Versus Networks: The Implications on Innovation and Social Change'. *American Behavioral Scientist* Vol. 50, No. 7, pp. 857–866

von Hippel, E (2005) *Democratizing Innovation*. Cambridge, MA: MIT Press

Lindhult, E (2005) *Management by Freedom. Essays in moving from Machiavellian to Rousseauian approaches to innovation and inquiry*. Stockholm: Doctoral Thesis in Industrial Economics and management, Royal Institute of Technology

Moulaert, F, Martinelli, F, Swyngedouw, E & González, S (2005) 'Towards Alternative Model(s) of Local Innovation'. *Urban Studies*, Vol. 42, No 11 pp. 1969–1990

Mumford, M (2002) 'Social innovation: ten cases from Benjamin Franklin'. *Creativity Research Journal*, Vol. 14, No. 2, pp. 253–266

Rogers, E (1995) *Diffusion of Innovation*. 4th ed. New York: The Free Press

Schumpeter, J (1947) 'The Creative Response in Economic History'. *Journal of Economic History*, Nov. pp. 149–159

Tidd, J, Bessant, J & Pavitt, K (2001) *Managing Innovation. Integrating Technological, Market and Organizational Change*. 2nd ed. Chichester: John Wiley & Sons Ltd

5. Partnership for Sustainable Work Environment Development

5.1 Introduction

What characterises a successful partnership and how is this kind of co-operation organised? A description is given here of a collaboration project that succeeded in solving a complex work environment problem in an entire sector. The partnership started in the brewery sector in 1994 and has been conducted since 2000 in collaboration between the trade association and the trade union that represents the drivers. The breweries have organised a work environment programme that consists of a steering group and regional networks in which all the occupational groups involved participate. As a result of this collaboration, the brewery drivers now enjoy a improved work environment. The collaboration of the breweries in the steering group is analysed on the basis of theories concerning partnership, but the interaction with the regional networks is regarded as being a decisive success factor.

The chapter begins with two short sections on background and method. In three more detailed sections we shed light on the owners' involvement, the forms for collaboration between the partners and the importance of external specialist support. This is followed by a summary of the results and conclusions.

5.1.1 Background

A partnership was started in the brewery sector in 1994 and this collaboration still exists. The brewery sector consists of relatively few players and a joint trade association.¹ The activities of the partnership are described here as an establishment phase (Phase 1) with external support (1994–99) and a Phase 2 in which the breweries conducted their development under their own auspices (from 2000 onwards). An evaluation was made after the sector took over responsibility for the development work entirely.

Arbets- och miljömedicin (Department of Occupational and Environmental Health)² took the initiative for the partnership when research showed a clear connection between the poor working environment of the drivers and ill-health. The problems appeared in the form of high sick-listing levels and a greater risk of early retirement as a result of problems with the neck, shoulders, back and knees. The problems also led to many drivers changing jobs (Stockholm County Council 1994). A questionnaire showed that principal work environment problems experienced by the brewery drivers were deliveries to goods reception points and steps at restaurants.

Wheeling brewery products up steps can involve lifts of up to 170 kg. At the photo there is 70 kg on the trolley.

1   *Sveriges bryggerier* (Swedish Breweries) is a trade association for the brewery sector that has been in existence for over 100 years. The organisation represents 20 breweries, which together produce some 90 per cent of the total volume in the country.
2   *Arbets- och miljömedicin* is part of the Centre for Public Health *(Centrum för folkhälsa)* within Stockholm County Council and is tasked with promoting public health in the county of Stockholm.

The members of the partnership were the breweries' trade association, the drivers' trade union and Occupational and Environmental Health (OEH). The project was financed by *AFA Försäkring*[3] and by the four largest breweries. The work was directed by a project group consisting of a human resources specialist from OEH, a driver actively involved in the trade union (a safety officer), a distribution manager and one of the trade association's managers.

It took a long time to build up effective co-operation within the partnership. It was gradually recognised that the work environment issues had to be linked to the operations and the work organisation. The work was formalised into regional networks. These consisted of representatives from all the occupational groups that were concerned with deliveries to restaurants, such as distribution managers, drivers and sales staff.

One concrete result of the co-operation was a national delivery standard 1999 that covered the entire sector: No deliveries stairs with more than five steps. This has subsequently been further developed on the basis of new requirements. The delivery standard resulted in the fact that a majority of those customers who were affected by the standard improved their goods reception facilities by conversion, installing lifts, hoists, ramps or other measures. In all, some 1 500 goods reception points were modified throughout the country, half of which were located in Stockholm.

The changes led to savings in costs for the breweries in the form of reduced sick leave and lower manning levels as a result of faster deliveries. At one of the breweries, short-term sick leave among drivers was almost halved following introduction of the delivery standard (from 6.9 per cent to 3.7 per cent). The drivers benefited in terms of an improved working environment as well as better health. In a follow-up questionnaire survey conducted five years later, (2004) it was confirmed that the changes had to a significant extent contributed towards reduced physical strain for the drivers with less problems associated with the shoulders, arms and back.

> We have eliminated one of the biggest delivery problems, have healthier drivers and have changed their attitude to the possibilities of improving the work environment. First of all they said: 'This is impossible!' Now they are saying: 'Can you fix this too?' I often meet drivers who say that the project has meant that they can stay in the brewery industry. (Project Manager, Phase 1 and Phase 2)

---

3   An insurance company tasked with administering contract insurances between labour market parties that are regulated in collective agreements

5.1.2 Method

Our chapter is based on empirical data that has been gathered by various methods over a long period of time (ten years), which can be regarded as a strength.

OEH participated in various ways in the different phases of the development work:

- Phase 1 (1994–1999): Active participation as an intervener/project manager (Målqvist).
- Phase 2 (2002–04): Evaluation with a focus on whether the process resulted in a sustainable development of the work environment activities (Parmsund).

The intervention in Phase 1 was based on action research theory (Gustavsen 1992). It included a close cooperation and a dialogue-based interaction with the participants during a long period. The researchers contribute mainly with strategic competence in change management.

The data collection in Phase 1 took place largely using the following qualitative methods:

- journal notes
- interviews with key individuals (five) at the breweries on two occasions (with the help of an external interviewer)
- interviews with project leaders and key individuals (six) at the trade association and from two breweries (external interviewers)
- interviews with 35 drivers six months after the new delivery standard had been introduced on how they experienced the changes in their work environment (external interviewers)
- continuous follow-up on how customers (restaurants) that were affected by the delivery standard had decided to solve their goods reception situation.

In addition, work environment questionnaire surveys were conducted on three occasions. The questionnaires were answered by drivers, above all in Stockholm in 1994 (78 per cent response frequency) and 1999 (i.e. six months after introduction of the delivery standard). The same questions were posed in 2004 to drivers from all over the country within the framework of the evaluation. This later questionnaire was supplemented by a series of open questions. The total response frequency was 61 per cent, but varied considerably both between regions and between breweries.

The evaluation in Phase 2 included the following:

- observations made at 35 meetings in five networks over a period of two years
- interviews with nine representatives of different occupations with experience of the first regional network that was started
- informal discussions with the project manager in which his reflections on his work and work situation emerged
- recurring informal discussions with the person who was the intervener/project manager during Phase 1.

Since the evaluation had an interactive element, the trade association steering group was also used as a reference group during the evaluation period. The evaluator took part in ten meetings of this type at which the evaluation was given a firm foundation and information was given on it. After this, the evaluator also asked a series of critical questions on the project, which led to discussion among the steering group participants. It can be claimed that these meetings with the steering group and subsequent feedback with a group of drivers who were active trade union members and network participants increased the validity of the results (c.f. Askerøi 2006).

5.2   Owners' involvement and driving forces

Research has shown that involvement on the part of the owners is important for the implementation of changes, which result in long-term effects in an organisation (Svensson & Jakobsson 2008). Here, the driving forces that were behind the owners' involvement in the project phases are described and analysed.

5.2.1   Phase 1

In the mid-1990s, the trade association was interested in working on work environment issues in order to strengthen their position among the member companies. Those responsible also saw the possibility of reducing the costs of sick leave and increasing the efficiency of the sector through the project.

The owners' involvement was expressed in a number of ways. The trade association's technical director played an active role in the project management and was the driving force behind the implementation of the common sector delivery standard on behalf of the Board. The individual breweries financed training in the project and participated in the steering group and the regional networks. In this way, the owners gave legitimacy to the partnership. The involvement was facilitated by the fact that the number of players on the market was few in comparison with other sectors. The improvement work became in this way competitively neutral between the breweries. There was also an individual involvement on the part of two of the leading managers.

The structure of the development work gradually became clear and distinct. Formally, the work was organised through different co-operation groups. The technical director was the chairman in all groups, a clear way for the employers to determine ownership. The trade association also had control over all resources (except for the salaries of the two project managers, which were financed externally) and over the communication channels out to the breweries.

The decisions during the development work were made in different ways in different stages of the process. Initially, the employers (distribution managers) and the two project managers co-operated with each other. The employers determined the goal and presented project plans and time schedules. After two years' work by the project managers on creating a firm foundation for the programme, the new delivery standard could be introduced. Thorough preparatory work meant that the actual introduction was completed quickly and basically without problems. The goal of implementing and maintaining the 'five stages' of the delivery standard was concrete and easy to measure in terms of the number of reported and improved goods reception facilities. The standard was based on a well-known and accepted principle within the breweries, namely the common pay system for drivers.

5.2.2 *Phase 2*

From 2000 onwards, the composition of the partnership was changed when OEH handed over the project entirely to the trade association. It then employed the internal project manager from Phase 1 as the only project manager. The project manager worked directly under the technical director. The latter was the chairman of the steering group and responsible for getting support and backing for the decisions of the steering group from the board of the trade association, to which he regularly submitted reports on the project.

The members of the steering group (heads of distribution and logistics) remained in several cases entirely passive until acute problems arose, which were then remedied. The administrative strain on the project manager was not relieved until he announced that he was to leave his post within a few months. When the project manager vacated his post, the steering group took greater responsibility for the partnership, which among other things resulted in a clearer structure for meetings and a better follow-up of decisions.

5.2.3 Conclusions on the owners' commitment and driving forces

According to Caplan and Scott (see Chapter 3), one reason for forming a partnership could be to share the risks in the venture. In this development project, the employers were the principal risk-takers. It is a difficult business creating agreement and trust in work environment issues *between* different private players, especially if there is a risk of the venture concerned having a negative impact on the financial result. This was also one of the reasons for the subordinate standing of the interveners and safety officers in the introductory stage. Inconvenient demands were made of the customers and an individual brewery could lose revenue unless all of the breweries adopted and observed the new delivery standard. The employers' only guarantee was their trust in each other, or in other words that they would all make the same demands and that no-one would use the agreements in the partnership to their own competitive advantage.

In this context, the responsibility of the employers meant that they had the primary right to determine what should be defined as a work environment problem, the right to decide on the limits in the activities the partnership carried out on work environment and the right to decide on the goal of the work environment work. Furthermore, they had the resources within their companies (through developed channels of communication, the right to give directives to subordinate managers and employees, and the right to make man-hours available) to implement and establish the intentions in the steering group. This meant that the project either lived or died with the commitment of the employers.

One important explanation for the successful outcome is the way in which the various players co-operated. In this 'partnership', it was the employers who were really able to implement the desired changes, but they needed the support of the interveners and the union representatives – for example in the form of the external resources and the change management expertise that they contributed, as well as the occupational expertise of the trade union representatives. Since the interveners recognised the necessity of their subordinate positions and the need for a non-confrontational approach at the initial stage in order to achieve a co-operative situation, a platform of trust was created which became the starting point for the partnership. The employers allowed the interveners and the trade union representatives to enter arenas which from the beginning they had no access to (in co-operation with the board of the trade association, at meetings with managers and sales staff at the breweries as well as with customers). This accord behind the project gave legitimacy to change standards, routines and behaviour towards these different groups, which it would otherwise have been impossible to achieve.

Another important explanation for the success of the project is the strong management exercised by the trade association in the introductory stage of the partnership, something that was decisive in persuading all the breweries and all the occupational groups (including the managing directors) to accept the decision to make the external work environment competitively neutral and to introduce a new delivery standard.

5.3 Partnership

The relationship between employers and employees is regulated on the Swedish labour market since 1977 in the Co-determination Act, in which employees are given a regulated influence over various management issues. The employees can demand information and negotiations on such issues. The Work Environment Act requires the employers to take responsibility for a good work environment. In this project, there was co-operation between employers and employees on grounds other than employees citing the legislation, and when an agreement was reached on the establishment of co-operation there was no negotiation situation, but instead a common learning process began (Målqvist 2003, 2005). This is described and analysed in the following section.

5.3.1 New forms of co-operation

In the project, a new form of co-operation was developed between employers, employee/union representatives and OEH's interveners. One reason for the employers to agree to a partnership was to comply with demands from the Work Environment Inspectorate, which required the four largest breweries to improve the drivers' work environment. The interveners negotiated with the employers for eighteen months before co-operation could be initiated and argued that local trade union representatives should be allowed to take part. To begin with, these were only allowed to serve as a reference group. Gradually, the trade union representatives were permitted to participate in the co-operation meetings together with the employers and the interveners based on the argument that it was unnecessary to have duplicate meetings. An element of trust had been generated.

Once the decision on the brewery sector's new delivery standard had been made, a process was started to get support and backing for the concept in the breweries. The participants in the steering group recognised that the sales staff – the occupational group that has first contact with new customers – had so far been left out of the discussions on how the delivery standard should be implemented. The steering group decided that from that point on the sales staff would be given responsibility for informing the customers about the delivery standard and checking whether goods reception areas complied with the delivery standard.

The project management realised that it would be difficult to change the duties of the sales staff simply by making decisions and issuing orders. It therefore became necessary to find scientific and pedagogical methods, which were base on participation and learning, in order to persuade the sales staff to accept something that was totally against their culture, namely to make demands of the customers. Gradually, a number of efforts were made to motivate the sales staff and their managers for the new duties. One feature was a form of problem-based training, which was provided for 600 senior managers, sales personnel, distribution managers and drivers in several parts of the country. In order to increase the level of understanding for the drivers' work situation, sales staff and senior management were asked to pull a two-wheeled barrow with three beer kegs (120 kg) up a flight of steps. This proved to be almost impossible for anyone who lacked the necessary experience. The feature became a competitive event that fitted into the male culture that existed among the sales staff. Attempting to perform a physical task under maximum strain creates a stronger impression than a set of information on loads and health risks. Another way of increasing the sellers' motivation was the argument that the new delivery standard would create profitability in the long term for the breweries as a result of rationalisation and lower sick-leave levels. As far as the sales staffs were concerned it would mean that they worked in a preventive way on cost saving in the long term. A third way was that the sales staff, if they encountered problems with the customer, could transfer responsibility to the distribution manager who would then handle continued contact with the customer. If a driver felt that a member of the sales staff had not informed the customer of the new delivery standard, he took over the task himself.

During Phase 1, the project also supported technical development since there was a lack of hoists on the market that could cope with the transport of heavy goods in staircases and flights of steps. Many customers received help from project managers and/or network participants to find practical solutions, which led to a better work environment at goods reception points.

5.3.2 A functioning organisation

In order to achieve sustainable results, constant reflection is needed on how the development work is to be organised (Argyris & Schön 1995). Within the project, the organisation changed shape depending on the needs that arose during the course of the process. The regional networks became an important base for the implementation of the delivery standard and contained representatives of the various occupational groups concerned. The networks had the following tasks:

- common problem solving
- monitoring to make sure that all breweries followed the delivery standard
- checking that all breweries implemented the necessary measures
- making sure there was a common policy in relation to the requirements and views of customers
- following up the measures.

During Phase 1, the network in Stockholm was led formally by the technical director of the trade association, but it was organised and followed up by the project managers. In the rest of the country, the networks were directed by distribution managers, who were either personally involved in the matter or were requested by the trade association to assume responsibility for it. These worked with no special support from the project managers. Only the network in Stockholm continued beyond 1999.

During Phase 2, a permanent work environment organisation was set up for the entire brewery sector. Under the Board of the trade association (which was made up of members from the management groups in the breweries) a national steering group was set up (consisting of the national distribution managers from the largest breweries, a trade union representative and the project manager). Each network has someone who is responsible for reporting to the steering group. The project is in other words built up on the basis of an organised form of co-operation on several levels (see Figure 1).

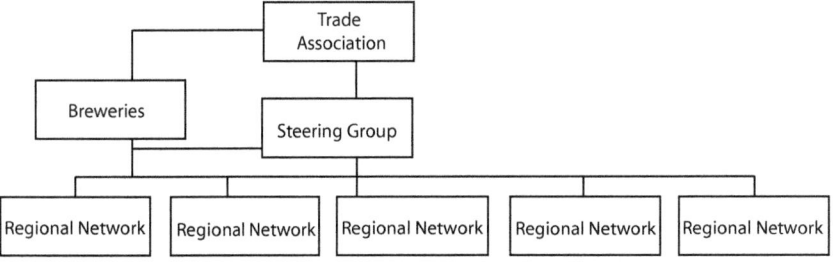

Figure 1. Organisation chart for the work environment organisation in the brewery sector (Phase 2).

The trade association decided that four new regional networks should be started in order to arrive at a uniform assessment of how the delivery standard should be applied. The evaluation conducted five years after the standard was introduced showed that the composition and commitment of the networks differed. One important factor governing the degree of commitment was the extent to which the delivery conditions were experienced as being a major problem or not among the breweries in the respective regions. Most occupational groups and companies took part in the metropolitan region networks, where the problem of transportation in cramped areas was greatest.

During Phase 2, the project manager had in practice the task of individually directing the work on implementing the delivery standard and serving as the sector expert in connection with the design of goods reception areas, interpretation of legislation and so on. The project manager often felt weighed down by the burden of work, and described his situation as follows:

> My role has grown all the time. It is a weakness of the project that so many people are dependent on me. I am the motor in the whole project and am expected to do everything. They are active out in the companies and come to the meetings with questions and discussion material, but they have not done that much to help in the meantime. I'm the one who has to inspect restaurants, meet The Work Environment Authority4 (WEA) and property owners, produce technical solutions and run the network meetings all over the country.

A project manager cannot do more than the organisation and resources he has permits him to do, but he could have asked the steering group to take more responsibility for activating the networks.

4   The Swedish authority for work environment issues.

5.3.3 Conclusions on collaboration

Can it be claimed that the collaboration that existed within the project and the steering group was a partnership? Based on the overall definition of partnership given in this book – in other words a collaboration that results in benefits for all parties, horizontal decision-making and a process-oriented approach – we are of the opinion that it was.

The collaboration that is described in this chapter is relatively complicated – with different organisations and players involved – which proved to be necessary in order to change the work environment and create long-term effects. What was it in the collaboration model that made it so successful? Some of the more important explanations are:

- Pressure from WEA made the employers open for suggestions from the interveners and the union representatives
- A clear and common goal with established deadlines for different measures
- A clear division of power and responsibility in the project organisation.
- A joint undertaking between employers and the union.

Together, the above factors contributed towards an action-oriented partnership. Activities were carried out which improved the work environment for the drivers. Concrete problems were solved by means of systematic efforts. We intend to take a closer look at the various explanations.

5.3.3.1 A joint undertaking

As with networks, (Moreno 1934, Kilmann 1977) a partnership is usually defined on the basis of a voluntary undertaking. The collaboration in this project was based on the fact that three parties made a voluntary agreement, but meant in practice that a number of companies and employees were obliged to participate in making sure that the goal was achieved. We are of the opinion that this collaboration is closer to the concept of joint venture, since representatives of the various occupational groups were enjoined to take part.

The trade union could have cited the Co-determination Act and the Work Environment Act to demanded collaboration. This, however, would probably have generated a sense of opposition and distrust, i.e. a negotiation situation would have arisen instead of co-operation. In Phase 1, the project management invested a considerable amount of effort in motivating the sales staff, since these could otherwise have made it more difficult to achieve the goal. The horizontal decision-making in the networks was subordinate to the decisions of the steering group and the Board of the trade association, and was therefore at the tactical and operational level. During Phase 1, the partnership had a process-oriented approach and an organisation that changed depending on the phase that the project was in. In this way, it is possible to talk about learning in the development work.

In general, the purpose of a partnership is not to exist on a permanent basis; instead, the work shall be gradually institutionalised (see Chapter 3). The breweries and the trade union also created a permanent work environment organisation for the entire sector once the intervener withdrew (Phase 2 see figure 1). In this respect, it is possible to talk about sustainable development work with long-term effects.

In their original sense, networks are based on voluntary participation, which means that it should be mutually rewarding and developmental for the participants and their organisations to take part. (Moreno 1934, Kilmann 1977). One critical success factor in the project was that it was based on a 'win-win' situation. In other words, all three parties would regard themselves as winners if the goal was achieved (Banke & Holsbo 2002). The distribution managers had the chance to work preventively with the drivers' work environment and in this way avoided having so many injured or worn-out drivers, which would otherwise have led to increased costs and requests for relocation. The drivers' union representatives could prevent injuries for themselves and their colleagues. The sales staff contributed towards an improved work environment and higher profits in their companies. The fact that each network participant can thus actually see opportunities for reward (preventive work) and development (mutual learning) places demands on the ability of the steering group and the trade association to provide support and motivation (Målqvist 2005, Parmsund 2006).

Access to time and resources is a necessary precondition for being able to become involved in a development-oriented network (Svensson & Jakobsson 2008). The decision on the introduction of a new delivery standard was founded at the highest level within the largest breweries. As a result, no major problems were encountered when it came to releasing employees and managers to take part in training or network activities (Parmsund 2006).

5.3.3.2 *A clear and common goal*

There are often hidden agendas associated with the common goal in a partnership (see Chapter 3). Researchers and union representatives were worried that the employers might have a hidden agenda, for example that the new delivery standard would mean that the drivers were forced to cope with more deliveries per day. However, an assessment was made that this would be better from the work environment point of view compared with heavy deliveries via steps and stairs. During the negotiation stage, the employers were worried that the researchers might have had a hidden agenda. They could have alleviated this concern by openly stating that their intention was to test a change method, not to favour or take a stand in support of a certain party in the development work.

The potential for attracting joint and strong support for a goal is undermined if there is imbalance in the partnership in terms of status. If the balance of power is uneven, the common goal formulation is of decisive importance. In our opinion, it is important to have as concrete and clearly defined a goal as possible when there are several parties involved. There shall be as little scope for interpretation as possible, and at the same time it must be possible to satisfy the individual interests of each party by means of the goal (see Chapter 13). If the goal is concrete in nature and has been reached in agreement, it increases the chances of achieving an action-oriented partnership rather than one, which becomes bogged down in a discussion phase. The next question is of course how the goal is to be achieved, i.e. an overall action plan is required, including a deadline. Our results show that it is important not to exercise detailed control but rather to allow the process to reveal the questions that need to be put on the agenda. The goal should also be realistic and measurable for the sake of follow-up. The project that we studied shows that very careful goal formulation is needed in order for a partnership to have a sustainable outcome.

Within a partnership, there is seldom agreement on how the goal for the collaboration is to be achieved (see Chapter 3), as different participants have different perspectives. Since neither researchers nor drivers in this project had specific demands or solutions, the development work was based on the actual situation in the brewery sector. Once the goal formulation was clear, there were only constructive discussions and full agreement was reached on the best way to approach the process of making changes. The Work Environment Authority which took part in a reference group, allowed the trade association to decide which work environment demands should be imposed on the customers.

5.3.3.3 *A clear division of power and responsibility in the project organisation*

When we examine the power perspective of the collaboration, we can see that the employers had the greatest power since they had the authority that was needed, the right to make decisions and the resources for the development work. According to Swedish legislation, it is the employers who have principal responsibility for the work environment, but also the right to direct and allocate the work. Consequently, the employers had both the responsibility for the drivers' work environment as well as the power to say yes or no to improving it. There was thus no dilemma as regards responsibility, which can be a problem in partnerships where the relationships are more equitable.

The uneven distribution of power meant that the interveners had to subordinate themselves to the employers' primary right of interpretation without violating their scientific and ethical principles. They accepted this subordination since the employers were anyway taking the main risks and meeting the costs of the project. Nevertheless, the researchers still had an interest in being able to influence the employers' arguments and attitudes, which required great tactical and strategic expertise on their part. In order to strike this balance and not need to withdraw from the project because of the uneven division of power, it was important for the researchers to be able to see the purpose of the partnership from the employers' point of view and to express their understanding for their underlying driving forces. In order to achieve collaboration, it was also important that the employers did not experience any sense of opposition, either to the interveners or to the drivers' union representatives. The drivers' safety officer found himself in the same subordinate position as the interveners when he endeavoured to develop some form of joint action between the employers in order to make the work environment activities competitively neutral.

If the participants find themselves to be at approximately the same organisational level, the chances of them being able to participate as equal parties in the network increase (Svensson & Jakobsson 2008). In this partnership, there were clear-cut own interests and an uneven division of power, among other things because the participants were on different organisational levels within the breweries. Socioeconomic affiliation and level of education also influence the power relations in a partnership (Chapter 3). These preconditions – particularly if there is an ambition for the empowerment of subordinate participants – indicate the risk of built-in conflicts in a partnership. Therefore, it was a challenge to the interveners to establish credibility in the eyes of the sector and its customers both through their actions and their language. Prior to the evaluation of the brewery project, a leading distribution manager took up the fact that he had misgivings about working with academics because of their high level of abstraction and theoretical language.

Participation in a partnership can be graded into four levels of influence (Stott & Keatman 2005):

1) to be informed
2) to be consulted (to take part in discussions, have the opportunity to express your opinions and provide feedback)
3) to have the chance to exert influence (to participate directly in decision-making and have the right to vote)
4) to have control (to initiate or lead activities).

The partnership began to take shape after two years of stiff negotiation. At the time, the trade union representatives were on Level 1 (were informed), since to begin with they did not take part directly in the collaboration work, while the researchers were on Level 2 (were consulted). Once the union representatives had joined the partnership and the project managers had been appointed, both the trade union and the researchers could work at Level 3 (had the chance to exert influence) and Level 4 (with control over certain activities) (Stott & Keatman 2005).

The drivers, who were the target group for the actual change management work, were the group who had the least influence over the stages prior to the introduction of the delivery standard. Afterwards, the drivers' reports on how the customers had reacted to the new delivery standard and whether or not they felt the new routines obstructed efficient goods handling were needed.

The interveners worked strategically on the drivers' participation and influence before the delivery standard was introduced in order to create an empowerment process that motivated the drivers to take the responsibility vested in them in the project. According to Caplan & Scott (Chapter 3), continuous follow-up is needed to see what the representation of the parties looks like – both on an organisational and an individual level – where the exercise of power is reviewed. This conclusion correlates well with our experience, which indicates the necessity of continuous support to the 'weaker' party. This process is still in existence (spring 2007) in the form of a supporting network between researchers and the drivers' union representatives from the regional networks.

In one of the networks, a sense of equality eventually arose between the parties despite the organisational inequality that existed between them. The drivers' union representatives were allowed to play the role that their knowledge of the work conditions, activities and goods reception facilities justified. This led to an increase in their status in the network, in which the representative of the trade association and several distribution managers also work. In time, one of the union representatives was appointed network manager.

During Phase 2, it was possible to discern disagreement in the steering group for the permanent work environment organisation. There is no disagreement between the employers and safety officers, only between employers about which new delivery standards are to be introduced, or in other words what demands can be made on the customers in order to create a good work environment for the drivers. This disagreement became apparent, for example, when a decision that was taken on a new delivery standard was subsequently reversed.

According to Shuell (1986) we remember considerably better what we have done compared to what we have read or heard. The purpose of allowing managers and sales staff to try wheeling beer barrels up a flight of steps was to try and create an inner motivation among those who could not directly see any individual benefit from taking part in a partnership. It represented an attempt to create an insight into the problem and group pressure on the subject by means of an emotional experience.

The 'power factors' of all the parties – i.e. the employers' resources and communication channels, the interveners' change management skills and external funds and the drivers' vocational skills – interacted in a fruitful way during the course of the process. With common resources, the parties were able to bring about changes that they would not have been able to achieve on their own.

5.3.3.4 Course of action

The goal set for the collaboration – the common sector delivery standard – meant that an entire sector was expected to change its behaviour on the basis of the goal and it proved to be very important to stick to this goal. The project thus had a clear course of action and it was the effort to achieve practical results that was the basis of the collaboration, both in the steering group as well as in the network.

This course of action did not mean that the project was driven by a clear planning logic. Instead, it was based on a process-oriented approach that was founded on a dialogue and learning from acquired experience. The strategic thinking was found in the steering group, whereas the practical work was organised in the network.

In order to achieve results, formal rules were used in combination with informal problem solving. The partnership acted within the rules and regulations that exist within the Swedish work environment area and referred to Swedish work environment legislation in relation to its customers, but the actual co-operation was unregulated. Extensive involvement on the part of the three parties was necessary, it became a constant task for the project managers to make sure that all the managers concerned (and sales staff) actually performed their appointed duties. The regulations served more as a means of support and a precondition than a driving force for change.

Our three most important explanations as to why the project was successful in producing concrete results are as follows:

1. the breweries' trade association served as a 'council of administration' and in this way neutralised the competitive factor in the work environment area and took a central decision on joining a common undertaking with researchers and the trade union
2. the fact that the individual interests were accommodated within the goal formulation and that there was no scope for different interpretations
3. that the division of power was known and that the independent party (the interveners) saw the importance of supporting the most vulnerable group.

5.4 External support

In order for development-oriented learning to take place in the network and the partnership, a stable platform is required with external support as an important precondition (Svensson & Jakobsson 2008). The external support in the project was designed as an intervention with a focus on solving work environment problems. The ambition was, in a latter stage, to generate research theory on the basis of the experience.

Initially, the interveners judged that it was possible to create a platform for a functioning partnership, but it became apparent that this required a lot of support on the part of the project managers to managers, customers and sales staff throughout the entire build-up stage. Phase 1 was run in project form with the two project managers who worked at OEH and were formally 'external' in relation to the brewery sector. One of the project managers was a driver who was active in the trade union and had many years' experience of the organisation and operations of the sector. The other project manager was an academic with knowledge of change management, the importance of involvement and the systematisation of a development project. The daily co-operation between the project managers contributed towards mutual learning, which was useful for the change management work and created credibility in relation to the participants and the brewery customers. The unconventional approach with one external and one internal project manager was a basic cornerstone for the successful change management work (Målqvist 2003).

The brewery sector participants were used to working on the basis of a 'top-down' strategy and this characterised the thinking of both the employers and the employees. One of the external project manager's contributions was to introduce ideas on the value of a 'bottom-up and collaboration' strategy which was based on participation and learning. The result was a combination of strategies that placed the emphasis on all three perspectives – planning, activating and networking – but with different focuses depending on where in the process the development work was located. The combination of strategies provided scope for directives, a high degree of participation, follow-up and – not least – mutual learning.

As a result of continuous contact with both breweries and customers, the project managers could assess that thorough preparatory work was needed before the delivery standard could be introduced. The project manager with an academic background assumed responsibility for introducing methods for participation and for taking part in meetings within different occupational groups and at the largest breweries in order to ensure support and understanding for the project and to gather views. In this way, she made sure that the preconditions for activation and network co-operation were created and maintained. The project managers realised that a complement was needed to the traditional top-down strategy of the breweries. It would otherwise have been difficult to know whether the network decisions could be implemented (in restaurants and shops). In order for the delivery standard to be maintained, it was necessary that all employees and managers should act in the same way towards the customers. Therefore, the project managers took it upon themselves to solve problems together with the individual breweries and at the same time start an informal learning process that prepared the managers for what the new delivery standard would mean for their operations and for their own role in the implementation.

One example of the bottom-up strategy is that the project managers could at an early stage take the initiative in setting up a union working group in the Stockholm region, which met regularly in order to follow up on whether the regional managers were fulfilling their undertakings out in the breweries. This could be regarded as part of an empowerment of those drivers who were active in the union. The external project manager also put a lot of effort into increasing the employers' awareness of the importance of the drivers' participation and influence in the development work. When network decisions appeared to be poorly founded, the project manager made informal contact with the managers and conducted a dialogue on how the preparatory work had been carried out. Those managers who felt estranged from the activation strategy were in this way given fresh knowledge on the value of participation. Both managers and union representatives who took part in Phase 1 emphasised the considerable importance of OEH in the implementation of the project:

> By attending our meetings the project managers gained an insight into what the problems were. They had an impact as a pressure group – it said in black and white that it was not only the suppliers who were negative to the goods reception facilities. (Distribution manager)

> They played a very important role in giving legitimacy and status to what we were doing, and gave perspective to our work. [...] They were driving forces all the time. Without that involvement, I don't think it would have been possible to implement. (Driver)

One purpose of the external support in the change work was that a sector with serious work environment problems needed support to initiate a long-term learning process that would lead to sustainable development. Insight regarding the necessity of linking the work environment issues to the operations and the structure of the organisation gradually increased. When OEH ended its co-operation after five years, the preconditions had been created for the sector to continue solving work environment problems and to further develop methods by themselves. Given that the project manager who came from the brewery sector was employed by the trade association in Phase 2, the change management methods could be kept alive within the sector and generate improvements reagarding other work environment problems. He summarised his experience in the following way when he left his post as project manager:

> We would never have come so far simply through the union, but it is a union issue that has come a long way [...] I have been insistent and unafraid, and it has gradually awakened respect among the employers and has gained another status. (Project manager, Phases 1 and 2)

The employees of OEH have continued to maintain contact with the brewery sector. During Phase 2, the evaluator partly had the role of providing external support by regularly participating (more or less) actively in steering group meetings. Since spring 2005, the project manager and evaluator have taken part twice a year in a network with brewery drivers who are active in the union.

5.4.1 Conclusions on external support

In our opinion, the most important contributions of the external support to the successful result and sustainability of the development work were the following:

- that the development work was not only planned and organised from the top-down
- that the internal support was not economically dependent on the other parties – it had its own funding
- that the development work was based on a process-oriented approach

By tradition, the breweries used only a hierarchical and Tayloristic approach in their change management projects, and the external support thus had an important function to play in introducing a 'bottom-up' perspective to the development work. A basic assumption for an impact of this type was that the external support was independent of both the other parties (employer and trade union). Another assumption was that the external support had its own principal interest (to test and analyse a change management method), and in this way it could base itself on a scientific approach. Otherwise there would have been a significant risk that the support from outside would only have been a practical resource or been forced to work as a consultant.

Earlier research shows that project management is a demanding task which often involves a lot of responsibility, but little authority, and that development work which is conducted in network form should have clear ground rules and concrete goals (Andersson et al. 2006). These research results concur well with the experience gained in the brewery sector partnership. Normally, one refers in partnerships to a co-ordinator rather than a project manager. The difference is that the co-ordinator does not run the development work on his or her own, but co-ordinates a joint assignment. It is, however, usual for the co-ordinator to anyway serve as a project manager and to assume the responsibility that the parties should take for driving the work forward (Andersson et al. 2006). In this partnership, the project managers undertook these functions initially in order to create success, but with the pedagogical intention of gradually handing over responsibility and management to the distribution managers at a later stage.

Trust is an important success factor for a partnership (see Chapter 3, Kramer & Tyler 1996). Right from the beginning, the project managers and union representatives carefully fulfilled the tasks they had undertaken and been given, and in this way gained the trust of the employers. On the other hand, there were a number of distribution and sales managers who failed to carry out what they had been asked to do, which meant that the confidence of the project managers in the distribution managers was relatively low in Phase 1. It is important to distinguish between the trust between individuals and the trust between organisations. Caplan & Scott (Chapter 3) are of the opinion that it is not likely that organisations from different sectors and with different aims can create trust between themselves. In our project there arose, on the contrary, a lack of trust within one of the participating organisations. The management of OEH demanded that the project managers should terminate the project (after the new delivery standard had been introduced) claiming that the work of the project managers could be likened to that of a consultant. This indicates a lack of confidence within one of the partner organisations, which is probably a result of the management not knowing enough about the project and a poor grounding of the project content on the part of the interveners.

The experience gained in this study shows that it was necessary for the project managers to accept the responsibility that in fact rested with the managers until they realised the importance of taking this responsibility themselves. Otherwise, in our opinion, the project would never have achieved success. The project managers even went in actively and made demands on – but at the same time supported – those managers who failed to take responsibility. The head of the trade association never noticed that the project managers took on this role, since the managers had often fulfilled their undertakings for the next meeting. The project manager role entailed active efforts to gain support and understanding for the project, the co-ordination of activities and administrative duties.

5.5 Conclusions

The partnership within the brewery sector is a unique example of collaboration between players in the private and public sectors for sustainable development work in connection with work environment issues. As a result of a strong commitment on the part of the owners, new forms of co-operation between different breweries, different occupational groups and the trade union, as well as external support in terms of methods and funding, the working conditions could be improved in the long term throughout an entire sector. New forms of collaboration arose within the partnership between employer and trade union. An effective and permanent organisation was a precondition for implementing and maintaining the delivery standard. The sector took responsibility for this by setting up a steering group and regional networks, and by employing someone with responsibility for the work environment.

The owners realised that the drivers' work environment was causing health problems and that long-term profitability could be improved by doing something about these problems. The awareness of the need to link work environment issues to operational factors and the structure of the work organisation gradually increased among the employers. The breweries gave legitimacy to the partnership by allocating financial resources and taking part actively in the work.

The form of collaboration in the project was not a pure partnership based on the definitions that we have presented, but the principles correlate well. The differences that we observed are primarily to do with the voluntary or compulsory nature of participation in the partnership. There may be voluntary principles on an organisational plane, but those individuals who have maybe had the task forced on them by their employer perhaps lack a personal commitment. As we see things, the question of voluntary principles or compulsion is not decisive – it is the participants' engagement in the task that is important. The project managers need, therefore, to analyse the driving forces for the participating organisations and their representatives in order to determine whether there is a difference in the level of engagement and, if so, what they can do to influence it.

The importance of careful goal formulation has been emphasised. In a partnership, it is likely that it is the rule rather than the exception that each representative comes into the partnership with his/her own interests. For successful co-operation, everyone's underlying interests therefore need to be considered in the goal formulation. If the division of power in the partnership is uneven, the project manager needs to make a special point of checking that the interests of the weaker party are satisfied. An uneven division of power may also mean that the stronger party can entirely steer the direction of the partnership. The experience gained from our project shows that the project manager needs to make sure that the bottom-up strategy is always kept alive, or in other words to make sure that everyone affected by the project is given the opportunity for active participation, i.e. that everyone who is affected by the process is given the chance to take an active part in it.

The external support was of great importance to the outcome of the partnership. The OEH intervener was an independent party (given the external funding and the external organisational affiliation) and served as co-ordinator, strengthened the possibilities for dialogue and supported the initiation of a long-term learning process in order to establish the communication channels needed to implement and maintain the delivery standard. The freedom of the intervener to ask critical questions affected the parties' behaviour during the build-up phase, but also once the work environment activities had become part of the normal operations. The independent party created the preconditions for a form of collaboration on more equal terms than was previously the case between the employers and union representatives. Through their independent positions, the project managers could work actively towards building up the confidence between the partners. This was especially important since the brewery sector by tradition works on the basis of a hierarchical approach.

The external support was of several types: financial, knowledge-related and technical (through new product development). The financial support came from research grants, while the knowledge-related support concerned, above all, the introduction of the bottom-up strategy and systematics in the project work. The project manager with sector experience, who was temporarily employed at OEH, contributed knowledge-related support on the basis of his knowledge of the internal operations and his technical know-how. The combination of these different types of support was an important critical success factor for the project.

The supporting empowerment process for the drivers is still in progress in the form of regular network meetings between the intervener, the evaluator and those drivers who are elected representatives of the trade union. This long-term support has meant that union representative drivers could co-ordinate themselves, and together with the intervener and the evaluator they have developed strategies in order to strengthen their positions in relation to the employers in the regional networks and the steering group.

On the basis of the project, which started in 1994, a work environment organisation has been established for the entire brewery sector, and the parties within the sector have now been working themselves with work environment issues since 1999. The results indicate that a sustainable system of work environment activities has been established within the brewery sector.

The collaboration on which the project has been founded is not a formal partnership, but it is nevertheless instructive and relevant for strategies and theories on partnership. The experience on driving forces, goal formulation, the empowerment process and external support are important and can generate general knowledge on strategies for sustainable development organised in the form of partnership.

References

Andersson, M, Svensson, L, Wistus, S & Åberg, C (2006) (eds.) *On the Art of Developing Partnership*. Stockholm: Arbetslivsinstitutet

Askerøi, E & Eikeland, O (2006) (eds.) *Som gjort, så sagt?: yrkeskunnskap og yrkeskompetanse*. Högskolen i Akershus: Oslo

Argyris, C & Schön, D (1995) *Organizational learning II: Theory, method, and practice*. Massachussetts: Reading

Banke, P & Holsbo, A (2002) 'Institutional support for developing SMEs'. In Docherty, P et al. *Creating sustainable work systems. Emerging Perspectives and Practice*. London: Routledge

Gustavsen, B (1992) *Dialogue and development: theory of communication, action research and the restructuring of working life*. Stockholm: Assen, Van Gorcum

Kilmann, R (1977) *Social systems design*. New York: North-Holland Publishing Co

Kramer, R & Tyler, T (1996) *Trust in organisation*. London: SAGE

Moreno, J L (1934) *Who shall survive?: a new approach to the problem of human interrelations*. Washington DC: Nervous and Mental Disease Publishing

Målqvist, I (2003) *Hållbar förändring: systematiskt arbetsmiljöarbete på branschnivå*. (Sustainable Change – Systematic Work Environment Management in the whole Brewery Sector.) Stockholm County Council: Dept. of Environmental and Occupational Health, Report 2003:2

– (2005) *Ledning för hållbar förändring: utveckling, rationalisering och arbetshälsa – kan de förenas?* (Managing Sustainable Change: Development, Rationalization and healthy Work Sites – are they possible to unite?) Stockholm County Council: Dept. of Environmental and Occupational Health, Report 2005:4

Parmsund, M (2006) *Att organisera för hållbar utveckling: utvärdering av nätverk som metod för arbetsmiljöarbete*. (To organize for sustainable change. An evaluation of networks as a method for work environmental development.) Stockholm County Council: Dept. of Environmental and Occupational Health, Report 2006:4

Shuell, T J (1986) 'Cognitive conceptions of learning'. *Review of Educational Research*, Vol. 56, No. 4, pp. 411–436

Stockholm County Council, Dept. on Occupational Health (1994) *Professional Drivers. Report on work environment and sickness among professional drivers in Stockholm County*. Stockholm County Council: Dept. on Occupational Health, Report 1994:5

Stott, L & Keatman, T (2005) Tools for measuring community engagement in partnerships. *BPD Practitioner Note*. London: BPD Water and Sanitation

Svensson, L & Jakobsson, E (2008) 'Learning in Networks – A strategy for Developing Workplaces?' In Johansson, M & Lundberg, H (eds.) *Strategic Networks*. London: Edward Edgar (forthcoming)

6. Advisory partnerships in a governmental mandated network

6.1 Introduction, background and aim

In recent years, a number of new approaches to organising development and innovation work have emerged. These include networks, innovation systems, the Triple Helix, clusters, and partnership. All of them can be regarded as examples of so-called system initiatives, i.e. they are based on the idea that 'a system' is required to change 'a system'. In this chapter, I intend to discuss one such system initiative that has become increasingly common in development contexts, especially in the EU, i.e. partnership. I will particularly focus on partnership within the framework of the Objective 3 programme in Sweden, which was part of the Social Fund in EU.

Most partnerships in Sweden receive funding from the Swedish State and/or the EU. In this context, we can say that partnership is a working method used in the course of social planning and development work in which actors with complementary and/or overlapping interests and responsibilities are involved in a joint planning, decision-making and implementation process. In the Objective 3 programme, much is expected of the regional partnerships. The idea is that the partnerships should act as bearers of the programme's vision and constitute a forum for regional coordination on issues relating to learning, training and skills development in the regions.

How then do the regional partnerships of the Objective 3 programme work in practice? How do representatives of the various partners view the partnerships' goals, tasks, roles and collaboration with other actors in the

Objective 3 programme? The aim of this chapter is, on the basis of a study of four partnerships, to analyse and discuss the preconditions and potential for partnership work within the Objective 3 programme.

6.2 Working with change and development in partnerships

Partnership and other forms of inter-organisational collaboration is often linked with concepts such as sustainable change and regional development. It is assumed that sustainable changes require organised collaboration between different actors and spheres (Malmborg 2003, Hudson et al. 1999). The partnership concept is also based on the notion that most have something to gain and few have anything to lose by cooperating on a broad front, and that such cooperation is assumed to lead to synergies, coordination and the spreading of risks (Elander 1999). On the hole it seems to be a tendency to present partnerships as a solution to problems that are otherwise difficult to solve (cf. Hudson et al. 1999, Malmborg 2003).

How then can one organize for change and development in a partnership context? Are there any criteria for the success of such collaboration between organisations? Well, that depends on what we mean by criteria or preconditions.

In the literature on partnership and other inter-organisational collaboration forms, certain aspects or preconditions are highlighted that are assumed to help or hinder successful collaboration. First, the importance of having clear objectives and a common vision is underlined (Brinkerhoff 2002, Elander 1999, Malmborg 2003). Brinkerhoff (2002) notes that it is vital that all of the members of a partnership understand and accept the partnership's objectives and that they share a common vision for the work of the partnership. Malmborg goes even further and claims that a shared vision of the objectives of the partnership is in fact an integral element of the concept of partnership. However, although the importance of joint objectives is highlighted, it is also noted that all of the individual members of the partnership must feel that they are gaining something from the partnership and that they can achieve their own goals by working within it (Malmborg 2003, see also Chapter 2).

Second, trust is often seen as a decisive success factor for partnerships (Billet & Seddon 2004, Brinkerhoff 2002, Mohr & Spekman 1994). Mohr and Spekman (1994) note that trust is based on the belief that the members of a partnership are reliable and that they will meet their undertakings. The authors therefore feel that trust is also closely related to the motivation and commitment of the parties concerned and their willingness to collaborate in a partnership context. Billet and Seddon (2004) point out that establishing a trusting relationship between the various actors is one of the major challenges that face a partnership. The authors note that time and scope for discussion and negotiation are important factors in the effort to generate a joint understanding of the work and trust in each other.

Third, the importance of mutuality is often emphasised in this context (Brinkerhoff 2002, Coulson 2005, Suff & Williams 2004). Brinkerhoff (2002) sees mutuality as a decisive aspect of all partnership collaboration. Indicators of mutuality identified in this context include responsibility, access, participation and equitable decision-making. In the case of responsibility, Brinkerhoff (2002) underlines the importance of all the partners accepting responsibility and being held accountable for their actions and the potential impact these actions may have on the partnership and its work. It is also important that all the partners have access to the information available and have the opportunity to participate in meetings, decision-making and other relevant programme activities. In this context it is important that relevant information is made available in an easily-understandable form and that the use of complex or specialised language that may exclude the full participation of one or more partners is avoided. Achieving equitable decision-making is a challenge to any partnership, according to Brinkerhoff, especially if there is an imbalance of power between different partners. Such an imbalance of power usually relates to the fact that one or several partners control the major part of the resources available. Such distortions in the balance of power can also easily undermine other important elements of a partnership's work, for example the exchange of resources and the allocation of authority (Brinkerhoff 2002, Coulson 2005). Malmborg (2003) also points out that it is important that all of the partners are able to influence the work of the partnership and that there is agreement on the roles that each of the partners will play in the partnership. The partners must be able to see each other as assets to the collaboration in the partnership according to Malmborg.

Commitment and competence are other aspects that are highlighted with regard to both partnerships and networks. Malmborg (2003), for example, notes that partnerships must have the relevant knowledge, expertise and know-how. Having the correct competence within the partnership can prevent imbalance and conflicts concerning the roles of the different partners. Brinkerhoff (2002) links competence and commitment together and sees the existence of so-called 'champions' as an important precondition for the development of a partnership. She describes champions as being entrepreneurially-minded individuals who work in a committed way with partnership-related issues within the partnership, in their own organisations and externally.

But even if the aspects mentioned above are believed to be important it is in general difficult to outline any precondition concerning successful partnership work. One problem is that it is difficult, despite a number of interpretations of the concept of partnership, to find a uniform definition of what constitutes a partnership[1]. There is also, in many respects, a lack of knowledge about partnership and the work that is conducted within partnerships. Furthermore, partnership work is often of an innovative, experimental nature, which means that different partnerships have to find and develop working methods that suit their particular needs (cf. Brinkerhoff 2002).

6.3 Partnerships as part of a larger development network

The concept of partnership and the search for collaborative advantages have also become something of a guiding light in political, policy and strategy contexts (Dahlsson 2000). In Sweden, partnership has become a central concept in the field of social planning and development. In this context, it is believed that partnership can help to promote interaction and power sharing between different decision-making levels in society (Dahlsson 2000). Specifically partnerships are believed to create opportunities for change and development at the local and regional levels (Dahlsson 2000, Gorpe 2006). The basic idea is that collaborating in partnerships at the local and regional levels will increase the chances of achieving both joint and individual objectives and lead to effective decision-making (Hallin & Lindström 1998).

Sweden's membership of the European Union and participation in the common regional and structural policy, which is partly funded by the EU's structural funds, is often presented as an explanation of the increasing interest in partnership in Swedish industrial policy (Dahlsson 2000). It is also common for Swedish partnerships to be linked to a larger programme or network with a link to one of the EU's structural funds.

---

[1] A common denominator in the descriptions of the concept is the *collaboration* between different actors (cf. Elander 1999, Brinkerhoff 2002, Malmborg 2003). For a more detailed discussion of the concept of partnership see chapter 3.

6.3.1 Objective 3 – a national programme for regional growth

Objective 3 is a programme within the European Social Fund. The aim of the programme is, by investing in competence development in different ways, to strengthen the position of the individual on the labour market and thus, in the long term, to contribute to growth and increased employment (SPD 2004, *Programkomplement växtkraft Mål 3*, 2005, 2006). The programme is particularly aimed at employees in small and medium-sized organisations and administrations. Another target group consists of individuals who are in a weak position on the labour market (Gorpe 2006, SPD 2004). By supporting competence development at the workplace and working to create links between newfound knowledge and practical application, it is assumed that organisations will be given the chance to develop so that they can meet increasing demands in working life.[2]

With regard to the implementation of the programme it is emphasised that the focus is on the regional level (SPD 2004). More precise, the intention is that the implementation of the concrete activities within the programme should be determined at the regional level in close collaboration with active partnerships and the labour market in the area concerned. In both the overall programme document and the programme complement for Objective 3, it is pointed out that having active partnerships at the national and regional levels is a precondition for the successful implementation of the programme. The tasks of the partnerships include providing information about the programme and advice and support to the regional ESF offices. Another important task for the partnerships is to develop regional plans on the basis of the needs identified in the respective regions. These plans should then act as the foundation for the concrete development work in the region. The programme document also states that the partnerships should continually follow up and revise these plans. Further it is assumed that the partnerships will be able to act as a forum for regional coordination and as a support for the implementation of the programme on the basis of the regional plans for Objective 3. The idea is that the regional partnerships will represent the labour-market partners and, given their networks of contacts and knowledge of regional conditions, contribute to legitimate the programme and reach the intended goals.

---

[2] For a detailed description of the Objective 3 programme, see the programme document for *Växtkraft Mål 3* (www.esf.se).

6.3.2 Regional partnerships – part of the Objective 3 network

Although the regional partnerships are expected to play a prominent role in the implementation of the Objective 3 programme, there are also other important actors in the programme that the partnerships have to pay attention to and are expected to collaborate with.

At the national level, for example, the partnerships are required to cooperate with the central ESF authority (the Swedish ESF Council) and the Supervisory Committee. The Swedish ESF Council is responsible for the coordination and administration of the programme. The Supervisory Committee follows events and developments within the programme and decides whether adjustments to the programme and the funding can be accepted during the programme period. The Supervisory Committee is supposed to collaborate with the regional partnerships and the Committee approves the regional plans drawn up by the partnerships. (Gorpe 2006, SPD 2004, *Programkomplement Växtkraft Mål 3* 2005, 2006).

At the regional level, it is assumed that the partnerships will cooperate closely with the regional ESF offices.[3] The idea is that the partnerships should have a strategic, supportive and advisory function in relation to the regional authorities and that the regional ESF offices should have a drafting and preparatory function in a dialogue with the partnerships. The regional plans drawn up by the partnerships are expected to act as a starting point for this cooperation. However the officials at the regional ESF offices are deciding authority.

In addition to the collaboration with actors at the national and regional levels as described above, it is assumed that the regional partnerships will also collaborate with various actors at an 'inter-regional level'. This collaboration came into focus in 2003 in connection with a reorganisation of the authority. The implementing organisation was divided (from 1 July 2003) into six administrative areas with a number of counties in each area. Previously, each county had constituted a unit with a regional/county manager. A new management structure was also introduced at this time. The managers at the regional ESF offices were replaced by a number of managers for the administrative areas. Each such manager is responsible for a number of offices.[4] Under the new organisation, the partnerships are expected to collaborate with the relevant administrative area manager as well as with the other partnerships in the area.

---

[3] The ESF authority is divided into a central and a regional organisation in which the ESF offices represent the regional authority level.

[4] In the present organisation each regional manager is responsible for at least two offices/counties and at most five offices/counties.

On the whole, it seems that the partnerships in the Objective 3 programme work within a complex organisational context, i.e. within a network-oriented context in which partnerships and authorities at different levels are expected to collaborate and learn from each other on issues relating to regional change and development.

6.4 Four partnerships in the Objective 3 programme

In this section, we will look closer at the practical work of some of the partnerships in the Objective 3 programme more closely. The empirical material presented in this chapter is mainly based on interviews with a number of representatives from four different partnerships.[5] The four partnerships are designated A, B, C and D here. The work of the partnerships is described on the basis of the representatives' views of a) objectives and strategy, b) organisation and work situation, c) the character and orientation of the work d) collaboration within the Objective 3 network and e) results and experience regarding the work done.

6.4.1 *Objectives and strategy*

The overriding objectives of the Objective 3 programme are presented in the programme documents. These objectives mainly relate to promoting competence development and contributing to increased growth and employment. In the case of the partnerships studied, there appears to be a relatively high degree of unity within the partnerships in terms of their view of the overriding objectives. The objectives highlighted by the partnership representatives are also well in line with the overriding objectives specified in the programme documents.

> That growth and employment should increase in the period [...] and competence development. (Org. 2, partnership C)

When asked about a strategy or an action plan to realise these objectives, the representatives primarily refer to the regional plans drawn up within the framework of the respective partnerships.

> Yes, that's what I think the regional plan is. (Org. 1, partnership B)

[5] The empirical data presented in this chapter constitutes part of the data compiled within the framework of a more extensive study of partnerships in the Objective 3 programme in Sweden for which APeL R&D and Linköping University are responsible.

Several of the representatives interviewed point out that a lot of the initial work was devoted to the regional plans and that these present the partnerships' visions and ambitions in relation to regional development needs. However, the possibilities to work according to these plans have been limited due to due to the rules and regulation set by the central authorities.

> We have drawn up a plan for our work. [...] but our freedom to do what we really want to do has been extremely limited [...] the money has been locked up in standardised figures decided on at the central level. (Org. 2, partnership B)

> I think that the regional plans have [...] legitimised this partnership. It's just a pity that they have been given such little value [...] accountants and others have almost [...] totally disregarded them and said that they are not important and that it is SPD and the supplement that matter. [...] This has been a disappointment during the period. (Org. 1, partnership C)

Although the importance of the regional plans is highlighted among the partnership representatives, it can be noted that several of the interviewed representatives find it difficult to describe their partnership's strategy in more concrete terms. In the case of one of the partnerships studied, the representatives explicitly say that strategy has not been discussed within the partnership. Further a lack of distinction between the partnership's objectives and the partnership's strategy can be noted among some of the representatives. Sometimes the regional plans for example are described in terms of both objectives and strategy.

6.4.2 Organisation and work situation

The partnerships in the Objective 3 programme are so-called advisory partnerships. In other words, the main role of the partnerships is to advise and support the regional ESF offices. Some of the partnership representatives indicate that the fact that the partnerships only have an advisory role in relation to the regional ESF offices can be frustrating and reduce motivation and commitment to the partnership.

> As the role is advisory and there are officials that ultimately decide I believe [...] that we lost a little of our enthusiasm in the second half because it felt a bit like, well, we can give our advice but in the end it's the other guy who makes the decisions. (Org. 1, partnership D)

If we examine the organisation of the partnerships more closely, it can be noted that all four have a chairperson who sets the agenda for the partnership meetings. Three of the four partnerships also have working groups that act as drafting committees. In general, the representatives say that the working methods and collaboration within the partnerships work well and that it is easy to reach agreement even though there may be a lot of discussion of certain issues. The frequency of partnership meetings varies from partnership to partnership, although most of the representatives say that, at least at the beginning, they met 4–8 times per year. The initial period of the work of the partnerships is described in positive terms by all of the representatives. They say that the work in this period was characterised by commitment and enthusiasm, questions of principle were discussed and the partnerships felt that they were able to exert influence in various ways. In this period, attendance at partnership meetings was also high.

> In the first half there was a lot of activity and we discussed a lot of questions of principal and what it was important for the partnership to influence and so on. (Org. 1, partnership D)

It seems, however, that the work situation of the partnerships has gradually changed. The representatives claim that freedom concerning the partnerships work has declined in general, as has the scope for exerting influence and testing new ideas within the framework of the programme. Central bureaucracy and control has increased according to the representatives, and regulations and the allocation of resources to the regional level can be changed at short notice. This creates major problems at the regional, operational level and over time affects the representatives' commitment to the partnership work. Several of the representatives have decision-making powers in their own organisations as well as previous experience of partnership and development work. They point out that their time is limited and that the work of the partnership must be seen as being meaningful if they are to give priority to it.

> We entered a period, after half of the programme period perhaps, when sometimes the money came to a dead stop and sometimes it was full speed ahead and we had to really step on it. Things were very uneven and some of the members began to wonder whether there was any point in going. After a while, decision-making also became more and more centralised. I would say that this practically killed off the interest of most of us. So there has been very little action over the last year or eighteen months. [...] we have felt that it doesn't really matter whether we are involved or not. (Org. 2, partnership D)

> They changed all the rules about what you could get money for [...] and it became really complicated [...] this has an effect [...] gradually you become a little quieter because you don't know when they will change things. [...] So what

> does it matter that I'm sitting here spending my time and energy on this [...] if I am to give priority to something and become involved I have to know that it means something. (Org. 1, partnership D)

The representatives seem to be primarily referring to the reorganisation of the authority carried out in 2003 when they talk about the increase in bureaucracy and control and the greater level of uncertainty and unpredictability in the programme.

6.4.3 *Character and orientation of the work*

What characterises the work of the partnerships and the issues they address? The programme documents for Objective 3 present a number of different tasks that the partnerships are expected to work with. First, it is stipulated that the partnerships in the Objective 3 programme should draw up plans for the regional development work and provide advice and support to the regional ESF offices. In the case of the partnerships studied, the results also indicate that the partnerships work with such tasks to a great degree.

> In the regional development plans, we in X (partnership C) have reached agreement on how we see the needs and what needs to be done. [...] we have largely become an adviser to the ESF office and a forum where issues that are perhaps not entirely straightforward, above all not to the management of the officials at ESF, can be brought up and discussed. (Org, 1, partnership C)

Second, it is assumed that the partnerships will work with the dissemination and follow-up of the work of the programme. The programme documents state, for example, that one of the tasks of the partnerships is to spread information about the programme. It is also pointed out that the partnerships should work on an ongoing basis to follow up the concrete work at the regional level. This applies particularly to the work on the regional plans and their implementation. The results in the case of the partnerships studied show that all of the partnerships have worked actively to disseminate information on the Objective 3 programme and on the opportunities for applying for support that exist within the framework of the programme. The results also indicate that extensive dissemination work has been conducted within certain projects. However, there does not appear to be a concerted or deliberate strategy for disseminating the results and experienced gained in the course of the work at the regional level. Responsibility for disseminating experience and results seems largely to depend on the initiative and ability of the individual representatives.

> It is up to every organisation in the partnership to disseminate result as well as they can and in the way they want. (Org. 3, partnership D)

A similar pattern emerges with regard to follow-up and evaluation. Some of the representatives say that they receive information on what is happening from the officials at the ESF office verbally, but on the whole it does not seem that the representatives have worked with follow-up and evaluation in any organised or planned way. Several of the representatives say instead that follow-up and evaluation are primarily tasks for the regional ESF offices.

> I don't think we have worked with this much. (Org. 2, partnership D)

> It's really up to the offices to follow up these things. (Org. 1, partnership A)

At the same time, the representatives point out that due to changed circumstances it has become increasingly difficult for the ESF offices to follow up what is happening in the projects initiated within the framework of Objective 3 in the long term.

6.4.3.1 Collaboration within the Objective 3 network

The governing documents for Objective 3 underline the importance of the partnerships' contacts and collaboration with various actors within the programme's network. To what extent and in what way do the partnerships then collaborate with other actors in the programme?

If we first examine the partnerships' contacts and collaboration with actors at the central authority level a relatively gloomy picture emerges. All of the interviewed representatives state that contacts with the central ESF authority and with the Supervisory Committee are practically non-existent.

> No, none at all. (Org. 4, partnership D)

A more positive picture emerges regarding the partnerships' collaboration with actors at the regional level. Here, the partnerships collaborate primarily with the regional ESF offices and this collaboration is described in general in positive terms by the partnerships. The representatives say that collaboration is well-established and that representatives of the regional ESF offices often attend partnership meetings.

> Yes, they attend our meetings. [...] My understanding is that we have had very good relations with them. (Org. 4, partnership A)

> Excellent. (Org. 2, partnership B)

Apart from the ongoing participation of representatives of the ESF offices in partnership meetings, the collaboration with the offices comprises reporting from certain projects and/or the discussion of regional plans. However, although the partnership representatives in general feel that the contact with the regional ESF offices works well, opinions differ on to what extent the partnerships can influence the work of the offices or decisions on concrete issues. Some representatives also say that the nature of contacts with the ESF offices has changed over time and that previously it was easier to work in a proactive way on a number of different issues.[6]

6.4.4 Results and experience

What then has been achieved by the work in the partnerships and what experience do the partnership representatives feel it is important to take with them to new partnerships?

When the representatives are asked to specify the results of the work of their partnerships, they first mention that networks and constellations for collaboration between the organisations involved in the partnership that previously did not exist have been developed.

> I think that having a forum where we can meet is much more important than people think [...] I can check thoughts and ideas there. [...] I think the consensus we create through this joint programme is important. (Org. 3, partnership A)
>
> I mean, the partnership will become a network in itself. (Org. 2, partnership D)

Second the representatives point out is that the work of the partnerships has contributed to increased investment in, and reflection on, competence development in those companies that have got support from the programme.

> Partly that we have got the companies that participated to reflect on their situation and how they can work with competence development issues in a more long-term way, and partly that the programme has helped to increase investment in competence development. (Org. 2, partnership B)

Overall the partnership members are doubtful, however, about whether the partnership work has had any more overriding form of structural impact.

---

6 In the case of the partnerships' contacts with actors at the inter-regional level, the results indicate that these contacts are more frequent than the contacts with the central authority level but not so well developed as the contacts with the regional ESF offices.

> I don't really think that we can see this as structural impact in that way. (County Labour Board, partnership B)

> Here we can be a bit critical I suppose and ask to what extent these projects have affected any of the structures in society. (Org. 1, partnership C)

But at the same time a few of the representatives mention that some of the projects have created potentials for structural impact.

> Through the partnership we have got a lot of support from business and industry for training and education in the county. [...] So this environment has contributed indirectly to the creation of other forms of cooperation [...] vocational training courses, technical college, nursing college and all the other things that are starting up. [...] There have been discussions here that have had ... such effects and structural impact. (Org. 2, partnership B)

> This (project XX) is a project that is now affecting the structure ... it is definitely affecting the education structure on the vocational side. (Org. 1, partnership C)

When asked about important experience gained and lessons learned from the work within the partnerships and the Objective 3 programme, the partnership representatives primarily take up the importance of reducing bureaucracy and of having a distinct structure with clear, simple and well-considered regulations that will endure throughout an entire programme period. They also express the desire for a more active and decision-making role for the partnerships in the future.

> I mean better support and different co-funding [...] training [...] clearer administrative regulations and approaches that are not changed during the period and especially not during the project period. (Org. 3, partnership C)

> You have to have this positive power in the partnerships of being able to be involved and make decisions, because as long as you only have an advisory role you feel as though you simply don't count in certain situations [...] A clearer structure, easier, become more accessible. That's probably what I would like to plead for most. (Org. 1, partnership D)

The representatives also underline the importance of creating better collaboration between the partnerships and actors at the central level.

6.5 Summarising analysis and discussion

In this section I will return to the questions posed at the beginning of the chapter. As the headline suggest this section focuses on a summarising analysis and discussion of the partnerships' work, preconditions and potentials within the framework of the Objective 3 programme.

6.5.1 The work within the partnerships

In the case of the work within the partnerships it can be noted that, at the overall level, there is a relatively high degree of agreement concerning objectives and visions. It is primarily the overriding objectives stipulated in the programme documents (SPD 2004)[7] that the partnership representatives describe as the objectives of the partnerships. However, the picture is not entirely unambiguous. There are some indications of ambiguity concerning what constitutes a partnership's objectives and what constitutes a strategy for achieving these objectives. Some representatives, for example, see the regional plans that the partnerships develop as objectives in themselves, while others describe the plans as a strategy or means of achieving the objectives. It is possible that the areas addressed in the regional plans are seen as a concretisation of the overriding objectives presented in the governing documents for the programme. The results indicate that there has not been much discussion of strategy within the partnerships, which may be one of the reasons for the unclear demarcation between the terms objectives and strategy. The importance of clear objectives, common visions and a meaningful task is highlighted in all the literature relating to partnership (Brinkerhoff 2002, Malmborg 2003). At the same time, it is pointed out that different expectations and interests often make it more difficult to agree on a common objective (cf. Malmborg 2003). In the case of the partnerships studied, it is, however, difficult to see that differences have led to any difficulty in agreeing on objectives and visions. One explanation of the unity that seems to prevail within the partnerships may be that the programme documents, which stipulate the overriding objectives, have had a governing impact and have thus made it easier for the partnerships to agree on overriding objectives and visions. It is also conceivable that the fact that the partnerships have mainly played an advisory role has made it easier to reach agreement on objectives and working methods. In many cases, it is only when the implementation phase is reached that conflicts and different interests concerning objectives and methods emerge

---

7   These focus mainly on increased employment, growth and competence development.

and have a noticeable effect on the practical work (cf. Klöfver & Nilsson 2007).

As in the case of objectives and visions, there is a high degree of unity concerning the working methods of the partnerships. The partnerships largely work with the type of task stipulated by the programme documents – such as providing support and advice to the regional ESF offices, developing the regional plans and providing information on the Objective 3 programme (cf. SPD 2004). Some partnerships have worked actively to disseminate information on selected projects, but there does not appear to be any overall strategy for the dissemination of experience and results. The same applies to the follow-up and evaluation of activities and programmes. None of the partnerships studied have any organised strategy for the follow-up and evaluation of the work of the ESF offices or the work of their own partnership. Several of the partnership representatives express the view that the follow-up and evaluation of the activities carried out is not one of the duties of the partnerships. Nevertheless, the programme documents for the Objective 3 programme (cf. SPD 2004) state that the partnerships should follow the implementation work in the regions and continuously adapt the regional plans to current trends and developments.

One problem relating to the lack of analysis and follow-up is that it is difficult to get a concerted picture of the results of the work and action taken by the partnerships. Although the partnership representatives state that the work of the partnerships has led to increased investment in competence development in companies and new opportunities for dialogue and collaboration between the members of the partnerships, it is difficult to see to what extent and in what way the work has contributed to new and more sustainable structure-related solutions (cf. SPD 2004). Continuous evaluations and follow-up activities can be assumed to provide valuable information and a basis for reflection and learning regarding what has been done and thus act as a starting point for the next steps in the work.[8] Continuous and documented follow-up can help in the long term to provide a concerted picture of the partnerships' work and the measures taken, which in turn can act as the starting point for continued regional development work within or outside the framework of the partnerships.

---

8 For example with regard to the development of regional plans and next steps, but also with regard to collaboration processes both within the partnerships and between different actors in the network.

6.5.2 The role and work situation of the partnerships in the programme network

When we examine the changes in the work situation of the partnerships, as described by the representatives of the partnerships studied, it can be noted that the first part of the programme period is generally described in positive terms. In this period, it seems to be possible to distinguish several of the aspects that, according to the literature on the subject, constitute characteristic elements of successful collaboration in partnerships. Besides unity on objectives and visions, the representatives also say that they feel that the partnerships were characterised by a relatively high degree of commitment and a bottom-up approach. It seems that the vision of combined bottom-up and top-down processes that was intended to characterise the work of the Objective 3 programme (see Chapter 2) to some extent is realised here. This is supported by the fact that there are signs of mutuality, for example in terms of access and participation, between different actors within the framework of the Objective 3 network (cf. Brinkerhoff 2002, Coulson 2005). The interviewed representatives say that in the early stages of the programme period,[9] the partnerships had a relatively high degree of freedom and influence with regard to the measures taken. The results also indicate that the work at the beginning of the programme period was based on a high degree of trust and confidence. The partnerships had confidence in the Objective 3 programme as a whole and in their own ability to contribute to regional change and development (cf. Brinkerhoff 2002, Mohr & Spekman 1994). On the whole, it seems that the role and work situation of the partnerships in the first part of the programme period generally contributed to commitment, enthusiasm for the work and a high level of attendance at partnership meetings.

However, the empirical results indicate that the work situation of the partnerships was changed during the course of the programme. The representatives point out that during the latter part of the programme it was increasingly managed in line with traditional, hierarchical principles while there was a steady decline in bottom-up processes in the form of influence and input from the partnerships in the programme. The representatives also claim that the authority at the central level does not take account of the plans developed by the partnerships or the regional needs expressed in these plans. There is a general perception that increased bureaucracy and regulation has reduced the scope for action and has made it more difficult

---

9   That is before the organisational changes in 2003.

to influence the regional development work. At the same time as control of the partnerships is strengthened there is a tendency for uncertainty concerning the work to increase as the central authority can, at short notice, change decisions on the resources available and this makes it difficult to plan the practical activities.

But, although there is apparent dissatisfaction with these trends, the results indicate that the partnerships as a whole have adopted a relatively passive, reactive attitude in relation to the changes initiated by the authority. This may, at least at first sight, seems surprising. Billet and Seddon (2004) have noted, however, that many partnerships that are tied to a strong structure in which the policy and the objectives have been set in advance and are defined by the sponsors of the partnership behave reactively in relation to policy problems and changes. The dissatisfaction of the studied partnerships was, however, expressed in different ways – in the form of a decline in interest and motivation and in attendance at partnership meetings. In such a situation, there is a risk that a partnership can lose competence and vitality in that 'champions' and other key individuals in the partnership prioritise other activities because the partnership no longer seems meaningful (cf. Brinkerhoff 2002, Pettigrew 2003).

Further it is also possible that the reactive attitude of the partnerships to the changes in the management and organisation of the programme is strengthened by the fact that there is no clear strategy for interaction and collaboration between the partnerships and the central authority level in the programme organisation. Even though the importance of dialogue and collaboration between the central and regional levels is highlighted in the governing documents drawn up for the work of the Objective 3 programme (cf. SPD 2004), it seems that these relations are in practice characterised by 'loose links' (cf. Weick 1976, Morgan 1986) in combination with formal top-down, one-way communication. It can be assumed that the lack of dialogue and discussion on the organisation and content of the programme's work reduces the level of trust between the partnerships and the central authority. Billet and Seddon (2004), for example, point to the importance of arenas for communication and negotiation as a way of generating trust, respect and insight into each others' work. The authors believe that providing time and opportunities for discussion is one way of developing trusting relations.

6.5.3 Some reflections and conclusions

What conclusions can be drawn from the analysis and discussion above? First, the results indicate that the partnerships studied have not acquired the prominent role in the Objective 3 programme that was planned. Even though there were signs of a bottom-up organisation with relatively good opportunities for the regional partnerships to exert influence during the first part of the programme period, it seems that over time the programme has increasingly been run on the basis of traditional, hierarchical and arbitrary principles.

Second, the lack of dialogue between the central and regional levels tends to create loose links between different actors in the programme network. These loose links in combination with a top-down steering can be assumed to have a major impact on the partnerships' work situation. The top-down related steering decrease the partnerships opportunities to act autonomously. At the same time there are little contact between the partnerships and the central authorities. The advisory role of the partnerships means that they are particularly dependent on a well functioning collaboration with other actors within the network. In a system where there is lack of dialog collaboration, advisory partnerships can easily become ineffectual and in the worst case there is a risk that they will be considered marginal and peripheral. In this study however, the results indicate that the partnerships studied have collaborated closely with the regional ESF offices on the regional development work conducted within the programme. It can be assumed that this collaboration has counteracted a marginalisation of the partnerships.

Concerning the work within the partnerships, the results indicate that collaboration between the representatives in the partnerships has developed and that networks of contacts have been established. Such networks can, if they endure, provide potential for continued collaboration on issues concerning change and development in the regions. But the advisory role of the partnerships may also have a limiting effect on the work within the partnerships. On one hand it can be assumed that it is easier to reach agreement on objectives and working methods in this type of partnership. But on the other hand the consensus exhibited in the partnerships may also be rather superficial (cf. Chapter 2), as unity is not put to the test when the time comes to give visions and objectives concrete form in terms of practical action. If this is the case, it may lead to more difficult issues being avoided as they may lead to the emergence of disagreement and conflicts of interest. The advisory role may also mean that tasks such as developing concrete strategy and follow-up activities are not seen as tied to each partnership's own working situation and are therefore neglected in the course of the partnership's work.

On the whole, the results indicate that the context in which the partnerships act is of great importance to the work of the partnerships. When, as in this case, the partnerships have an advisory role and are tied to a strong, regulating network, they become highly dependent on effective dialogue and interplay within the network.

References

Billet, S & Seddon, T (2004) 'Building Community through Social Partnership around Vocational Education and Training'. *Journal of Vocational Education and Training*, Vol. 56, No. 1, pp. 51-67

Brinkerhoff, J M (2002) 'Assessing and improving partnership relationships and outcomes: a proposed framework'. *Evaluation and Program Planning*, Vol. 25, Issue 3, pp. 215-321

Coulson, A (2005) 'A plague on all your partnerships: theory and practice in regeneration'. *International Journal of Public Sector Management*, Vol. 18, No. 2, pp. 151-163

Dahlsson, H (2000) *Regionalisering och flernivådemokrati. Partnerskap som profylax.* Statsvetenskapliga institutionen, Lunds universitet, Lund.

Elander, I (1999) 'Partnerskap och demokrati: omaka par i nätverkspolitikens tid'. In *Globalisering*/Anna Brink ... Amnå, E (ed.) Statens Offentliga Utredning (SOU) 1999:83

Gorpe, P (2006) *Svenska partnerskap: en översikt: rapport 1 till Organisationsutredningen för regional tillväxt.* Statens Offentliga Utredning (SOU) 2006:4

Hallin, G & Lindström, B (1998) *Det ouppklarade partnerskapet: om svensk regionalpolitik, strukturfonderna och den territoriella utmaningen.* SIR, Östersund, Rapport 108

Hudson, B, Hardy, B, Henwood, M & Wistow, G (1999) 'In pursuit of interagency collaboration in the public sector'. *Public Management*, Vol. 1, No 2, pp. 235-260

Klöfver, H & Nilsson, B (2007) *Mångfaldens Ansikten – mellan vision och praktik.* Institutionen för beteendevetenskap och lärande. Linköpings universitet, Linköping

Malmborg, F (2003) 'Conditions for Regional Public–Private Partnerships for Sustainable Development – Swedish Perspectives'. *European Environment*, Vol. 13, pp. 133-149

Mohr, J & Spekman, R (1994) 'Characteristics of Partnership Success: Partnership Attributes, Communication Behavior, and Conflict Resolution Techniques'. *Strategic Management Journal*, Vol. 15, No. 2, pp. 135-152

Morgan, G (1986) *Images of Organization.* London: Sage Publications

Pettigrew, P J (2003) 'Power, Conflicts, and Resolutions: A Change Agent's Perspective on Conducting Action Research Within a Multiorganizational Partnership'. *Systemic Practice and Action Research*, Vol. 16, No. 6, pp. 375-391

Programkomplement för Växtkraft Mål 3 i Sverige. (2005). Svenska ESF-rådet, Stockholm

Programkomplement för Växtkraft Mål 3 i Sverige. (2006). Svenska ESF-rådet, Stockholm

SPD (2004) Samlat programdokument för Växtkraft Mål 3, 2000-2006, Sverige. Svenska ESF-rådet, Stockholm

Suff, R & Williams, S (2004) 'The myth of mutuality? Employee perceptions of partnership at Borg Warner'. *Employee Relations*, Vol. 26, No. 1, pp. 30-43

Weick, K E (1976) 'Educational Organizations as Loosely Coupled Systems'. *Administrative Science Quarterly*, Vol. 21, pp. 1-19

7. You're welcome to participate – but on whose terms? On empowerment and structural impact

7.1 Background, aim and content

Is it possible to combine empowerment for vulnerable groups with a structural impact within the framework of a development partnership? In my study, I have followed the way in which a group of women on long-term sick leave have found their way back into working life. We have together tried to understand and explain the processes that led to sick listing, but also what is needed for a return to working life. The women were members of a development partnership within the EQUAL Programme, where they were regarded as experts on their own problems by the partnership. Two of the women on long-term sick leave participated in each meeting of the partnership to the extent that they had the time and energy needed, even though they had no formal influence on any of the decisions that were taken. So what can we learn from a target group that is a member of a partnership if it is not a full partner?

One important question in this chapter is whether the potential for a meeting on equal terms exists in a partnership when the preconditions for participation are so varied (cf. Chapter 9). Were the individuals on long-term sick leave regarded as players or did they become 'hostages' in the work of the partnership? Can problems really be solved simply by transforming 'exclusion' into 'inclusion' by setting up a partnership? This chapter sheds light on the problem of the double goals in the EQUAL

Programme – empowerment and structural impact – and the importance this has from the point of view of the person who is on long-term sick leave. Empowerment presupposes disempowerment (cf. Kabeer 2001), which indicates that there is a group that has to remain on the outside. The priority of the partnership in terms of time at the beginning of the period of support was therefore to support the women in breaking the process of powerlessness, which at the same time affected the chances of working in a structured way.

I begin by describing why a partnership is necessary for the target group of women on long-term sick leave and discuss how a partnership can be organised. This is followed by the participants' perception of disempowerment and empowerment, which was clarified in the interactive research process. In order to understand the importance and necessity of the work of the partnership in transforming exclusion into inclusion – i.e. changing disempowerment into empowerment – I describe in considerable detail what empowerment means for this group of women. The chapter ends with a discussion on the possibilities and difficulties of combining empowerment and structural impact.

7.2   Why is a partnership with this target group needed?

In Sweden, exclusion from the labour market means that some 1.4 million of just over five million people who are of an employable age fall outside the labour market. The figures include those individuals, who are openly unemployed, or those who are in some form of re-employment programme, early retirement or who have been sick-listed for more than ninety days (von Otter 2004). There was a significant increase in sick leave between the latter part of the 1990s and 2002, and above all in the case of long-term sick leave. In recent years, absence due to illness has begun to decline, although the level is still historically very high. During 2005, 11.2 per cent of the population aged between 16 and 64 received sickness allowance, sickness or activity benefit (converted to full-time employees). 595 000 new cases of sickness were registered during 2005, of whom 419 000 had a job (SOU 2006:107, p. 71). In 2006, the ill-health rate dropped from 41.3 to 39.9, the decrease being attributable to a reduction in short-term sick leave[1]. Why is the problem so great in Sweden?

---

1   See Swedish Social Insurance Agency *(Försäkringskassan)* Press Release 2007-01-19. Each tenth part of the ill health rate represents approximately 600 000 days' absence for reasons of sickness.

One explanation is the fact that increasing demands are being made on individuals to accept responsibility, in both their working and private lives, at the same time as cuts are being made in the welfare systems. Individuals are expected to take greater responsibility for their working environment, their rehabilitation and their employability, to name only a few areas. Collective responsibility is becoming less and less visible, at the same time as exclusion is increasing. Many people 'grow' with individual responsibility, but for someone who is already in a strained position it may prove to be 'too much'. Downsized organisations in the public sector and a weaker welfare system cause more problems for women than for men with the balance between paid and unpaid work.[2] Women are also the predominant labour force in the public sector in that the Swedish labour market is strongly gender-segregated. Women still carry the greatest level of responsibility for unpaid work, even though men have increased their relative share of unpaid work somewhat during recent years (Nordenmark 2004). The growing demands and decreasing resources – within both working and private life – mean that it is becoming increasingly difficult to strike a balance between the different spheres (cf. Johansson 2002). In the longer term, and under certain circumstances, this can have an effect on health.

An increase in equality in both working and family life is mutually beneficial, but the efforts need to be made in both directions in order to improve the situation facing women (SOU 2005:73). On the face of it, Sweden has a generous system of social insurance that supports the combination of work and family. It is perhaps for this reason that the social demands for women to be successful in all spheres are so high and that Swedish women feel they have to succeed as employees, partners and parents (Guest 2002). Johansson (2002) is of the opinion that one consequence of these demands is the high figures for sick listings with psychiatric diagnoses, for instance depression. Kilbom (1998) maintains that there is no other country in the western world with such long experience of having a large number of women on the labour market, at the same time as women still have the greatest share of responsibility for the family.

---

2   See also the work-life balance discussion. The ideal worker is still regarded as someone who does not allow the family or other commitments to disturb their paid work (Gambles et al. 2006). The term work-life balance indicates a wider attitude to the conflict between work and family than, for example, a traditional focus on a family-friendly policy. The discussions regarding work-life balance ignore the difference between paid and unpaid work and introduce the importance of leisure time. Striking a balance in life is good for one's health, and bearing in mind the pressure of today's work situation it should be an important consideration for all players in working life, says Kodz (2002).

The changes on a social level have clearly had an indirect impact on women's health. On the other hand, the changes are difficult to study and analyse on an individual level. The individual consequences of ill health are clearer and more direct at an organisational level when it comes to changes during recent years. The mechanisms that I have taken up above cannot – either individually or together – provide a full explanation as to why women suffer such a high level of sick listing. However, each sub-explanation may be a piece of the puzzle, and therefore contribute towards an explanation. Changes in the organisation of welfare are leading to a more stressful working life. When the workload becomes too much, the rest of life is also affected, which could have a negative affect on health (cf. Härenstam et al. 2003).

In my study, the focus is on the situation facing women who are sick listed over a long period of time, but the changes at the social level and their consequences at an organisational level during the 1990s affected a large group of people. Discrimination and inequality in working life were regarded as a serious problem throughout the whole of Europe. It was in view of this that the EQUAL Programme was started, the largest programme ever launched within the EU with a total budget of SEK 40 billion. It was on the basis of this programme that the development partnership studied in this chapter was set up.

7.3   The development partnership

The EQUAL Programme is a Community initiative within the EU that is administered by the European Social Fund (ESF). The programme aims at developing methods for combating discrimination and exclusion in working life, but above all at influencing structures, organisations, approaches, values, etc. that exclude and discriminate. The competence and development potential of individuals shall be utilised irrespective of gender, age, ethnic affiliation, sexual orientation or functional disability.

My study focuses on a target group of individuals who are on long-term sick leave, most of whom were employed in the public sector. The majority of these people suffered from fatigue-related depression, even though several of the participants at the start of the support period did not have a definite diagnosis. The organisation in the form of a development partnership was, for all the organisations and players involved, something new, and to start with there was only limited knowledge of this form of organisation. Therefore, the partnership was organised in the traditional form with a steering group and a reference group, and was based on an activation strategy, i.e. the involvement and driving force of the participants were regarded as being of central importance for the success of the project (see Chapter 1).

The steering group consisted of representatives from the employer (local authority and county council), social insurance agency, job center, learning centre, a co-ordinator and two participants. The co-ordinator and a study counsellor were employed at the learning centre. The reference group consisted of a corporate health care body, trade union representatives, a study counsellor, health developer, co-ordinator and two participants.

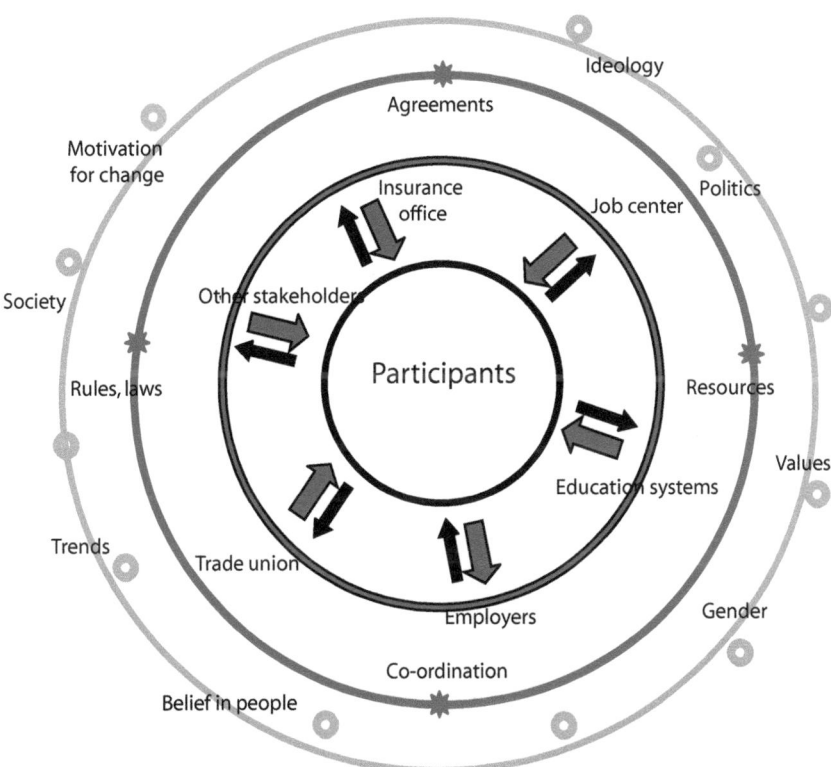

Figure 1. Complexity in organisation of the partnership

The complexity in the organisation of the partnership can be seen in Figure 1. The circle in the centre containing 'participants' symbolises the fact that the participants are to be regarded as experts in their own problem areas and that the players involved should base their approach on this fact. The project is in other words founded on a 'bottom up' perspective.

The second circle describes the players who participated in the partnership, and the arrows from the various players and participants[3] indicate that they should contribute towards the common task of the partnership. The arrows pointing to the players and the participants signify that they also want something for their own part. This way of looking at contribution and outcome is part of the stakeholder model. Already at this stage, one of the problems and difficulties concerning the representation of groups that are suffering exclusion can be identified – the participants should have been included in the second circle if they were full representatives of the partnership.

The third circle shows that all players are surrounded by a system of rules, agreements, routines and approaches. Since the players come from different authorities and different organisations, the systems of regulations are not always compatible. The potential for influencing matters 'upwards' and outside one's own organisation tend to differ depending on where in the hierarchy the players are located in their own organisation and what network of contacts the players have access to outside their own organisation.

The outer circle shows that there is an external system that influences the inner circles. Society is largely developed irrespective of what happens in the inner circles, and this affects the scope of action that is open to the various players and participants. Social structures are sluggish systems that are difficult to influence in the short term. The complexity in the organisation of the partnership indicates difficulties in influencing structures and achieving effects that move in the opposite direction. In addition, most of the players have a political direction, which could influence their approach in the longer term, for instance in connection with a transfer of power.

The R&D centre APeL, where I was employed, was organised formally under 'other stakeholders'. Research and development processes are operated traditionally on the basis of an outside-looking-in perspective. At APeL, attempts are being made to link together theory and practice in

---

3   When I write players, I refer to the representatives from the various authorities – social insurance offices, job center, training co-ordinators, and from the employers. The term participant refers to those individuals who are long-term sick-listed, even though they may, of course, also could be players.

a common learning process, and the interactive approach in the research work means close co-operation with 'practice' – or in other words an ambition to conduct research 'with' the participants (cf. Svensson & Aagaard Nielsen 2006).

7.4 The interactive research process

The interactive approach has been important to my research results. It is based on joint learning – or in other words the fact that participants and researchers together create an understanding of the problem (c.f. Aagaard Nielsen & Svensson 2006). In my study, in which the focus is on an understanding and explanation of the way in which women find their way back into working life, the joint learning became part of the empowerment processes for the participants.

It is difficult to describe in simple terms what characterises interactive research. Interactive research cannot be described solely in terms of the methods used. Interactive research is more of a perspective – a certain way of understanding and conducting research. The involvement of the participants in the analytical work is the essence of an interactive approach. Different methods can be used depending on the situation and the matter under research. The combinations of qualitative and quantitative methods will strengthen the research findings.

In figure 2, I have illustrated joint learning as a focal point in an interactive research approach. The participants and the researcher enter this process with different experiences and anticipations. These differences must be articulated and discussed before the learning process can take place in an open and trustful atmosphere. The joint learning should (in an ideal situation) continue throughout the whole research process – from the definition of the problem to the presentation of the results. But what happens to the role of the researcher in this joint learning approach? Is every participant a researcher? The answer to this is both yes and no! In seeking new explanations, the participants have a similar role to that of the researcher. But the motives for being involved may differ. The participants approach the joint learning process with different motives and anticipations. The outcome of the joint learning process will also differ – academic results on the one hand and practical usefulness on the other. The participants are seldom interested in gaining academic merits, but in finding new explanations and practical solutions (see Figure 2).

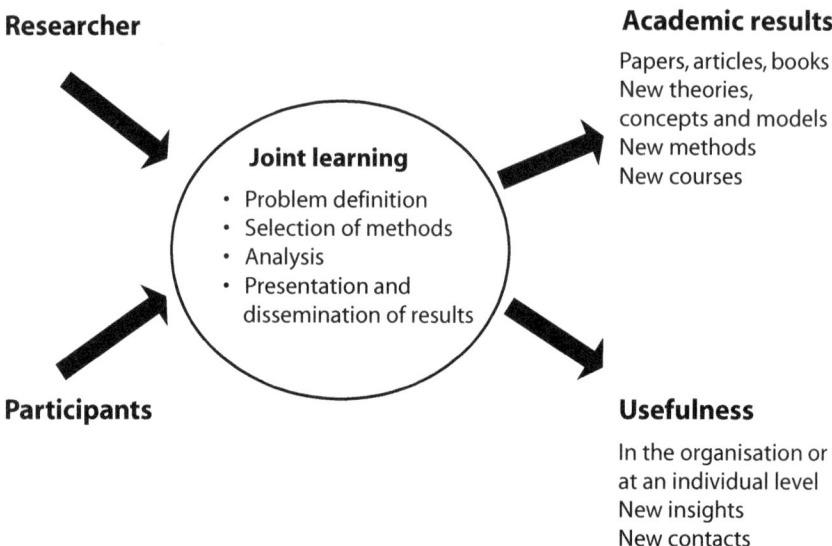

Figure 2. An illustration of an interactive research process with different roles and interests (Larsson 2006, p. 245).

Interactive research should not or could not be used everywhere. Joint learning is a time-consuming process, especially for the participants (Elle 2006). A necessary thrust must be established (Herr & Anderson 2005) and the researcher must feel comfortable with having such a close relationship with the participants. There must also be room for a critique of the situation, and of the organisation that is being investigated. A supportive structure is therefore necessary (Larsson 2006).

In my case study, many of these requirements were present or established in advance. The use of an interactive research approach was thus a natural choice for me. The participants had considerable time for involvement in the joint learning process. They were on sick leave and often found the meetings stimulating and encouraging. The project leaders accepted a critical approach, which sometimes led to a development in the project activities. I was free to use the data and to present it in my own way. It is important that the entry process is anchored at all levels in the project. Personally, I preferred to treat the participants as subjects in the whole research process – especially in the presentation of the data. I enjoyed the informal contacts, which to some extent will probably continue after the research is completed. The research process is to a very high degree collaborative (Figure 2), but the dissertation process is an individual enterprise (Herr & Anderson, 2005).

The joint learning process sometimes meant that we increased our understanding of the problems involved and saw that there was not merely *one* explanation for why the women had been long-term sick listed. What they had in common was the fact that in some way or other they found themselves in different stages of powerlessness.

7.5   From powerlessness to empowerment?

How did the partnership support the development of the participants towards empowerment – or in other words help them to reverse the feeling of powerlessness? This feeling of powerlessness had on the one hand developed as a result of increasing demands and decreasing resources in the working lives of the women, but also through the impact the growing demands and decreasing resources had on their private lives, through a cutting back of welfare resources. The first step in an empowerment process was for these women to retain control over their own lives. The women described this as increasing their resources in different ways. From our discussions, seven different resource categories were defined:

- Social resources
- Learning resources
- Physical resources
- Mental resources
- Emotional resources
- Institutional resources
- Financial resources

The term resources is frequently criticised because it focuses on emotional and cognitive dimensions of powerlessness but neglects social and political dimensions of power (Prilleltensky et al. 2001). However, access to material and psychological resources can be regarded as being necessary for gaining power and control over one's own situation – something which is in turn necessary for creating a sense of wellbeing and health, according to Prilleltensky (2001). For the women in my study, these changes were the first step in breaking a downward spiral of powerlessness, which among other things affected their psychological resources, for example through a lower level of self-esteem.

The work in the partnership led to the participants changing their resources in several respects. The resources, activities in the partnership and results achieved on an individual level are presented in Table 1.

Table 1. Changed resources, activities and results.

Aspects of changed resources	Activity	Result for individual
Emotional resources	Group discussion Individual discussion	From chaos to balance?
Social resources	Group meeting Guidance practice Other activities	Support in group New network/relations
Learning resources	Lectures, courses Group discussion (Vocational) guidance	Ability to handle stress Reflect yourself in the group Find new ways back into working life
Physical resources	Physical training	Take up leisure interests again Making new friendships Better physical health
Mental resources	Group support Individual discussion	Better self-esteem 'New' identity Learn to say no
Financial resources	Group discussion	Re-evaluation of material factors Financial pressure negative
Institutional resources	Participation in strategy and reference group Participation in research environments	Feedback on seminars, conferences, increasing the possibility for reflection

The importance of the various resources is different during different support periods depending on where the individual is on his/her way back into working life. Several of the resources overlap each other. What most people emphasise as being very important is having the opportunity to increase their social resources, primarily being able to receive the support of 'like-minded' members of the group. The partnership's view of the participants as being experts in their own problem areas creates dynamism in the group. The value of being listened to and being able oneself to decide what is important for one's own development was experienced positively, even though several of the participants initially reacted by deciding themselves which activities they wanted to have and take part in. Most of them were used to having a schedule with fixed activities and not to being able to make decisions themselves. To start with, the physical resources were emphasised, both in the sense of beginning with something that is not so demanding, but also as a means of improving their wellbeing and getting to know each other. Learning and mental resources were increased and changed for most of the participants. Learning resources are mainly increased through access to a formal raising of competence, but also through a more informal learning process at different group meetings.

Those areas that have been affected to the least extent are the financial and institutional resources. The financial resources have in the short term deteriorated, but in the longer term, once the participants have returned to working life again, a financial improvement takes place. The institutional resources have consisted of the fact that the participants have had access to various arenas, which they would otherwise not have had the possibility of accessing. Apart from participating in the partnership, they have also taken part in various research environments in order to be able to talk about their problems themselves. This has been experienced by most of them as positive.

It is not only access to resources on an individual and collective level that counts in an empowerment process. The other dimension of power is the capacity to act (agency), or in other words the ability to define our goals and to achieve them. The capacity to act does not refer only to observable behaviour but also to the degree of motivation, the feeling of meaningfulness and the purpose of the action (power within). The capacity to act, coupled with power aspects, can be something positive as well as something negative. It could be positive (power to/for) in the sense that individuals form their own life styles and goals, sometimes despite being questioned by those around them. It could be negative (power over) if it involves using violence, threats and coercion in order to dominate other people (cf. Williams 1994).

Resources and the capacity to act together constitute the capacity for how people can shape their lives – to be and to do. This is the third power dimension in the disempowerment/ empowerment process (Kabeer 2001). Prilleltensky (1994) considers that access to increasing material resources for vulnerable/oppressed groups is a necessary stage in the empowerment process.

The next stage in the power and control dimension is the possibility for active participation and self-determination at all levels. The third stage concerns the opportunities for competence development and self-efficacy, or in other words that the individual believes that he/she can control the results of his/her behaviour. There must be support and potential for this on a society, community and family level (Prilleltensky et al. 2001). Criticism has been voiced against the self-efficacy theory since it may give the impression that the individual alone changes his/her life. Critics feel that there is a risk of social problems being explained on the basis of a 'blame-the-victim' perspective (Franzblau & Moore 2001).

A tangible result of the study, and the one which most participants consider as being an important aid in moving from thought to action, is the social support from each other and from the co-ordinator and study counsellor during the group meetings. If access to the perceived resources is the first step in an empowerment process, the second step is the capacity to use this perception in order to act. Empowerment must express itself in the form of observable actions, but the capacity for action is associated with motivation, a sense of meaningfulness and the purpose of the action (c.f. Kabeer 2001).

The way back into working life began by recapturing time for oneself – or finding a 'room of one's own[4] '– and became an expression that was used in the partnership. For one of the women, 'a room of her own' involved singing in a choir, another woman took part in amateur theatrics, another sewed an evening dress while others went on walking trips. Forssén and Carlstedt (2006) emphasise the importance of women finding their own strategies for protecting their health – finding rooms of their own – irrespective of what experts and specialists think.

The individual development was positive for many of the participants in the partnership and was essential in order for them to be able to return to working life. However, when it comes to the structural impact, which was one of the goals of the EQUAL Programme, things were not quite so successful. Why was this? For most of the women, the empowerment process involved increasing their resources and regaining control over their own lives – in other words breaking the sense of powerlessness they found themselves in before and during their period of sick leave. The next step was to take action, both individually and collectively. The common reflection in the group has resulted in the participants being able to move outside themselves and to see things more from the outside. It is not until they have reached this stage that the participants can see that acquiring a sustainable working life is not solely dependent on them as individuals. It is only then that the desire can be awakened to 'have the energy' to act and influence structures. The problem is that this process takes time and the participants have attended meetings in the partnership from the beginning of the support period, which has given them an inequitable position right from the start. Is it perhaps the case that it is not until the support period begins to come to an end that the participants are 'fully charged' to be able

---

4   The expression 'a room of one's own' is taken from a Virginia Woolf (1945/1977) essay, which expresses the importance of having one's own space to female emancipation. This space, or room, can be of a physical or mental nature.

to and want to be involved in influencing structures? In the next section, a description is given of some of the collective actions that have actually taken place and which can lead to a structural impact in the long term.

7.6 From individual development to collective action via the partnership network

For most of the women in my study, it was an individual process of activation, while the collective process took place in group discussions through reflection on, and a mirroring of, each others' experiences. But according to several researchers, individual development is not enough to achieve long-term empowerment, (see for example Cooke 2002, Gutiérrez 1995, Herrick 1995, Ware 1999) since social relations are built on a super- and sub-ordination of groups and collective bodies. Therefore, individual development needs to be combined with collective action, for which the partnership offered an arena. The reflection in the group created a critical awareness, both towards each other and towards the world around them (c.f. Giddens 1991[5]). The greater awareness expressed itself among other ways in the list of approximately 40 'collisions with reality', or in other words the obstacles, which the participants felt hindered a return to working life. The list was created together with the co-ordinator and the study counsellor. One example of an obstacle is the fact that you cannot test studying at a university while at the same time retaining your sickness benefit, whereas it is possible to try studying at an upper-secondary school. The list led to collective action in the form of the dialogue seminar that was conducted with the entire partnership, at which the participants presented obstacles and/or collisions in different regulatory systems that they experienced during the course of their return to working life. However, this seminar did not result in any form of follow-up or continued discussion, and nor did it lead to any concrete results for the participants. However, it was one way of directly presenting views to the relevant organisations at the local level. It also provided a way for the participants to be regarded as representatives of the group of women on long-term sick leave and not as single individuals.

Another example of collective action was the meeting that was held with the County Insurance Delegation. This meeting resulted in a motion

---

5 Compare Gidden's (1991) division of human consciousness: the unconscious, practical consciousness and discursive consciousness. We use practical consciousness in our daily lives, often without reflecting on our actions, and it often consists of so-called tacit knowledge. Discursive consciousness constitutes discussion of and reflection on our actions.

to the Government on flexible health insurance, including a proposal for a variable return to working life. At present, any return to working life must be made in 25 per cent stages in compliance with social insurance office regulations. For many of the women, these steps were far too large, which they told the delegation.

A motion entitled 'Improve the re-adaptation of employees to working life after long-term sick leave' has also been submitted to the County Board. The motion takes up current issues that have been raised in dialogue with the participants, including how employees are received by employers on returning to work after long-term sick leave, and how they follow up on those employees who have returned to work.

Even if the women have been involved in certain collective processes aimed at changing regulations, they see no concrete results for their own part of the work they have done. The lessons that the 'recipients' learned, however, may provide a basis for working differently with preventive healthcare in the future. However, the collective action of the women on long-term sick leave indicates the benefit of the partnership. The experts – the women themselves – gained access to the social insurance office network, which would not have been possible without the partnership. Nor would the authorities have gained access to the knowledge of the women without their participation in the partnership.

7.7 Conclusions and discussion

My research shows that groups that find themselves in a situation of exclusion immediately and in the short term need individual development – which I have referred to in this context as empowerment – in order to end their feeling of powerlessness. After this, they can take action – individually and collectively. Participating in a partnership requires scope for action in order to be an equal partner. Dependency limits the scope for action. The participants also need to represent a group or an organisation, and not be regarded as representatives of their own individual cases.

Caplan and Stott (see Chapter 3) discuss how partnership literature is peppered with 'participatory language'. If the words are to have any credibility, they must be transformed into action or else the participants risk continued exclusion or being taken hostage. Being used as a hostage can in the worst instance mean being used as a legitimacy-creating partner, thus increasing the external credibility of a partnership. Another way of treating a group as a hostage is to reproduce the existing super- and sub-ordinance that exists in society.

In order to understand the roles in a partnership, positions of power must therefore be analysed. The importance of conducting a power analysis in order to find out how best to avoid reproducing prevailing power structures should be an important item on the agenda of a partnership that also has empowerment on the agenda (see Chapter 3). One lesson to be learnt, as pointed out by the co-ordinator, is that 'sitting at the same table does not automatically entail an equal division of power'. Figure 1 indicates the complexity in the organisation of the partnership. However, it does not show any power structures, which are often difficult to visualise theoretically since they are not explicit. Power can be explained on the basis of status, gender, contacts and, as in the case described, exclusion compared to inclusion. In the case described, it is perhaps fairly easy to illustrate inequalities when it comes to gender and professional status, whereas other power structures are more difficult to illustrate. Therefore, it is very important to work towards making the relations more equal so that all parties can experience the same value from taking part in a partnership. Otherwise, well-known power strategies will soon be repeated. Access to resources, the capacity for action and the ability to shape one's own life may serve as a platform for discussing the division of power in a partnership. Visualising power aspects in terms of power within, for and power over, gives a more varied picture. The development from powerlessness to greater control over one's own life gives, for the participants, an empirical understanding of the concept. This understanding must be followed by action, because without action the power aspect of empowerment is not visible. The dimension of the action will therefore be central. It is only when (collective and individual) action processes take place that the women experience resistance, which could be a sign that power structures are being challenged (c.f. Foucault 1980).

Is it then possible for a group of women on long-term sick leave to take part in a partnership and be able to contribute towards structural impact? They are in a position of dependency in relation to their employers and the social insurance office, and have lower positions in their working lives. They are women who are in poor health. They have no organisation that offers them support. Above all, they have lower self-esteem since they have been in a position of exclusion for a long time. Svensson (see Chapter 2) describes the risk of exclusion processes, such as gender and power positions, being reproduced in the partnership unless the partnership is transparent, non-hierarchical and based on a participatory concept. To this should be added the aspect of dependency (see also Chapter 9).

The concept of partnership is based on equal relations between the various organisations and players (see Chapters 2 and 3). If one party – in my study the women on long-term sick leave – is in a position of dependency on another party, the meeting will never be fair. My study shows that in the case of the women on long-term sick leave, their actions have personal and private consequences, whereas the actions of other players have organisational consequences. In the case of the women, a 'wrong' action has consequences on a personal plane since they do not represent an organisation. If, at the same time, they are dependent on other players this could have major consequences as regards their future working lives. This group of participants in the study would perhaps have experienced a greater sense of confidence and belief in other players in the partnership if they had not belonged to the same municipality. In other words, their dependency in terms of earning a living and their future working lives would not have been quite as important. They would have been able to act as representatives for a group of people on long-term sick leave instead of being regarded as separate individuals. They would then have been regarded more as a discussion partner and perhaps as a more 'fully qualified' representative of the partnership. The situation would also have been more supportive if they had been regarded as a large group with a shared view rather than as separate individuals representing only themselves.

> I feel, however, that we have not been taken seriously by the partnership. (participant)

One way of being able to exert influence in structures is to have access to a dialogue with those in power, or what has been referred to in the study as a change in the participants' institutional resources. Above all, the representative of the social insurance office stated clearly that it was positive to have direct contact with the participants and requested separate meetings with them, which was also experienced positively by the participants.

One proposal that was put forward by the participants was to invite other members of the partnership to attend meetings that were held by the participants – in other words, meetings where the participants would be in a majority as regards numbers and, for example, a representative of the employer would be invited to attend the meeting. This would have meant that the women could have supported each other in the group, at the same time as the employer would numerically have been 'the underdog'.

> A representative from each player should have been at our group meetings. If this had been built into the partnership, there would perhaps have been a completely different tempo at them or they would perhaps have ended in a completely different way. More would have happened, perhaps. (participant)

In Chapter 1, the question was raised as to whether the partnership organisation represents a new kind of strategy, which may overcome the limitations of earlier strategies. A bottom-up strategy based on activation of the participants is not useful in creating long-term effects, and the traditional top-down strategy is not effective for a variety of reasons. The partnership organisation can be seen as representing a 'dual strategy' for change, which includes both a strong representation 'from the top' (a system approach for change) and a participation 'from below' (an activation strategy).

My study shows that for those taking part, participation in the partnership was a paradox. It was an expression of a bottom-up strategy in a more traditional and short-term sense – in other words not in line with the intentions of a partnership, but more as a project based on an activation strategy. The participants were present at the meetings and were able to make their voices heard if they wanted and 'dared' to, and they had access to an arena, which they would not have been able to create themselves. But the strategy in the partnership also aimed to have a structural influence and thereby create changes in the long term. However, there have been no concrete changes for the women on long-term sick leave in this respect. On the other hand, changes have been made in the rehabilitation work and preventive health care work of the participating organisations.

A first sign of change which indicates a move from an activation strategy to partnership as a development strategy was the change in the language used that developed over the course of time, e.g. the steering group was called the strategy group during the latter part of the support period. The co-ordinator has pointed out that the major shortcoming in the organisation of the partnership was that the problem was not owned together, but that 'someone else' was expected to solve the problem of long-term sick leave in the municipality. The co-ordinator has also identified deficiencies in the grounding work which, after the event, we can see were partly the result of a lack of knowledge about the problem and partly of not knowing enough about the difference between running a project and organising a partnership (c.f. Chapter 3).

The reason for participating in the partnership – i.e. contributing to a sustainable working life in the long term – was not made sufficiently clear to the women on long-term sick leave. They had understood the purpose to be of a more short-term nature. They wanted to return to working life and their intention was to use the partnership as a player in order to test more unconventional ways of returning. The aspect the participants are most disappointed with is that fact that they did not succeed in influencing the partnership so that the work gave any concrete results for their own part, or in other words that more non-traditional ways were tested for getting back into working life. On the other hand, they can see in retrospect that they have nevertheless been able to contribute towards spreading knowledge about their problem, which other people on long-term sick leave can benefit from in the longer term.

In order for the participants to be able to cope with returning to work, radical changes need to be made in their working lives, as well as better chances to combine working life, family life and leisure time. The relatively extensive description of the process of powerlessness aims to reveal the forces and mechanisms that have to be addressed in order to create more basic changes for vulnerable groups in working life. In order for different activities in the project to lead to sustainable development, proper analysis needs to be conducted of both the powerlessness and the empowerment processes, as well as of those systems that restrict and make these processes possible. Changes that are based on a critical analysis provide the potential for learning and reflection, which are an important part of sustainable development work. The analysis that I have made shows that the conditions in workplaces must be changed in order for the participants to be able to cope with returning to work. Even if the co-ordinator realised this fact, it failed to penetrate the entire partnership, which meant that the most important piece in the jig-saw puzzle in a system for a sustainable working life was missing. The experience gained and the good results on an individual level meant that the development partnership applied for permission to continue with their work in the second part of the EQUAL Programme. The idea was to work pro-actively directly in certain selected workplaces and to guarantee homogeneity for the participants, i.e. in line with the definition of sustainability, but supplemented with a view of both paid and unpaid work. The application was based on the fact that employees at the workplaces and the people on long-term sick leave would co-operate. The participants were regarded as experts in the problems surrounding ill health and would serve as resources in the development work performed at the workplaces.

One conclusion is that the participants have increased their resources through the various activities in the partnership. I consider the fact that the organisation took place in the form of a development partnership to be of less importance for the development of participant resources. On the other hand, the collective action – which above all took place at the end of the support period – indicates the development potential of partnership as an organisational form. The participants were given access to various arenas, for example the Insurance Delegation, where they were able to make their voices heard and this was something that could eventually contribute towards more long-term development. The question is whether this could have happened if the change management work had been organised on the basis of an activation strategy. Hardly, but the real problem still remains: the partnership failed to contribute to the development of a strategy for influencing conditions at the women's workplaces in the long term. This is necessary in order for them to be able to return to work and – above all – to avoid new individuals being forced to take long-term sick leave. Sustainable development is namely a question of not consuming human resources, but instead creating and developing them (cf. Gatu 2005).

References

Aagaard Nielsen, K & Svensson, L (2006) (eds.) *Action Research and Interactive Research. Beyond practice and theory,* Maastricht: Shaker Publishing
Cooke, H (2002) 'Empowerment'. In Blakeley, G & Bryson, V (eds.) *Contemporary Political Concepts. A Critical Introduction.* London: Pluto Press
Elle, J C (2006) 'Other Futures are Possible'. In Aagaard Nielsen, K & Svensson, L (eds.) *Action Research and Interactive Research. Beyond practice and theory,* Maastricht: Shaker Publishing
Forssén, A S & Carlstedt, G (2006) 'It's heavenly to be alone!: A room of one's own as a health promoting resource for women. Results from a qualitative study'. *Scandinavian Journal of Public Health*, Vol. 34, pp. 175–181
Foucault, M (1980) *The History of Sexuality* New York: Vintage Books
Franzblau, S H & Moore, M (2001) 'Socializing Efficacy: A Reconstruction of Self-Efficacy Theory within the Context of Inequality'. *Journal of Community & Applied Social Psychology*, No. 11, pp. 83–96
Gambles, R, Lewis, S & Rapoport, R (2006) *The Myth of Work-Life Balance: the challenge of our time for men, women and societies,* Chichester: John Wiley & Sons Ltd
Gatu, H (2005) *Hållbara arbetsplatser. Botemedel mot ett sjukt arbetsliv.* Stockholm: Arbetslivsinstitutet
Giddens, A (1991) *Modernity and Self-Identity. Self and Society in the Late Modern Age.* Cambridge: Polity Press
Guest, D E (2002) 'Perspectives on the study of work-life balance. *Social Science Information'*, Vol. 41, No. 2, pp. 255–279
Gutiérrez, L M (1995) 'Understanding the empowerment process: Does consciousness make a difference?' *Social Work Research*, Vol. 19, No. 4
Herr, K & Anderson, G L (2005) *The Action Research Dissertation. A Guide for Students and Faculty.* Thousand Oaks: Sage
Herrick, J (1995) *Empowerment Practice and Social Change: The Place for New Social Movement Theory.* Working draft prepared for the New Social Movement. www.interweb-tech.com/nsmnet/docs/herrick.htm 2005-05-27
Härenstam, A, Karlqvist, L Bodin, L, Nise, G, Schéele, P and the MOA Research Group (2003) 'Patterns of working and living conditions: a holistic, multi-

variate approach to occupational health studies'. *Work & Stress*, Vol. 17, No. 1, pp. 73–92

Johansson, G (2002) 'Work-Life Balance: the case of Sweden in the 1990s'. *Social Science Information*, Vol. 41, No. 2, pp. 303–317

Kabeer, N (2001) 'Resources, Agency, Achievements: Reflections on the Measurement of Women's Empowerment'. In Sevefjord B & Olsson B (eds.) *Discussing Women's Empowerment – Theory and Practice*. Sida Studies No. 3, Stockholm

Kilbom, Å, Messing, K & Bildt Thorbjörnsson, C (eds.) (1998) *Women's Health at Work*, Stockholm: National Institute of Working Life

Kodz, J, Harper, H & Dench, S (2002) *Work-Life Balance: Beyond the Rhetoric*. The Institute for Employment Studies, Report 384

Larsson, A-C (2006) 'Interactive Research – Methods and conditions for joint analysis'. In Aagaard Nielsen, K & Svensson, L (eds.) *Action Research and Interactive Research. Beyond practice and theory*. Maastricht: Shaker Publishing

Nordenmark, M (2004) 'Balancing work and family demands. Do increasing demands increase strain? A longitudinal study'. *Scandinavian Journal of Public Health*, No. 32 pp. 450–455

von Otter, C (2004) *Aktivt arbetsliv. Om dagens behov och framtidens möjligheter – en trendanalys*. Stockholm: Arbetslivsinstitutet

Prilleltensky, I (1994) 'Empowerment in mainstream psychology: legitimacy, obstacles, and opportunities'. *Canadian Psychology*, No. 35, pp. 358–374

Prilleltensky, I, Nelson, G & Peirson, L (2001) 'The Role of Power and Control in Children's Lives: An Ecological Analysis of Pathways toward Wellness, Resilience and Problems'. *Journal of Community & Applied Social Psychology*, No. 11, pp. 143–158

SOU 2006:107 *Fokus på åtgärder – en plan för effektiv rehabilitering i arbetslivet*. Statens offentliga utredningar

SOU 2005:73 *Reformerad föräldraförsäkring: kärlek, omvårdnad, trygghet: betänkande*. Statens offentliga utredningar

Svensson, L & Aagaard Nielsen, K (2006) 'A Framework for the Book'. In Aagaard Nielsen, K & Svensson, L (eds.) *Action Research and Interactive Research. Beyond practice and theory*, Maastricht: Shaker Publishing

Ware, N C (1999) 'Evolving consumer households: an experiment in community living for people with severe psychiatric disorders'. *Psychiatric Rehabilitation Journal*, Vol. 23, No. 1

Williams, S (1994) *The Oxfam Gender Training Manual*. Oxfam UK and Ireland

Woolf, V (1945/1977) *A room of ones own*. London: Grafton

8. With the Target Groups as Partners

8.1 Aims and content

This chapter deals with the third problem area addressed in the book – partnership in relation to democracy. One way of striving to promote democracy in the work of partnerships may be to give the target groups a real chance to participate. The guidelines for the EQUAL partnerships emphasise the importance of excluded groups – for example the unemployed or those on the long-term sicklist – being able to make their voices heard, of the activities being run in line with a bottom-up perspective and of basing the activities on initiatives and ideas from the players and the target groups themselves, i.e. from those affected by the problem that the partnership has been set-up to solve (EQUAL 2000). This is why the development partnerships are encouraged to ensure that target groups and target-group organisations have the opportunity to participate in decision-making processes and in the running of operations.

One of the ambitions of the EQUAL programme is thus that the target groups should participate in the work of the partnerships, but how does this actually work in practice? Do the target groups participate on the same terms as the other partners? This chapter focuses on how ideas on the participation of the target groups are translated into practice in the local context. I will discuss the potential and the possibilities of the target groups to function as equal partners (in relation to the other partners involved) in a development partnership. In the development partnership I have studied, the target group is actually a partner, which is unusual in the EQUAL context.

The development partnership that forms the empirical basis of my study is introduced at the beginning of the chapter and the method used is then described. This is followed by a section that links ideas about partnership to the translation concept. The internal preconditions for the target group as a partner in the development partnership are highlighted in the following sections, and then the external preconditions for the target group's representatives at the individual, organisational and community level are examined. The chapter concludes with a discussion of the target group's participation as a partner and the obstacles and opportunities this may entail.

8.2 Members and activities in the development partnership

The development partnership studied, which is an EQUAL project, aims to find new ways back to the labour market for the long-term sicklisted and the long-term unemployed, and to identify obstacles to their rehabilitation. The idea is that new routes for a return to work can be demonstrated by creating and testing new models. An important basis for the birth of the project was a report written by a group of individuals on the long-term sicklist who had exhaustion symptoms. Their report called for changes in rehabilitation work for such individuals.

There are nine partners in the development partnership. These are representatives of the public sector (the Social Insurance Office, the County Labour Board, the County Council, local authorities and local authority associations), the private sector in the form of organisations that represent employers (one employers' organisation) and employees (one trade union organisation), the third sector (Coompanion, which supports co-operative development) and of the target group (made up of the long-term sicklisted and the long-term unemployed). The target group has eight representatives, which constitutes half of the development partnership, while the remaining organisations each have one ordinary representative – making a total of sixteen representatives. Five people are employed on a project basis in the EQUAL project and trainees are also involved for varying periods of time.

In the activities run by the partnership in 2006, 250 individuals are recorded on the list of participants, of which 150 belonged to the target group of long-term sicklisted. This list contains people who expressed an interest in participating in the partnership's activities irrespective of whether they actually participated in an activity or not. In 2006, 62 short-term activities were carried out with a total of 885 participants, and sixteen longer activities with a total of 149 participants.

The short-term activities included many 'try it out' activities such as yoga, expressive art, rhetoric in connection with job applications and training for job interviews. The longer activities ran for several weeks and included identifying possibilities and options, personal planning for the future and training in rhetoric. Psychodrama, group coaching and mentor programmes were other elements of the longer activities carried out.

The activities were largely planned on the basis of the wishes of the participants. A large proportion of the participants are women on the long-term sicklist and it has been difficult to recruit men to the activities. There are only 53 men on the list of participants, and not all of these can be said to have been active. As the bottom-up perspective has been central in the design of the activities, members of the target group have been able to request activities that they feel would strengthen them. It has sometimes been difficult, however, to clarify the link between participation in enjoyable activities and the testing of different ways (innovative ways) of returning to working life.

8.3 My method

A longitudinal case study of the development partnership was conducted in 2006 and 2007. The methods used included document studies, interviews and observation. The documents used for this chapter are mainly the partnership's implementation plan, the partnership agreement and the minutes of meetings. Interviews were conducted in June 2006 and February 2007. One person from each partner organisation, two people from the target group and two members of the project personnel were interviewed. The interviews have been transcribed and the interviewees are given fictitious names when their comments are presented in this chapter. There were also informal discussions, for example in connection with the observation sessions, which provided useful information. The observation sessions that primarily constitute the basis for this chapter entailed observation of the monthly development partnership meetings.

I was able to gain access to the development partnership due to my role as an external evaluator, work which was funded by the partnership although I was employed at a scientific institution. Evaluation reports, both written and verbal, were submitted in connection with the monthly partnerships meetings. These reports formed the basis for discussions within the partnership on issues of interest at the time. About a week after the partnership meetings, reflection meetings were held together with the personnel and the partnership's chairperson.

Below, the term 'organisational representatives' is used to designate those who represent the various organisations in the partnership, while those who represent the target group are designated 'target group representatives'. The text contains quotations in which people from the target group have different designations: clients, experts and participants. These designations are dealt with in the section 'The representative role'.

8.4 Ideas about partnership are transported and translated

Ideas about partnership can travel – for example from the Continent to Sweden – and eventually reach the local level where an individual partnership interprets these ideas and translates them into its own context. The European Commission has drawn up guidelines for successful private-public partnerships (EC 2003), and in Sweden there is the Community Initiative Programme for EQUAL 2000–2006 (EQUAL 2000) which, among other things, highlights the importance of the participation of the target groups. These documents are then interpreted and translated in the partnerships.

The translation concept (Callon 1986, Latour 1986, 1987) is central to the study of the transportation and translation of ideas. Characteristics of this concept are that active players are involved in the translation of an idea and that ideas are moved and changed in a translation process. How ideas are translated varies depending on how the players involved act and how the ideas are packaged for the move. The players can choose to change an idea, add something or simply reject the idea (Latour 1986). Several studies have demonstrated local variations when ideas are translated in a local context (Blomquist 1996, Fernler 1996, Hwang & Suarez 2005). Erlingsdóttir's (1999) study shows that an idea that is loosely packaged is translated by means of reinterpretation, while an idea that is ready-packaged, in the form of a model, is translated by means of copying. The loosely-packaged idea is also moved between different organisational fields, which may have an impact on reinterpretation. Ideas that lack a clear model for application thus provide great scope for action at the local level, while ideas that have a distinct application model limit the interpretation options of the local players (Johansson 2002).

In connection with the translation concept, the concepts of the 'obligatory passage point' (Callon 1986) and the 'black box' (Latour 1987) can also be applied. An obligatory passage point is a form of control, or a means of exercising power, that players must pass to achieve their objectives and move on (Callon 1986), such as an exam or an economic crisis (Blomquist 1996). The economic crisis is described in terms of 'the organisation bleeding', which calls for rapid measures. The black box represents something complex that we know little about, other than its input and output, and which is not questioned (Latour 1987).

A constructivist approach can be applied to the use of translation as a theoretical concept. Language and its importance in constructing our reality is emphasised, and language can be seen as a form of action that constructs our reality (Kristensson Uggla 2002). A constructed category can be seen as an interactive category, where interaction takes place between the idea of a certain category and the people categorised (Hacking 1999). People can become aware that they belong to a certain category and begin to act in line with this. When new knowledge about a category becomes known to those categorised their behaviour may change, which means in turn that the categorisation must be changed, the so-called feedback effect (Hacking 1999).

Aspects of the translation concept and the constructivist approach can be found in the 'conceptual model' that Czarniawska and Joerges (1996) have formulated concerning how ideas are transported in the world and translated in their new context in order to be of practical benefit. Ideas are translated and materialised in the form of an object – for example a text or an image – and as such the idea can be transported further. The object is then translated into action and is repeated and stabilised before gradually becoming institutionalised. At the new location reached by the idea, it is in turn translated into an object that can be sent on its way.

This conceptual model is used as a starting point in my study of ideas about partnership. Co-operation in development partnerships is, in my view, an ambiguous and complex process for which the translation concept, with its focus on processes and the actions of the local players, provides a relevant starting point. In partnership work, I also see the process as a learning process in which events during the course of the process provide insights and new knowledge. The next section deals with how ideas on the participation of the target groups are translated into action by the local players in the development partnership studied.

8.5 Ideas on the participation of target groups are translated

The ambition of the EQUAL programme is thus that the target groups should participate in the development partnerships. In Chapter 9, it is noted that there are few partnerships in which the target groups are represented, while this chapter illustrates an example of the opposite. Here, the translation of ideas on the participation of target groups in the local context is mainly addressed on the basis of the internal situation in the partnership, and I begin by highlighting the governing documents.

8.5.1 Governing documents

The governing documents for the work of the partnership stress that the target group is an important player. The vision, for example, speaks of 'creating more new routes back to working life that are client-controlled' and says that the project will help to 'make decision-makers at the national level aware of the clients' knowledge and experience as expert resources in the field of rehabilitation back to working life.' The implementation plan says that the unique feature of the project is 'the controlling function of the clients in the project which is guaranteed by the fact that they constitute half of the development partnership.'

All of the partners in the partnership are expected to contribute to the development and implementation of the project. The partnership agreement says that 'everyone's participation and involvement is equal. No partner should carry more weight than any other and the expertise and knowledge of all the partners should be respected and utilised.'

The implementation plan for the project states that those who represent the target group as a partner in the development partnership should have a larger group of clients who act as a form of reference group. The clients should also constitute a majority in a planned management group for the project's activities.

During the planning of the project itself, there were eight representatives of the target group, but in connection with the actual start of the project several of these dropped out, partly because of uncertainties about whether their sickness benefit would be affected by their participation in the project, and the acting project co-ordinator had to try to get replacements from the target group. Without the active participation of the target group many of the ambitions of the project would be unattainable.

On the basis of the intentions of the EQUAL programme to involve target groups, this development partnership thus chose to include the target group as a partner and to see the knowledge and experience of the target group as assets. There is nothing explicit in the documents to say that the target groups should participate as partners, only that it should be possible to utilise their expertise in various ways. In the partnership studied in Chapter 7, some members of the target group sometimes participated in the partnership meetings depending on whether they had the time and energy to do so. The scope that exists for interpreting the intentions of the EQUAL programme regarding the participation of target groups is rather considerable. The idea that the target groups should participate can be seen as loosely packaged, as it is up to the individual partnerships to interpret and translate how the participation of the target groups should take place. The governing documents make it clear that the target groups should be seen as valuable representatives in the partnerships.

In the case of the development partnership studied it was important to include the target group and this was stipulated in the governing documents. The fact that there were too few target group representatives at the start of the project itself demanded a great deal of commitment on the part of the project management. This could be seen as an obligatory passage point as far as the project is concerned. Without target group representatives it was difficult to run the project in line with the original intentions.

8.5.2 The representative role

The role of the target group in a partnership is not entirely given. First, the target group is made up of individuals who are covered by the activities run by the project and, secondly, they are a group of individuals with different backgrounds and experience. The target group thus becomes both a recipient of the project's activities and a bearer and transmitter of its members' experience of what it is to be sicklisted or unemployed in order to thereby influence the activities of the project.

Initially, the target group's representatives in the development partnership consisted of individuals who had been involved in writing the report that was an important basis for the setting up of the EQUAL project. During the course of the project, the representatives of the target group were appointed as a result of the personnel asking interested and committed individuals to take on this role. Members of the target group also asked certain individuals to become new representatives.

Those who represented the target group in the development partnership, as well as those who participated in the project's activities, were designated differently during the course of the project. Initially they were called beneficiaries, then experts and finally participants. The term 'beneficiaries' predominated in the early stages and was used at meetings and in documents. The report that formed the basis for the project was, for example, commonly referred to as 'the beneficiaries report'.

The term 'experts' was introduced by members of the target group in early 2006 as they felt that they were the experts at being ill and unemployed. Their expertise, in terms of their knowledge about their own situation, was highlighted in this way. The name change was also adopted at the transnational level where 'The Beneficiary Group' became 'The Expert Group'. Experts is still the term used transnationally, while in Sweden it was only used for a short time.

Not all of the members of the target group wanted to call themselves experts so it was decided to use the term 'participants' instead. Being an expert can be perceived as being more demanding than being a participant, which may be one of the reasons for the name change.

Some people were 'lured' to accept the role as a representative of the target group at development partnership meetings by being told that 'you only need to represent yourself and it is important that you share your experience with us'. In other words, recruitment was based on the experience of the individual. An organisational representative, Ulf, said at a development partnership meeting that it was good to have many target-group representatives as this provided a broad spectrum of views. Another organisational representative, Anna, pointed out that it was good to involve new target-group representatives in the development partnership and that the members of the partnership must not become 'expert experts'.

The fact that the target group must be represented in the partnership is concrete, but exactly how the target group should be represented and what role it should play are factors that are open to interpretation. Here too, there is a lot of room for manoeuvre. The designation of the target-group representatives is an example of something that was reinterpreted during the process. What do the different interpretations of the designations used entail? For example, does the term beneficiary suggest a relatively passive role? My understanding is that the term beneficiary is widely used in the vocabulary of the Social Insurance Office, and representatives of this organisation played an active role in the early stages of the project. The term expert may suggest a more active role and indicates expertise and someone who can be subjected to higher demands. On the other hand, not as much may be demanded of a participant. As I see it, this reinterpretation of the term used for people from the target group, irrespective of whether they only participated in the activities or were target-group representatives in the developed partnership, indicates a degree of uncertainty about what the role must and should entail. There are different expectations regarding the role and different interpretations of what it entails.

It can be said that the designation of the target group and the target-group representatives underwent a translation process during the course of the project. The sense of the language used in connection with the construction of a category for the target group in the partnership have been factors here, and the target group can be seen as an interactive category.

8.5.3 Being heard

The importance of being heard has been addressed in Chapter 9, and this can be seen as an important factor in the creation of equal relationships. In the partnership studied, one of the measures taken to ensure that the voice of the target group was heard in the development partnership meetings was to list this as a separate item on the agenda. From and including the meeting held in March 2006, an item headed 'The Participants' was reserved for members of the target group. Initially, they took up issues such as the 'us and them' atmosphere they perceived to exist between the organisational representatives and the target-group representatives. They also pointed out that the language used by personnel from public authorities can be difficult to understand and that it was necessary to appreciate that people suffering from burn-out sometimes lose track when speaking. Subsequently, they asked what the organisational representatives were doing to disseminate information about the project in their own organisations. The target-group representatives took the opportunity to relate their own experience and portray their own situation. This could, for example, relate to an individual who had ended up in a no-man's land between the sickness insurance and unemployment insurance systems.

At the beginning, it was no simple matter for the target-group representatives to make their voices heard. The two representatives Britta and Karolina both say that it was difficult to follow the discussions on the completion of the application for the implementation phase, and they felt that the discussion got bogged down in petty details. The meetings also went on far too long without a break. The uncertainty felt by the target-group representatives at the beginning was described by Karolina as follows:

> At the start I just sat there wide-eyed and looked around me wondering if I would ever dare to say anything.

The organisational representatives also describe how the target-group representatives seemed to be uncomfortable in their role:

> I'm sure they had a lot that they wanted to say, but they never said anything and I was extremely frustrated because they didn't say what I thought they were thinking. [...] I though the meetings were frustrating. (Gunilla, an organisational representative)

The difference between the organisational representatives and the target-group representatives is described by Håkan (an organisational representative):

> We didn't listen to them and we were very intolerant of their way of working and reasoning, that is that they were slower than us hyper-efficient public officials.

As the members of the development partnership got to know each other, the atmosphere at the meetings gradually became more open. The officials from the public authorities tried to simplify their language and the target group representatives were able to speak and were listened to.

> I actually think that we taught the other participants to listen to what we had to say. [...] People rub off on one another after a while and [...] perhaps we learn a little more that we should wait for our turn to speak [...] so it's a kind of evening out maybe. (Karolina, a target-group representative).

The differences between the representatives from the target-group and those from the organisations were initially very noticeable, for example in the way that they behaved and expressed themselves. A form of categorisation of the respective groups therefore took place in the interplay between the representatives. The two constructed categories can then be seen as interactive categories.

The fact that the target group had its own item on the agenda, which was a means of highlighting their experience, may in my view have directed focus away from other items on the agenda. The interest and involvement of the target-group representatives became focused on this item, while other items on the agenda did not receive the same attention from them.

8.5.4 *Responsibility and powers*

How were factors such as responsibility and powers for the target-group representatives translated in the partnership? If we see activity in meetings as an aspect of taking responsibility, then we can say that the target-group representatives were well represented in the development partnership meetings. In the nine meetings observed in the period May 2006 to March 2007, the target-group representatives were fewer than eight (six or seven) on only three occasions. At one meeting there were exactly eight and on the other five occasions there were nine to eleven target-group representatives at the meetings. On those occasions when the target group had more than eight representatives, ordinary members with voting rights were appointed on site among those present.

In the late autumn of 2006 and the winter of 2007, there were always more target-group representatives than organisational representatives at the meetings. Despite this, the organisational representatives have always had more to say. The target group, which constitutes half of the partnership, accounts for only one quarter of the statements made at meetings.

There was a lack of consistency among the target-group representatives in the development partnership. At six of the meetings I observed in 2006, a total of seventeen different individuals represented the target group. Of these, only three participated on all six occasions. As mentioned above, target-group representatives to the development partnership were not appointed democratically in an election process. Instead, interested people were approached by the personnel and by other target-group representatives. An advantage of the addition of new target-group representatives is that it made it possible for the partnership to learn from the experience of more individuals, a fact that was welcomed by some of the organisational representatives (see the section on the representative role).

Prior to the development partnership meetings, the target-group representatives met for a few days to prepare, primarily for their own item on the agenda. Not much time was devoted, however, to preparing for other items on the agenda.

Apart from participating in development partnership meetings, the target-group representatives were also members of various working groups. There was a tendency for operative working groups, for example the group that worked with operational planning, to find it easy to attract target-group representatives, while more strategically-oriented groups found this more difficult. A clear difference between the genders was evident in this context. The operational planning group contained only women (mainly target-group representatives), while men (both organisational representatives and target-group representatives) were members of the more strategically-oriented working group. In the highest decision-making body of the partnership, the organisations were largely represented by men, while the members of the target group (the sicklisted and unemployed) were mainly represented by women.

The fact that the target-group representatives were involved in decision making within the partnership may at first glance be perceived as positive as the target group was well represented in the highest decision-making body, namely the development partnership meetings. However, a closer examination of the type of decisions taken at the meetings and the drafting process reveals a different picture. One example is when representatives of the main funders of the partnership (all men) were commissioned in the autumn of 2006 to review the financial situation and employer responsibility in the partnership or, as the target-group representative Britta puts it – 'that was when the budget bomb was dropped'. None of the target-group representatives were involved in the discussions conducted by the funders. The formal decision on the measures proposed by the funders was, on the other hand, made at a development partnership meeting in which the target-group representatives did take part.

Where were the operational decisions made? Many of the decisions were made by the personnel group, under powers delegated by the development partnership, and the target group was not represented here. When the project was designed, a management group in which the target-group representatives would be in the majority was planned. The intention was that this management group would be subordinate to the development partnership and act roughly as an operative steering group. Such a group was never appointed.

If we examine the possibilities of the target group to take responsibility as representatives in the development partnership, then we can see certain problems connected with the addition of new representatives who were perhaps unclear about what being a member of the partnership meant and not always aware of the objectives of the project. Moreover, new members of the development partnership were perhaps not always updated about previous events. This may have made it difficult to understand the implications and effects of some of the decisions made. Another aspect concerning responsibility in the partnership is that it may have been unclear to the target group representatives exactly where overall responsibility lay – with the development partnership, the chairperson or the personnel. The arrangement with a rolling chairpersonship – a new chairperson every six months – and the lack of discussion on common objectives may have contributed to a degree of uncertainty on the issue of responsibility.

Ideas concerning the participation of the target group in meetings were translated in this partnership in terms of it being important to 'fill the seats' for target-group representatives at the partnership meetings. The importance of the target group being well represented tended to become more important than the continuity that may be required to learn about the operations concerned and exert influence.

Another tendency that can be discerned is that the target group was involved in the 'easier' working groups while the strategic working group, for example, was not attractive at all. It may be that it is seen as more demanding to participate in groups that work with strategic and financial issues, which may be seen as a type of black box. The fact that the financial crisis in the project was described as 'the budget bomb' by one of the target group representatives is perhaps an indication that the target group was not familiar with the financial aspects of the project. When the news about the financial difficulties emerged, it therefore came as 'a bombshell'.

The focus on the 'participants' item during the meetings may have been perceived as a 'safe harbour' in the midst of the complicated whole represented by all the items on the agenda – a whole that the participants had neither the energy nor the desire to address. This brings the question of responsibility to a head in terms of whether the target-group representatives wanted to shoulder full responsibility or whether they were satisfied to concentrate on their own item and the presentation of their own experience.

8.6 The significance of the context

Above I have examined how the participation of the target group was translated in a specific partnership. In this section, I would above all like to discuss in more detail the significance of the context for the target group as a partner. Here I take up examples of external conditions outside the specific partnership that may affect target group representatives in their role within a partnership. I do not claim, however, that this is a comprehensive discussion of contextual impact factors. Gender, for instance, is an example of a power structure in society that is dealt with in more detail elsewhere in this book. The context as discussed below is viewed especially from the target-group representatives' point of view and I have chosen to deal with this at the individual, organisational and social levels.

The Context

Society	→	The Context	←	Society
Organisation	→	Development partnership	←	Organisation
Individual	→	Target group representative	←	Individual

Figure 1: The context within and outside the partnership.

8.7 The individual level

At the individual level I see the individuals' own situation, state of health, financial status and competence as factors that can influence them in their role as target-group representatives. People who have been sicklisted or unemployed for a long time may be unsure of their own ability to cope with the tasks involved. They may not be ready to shoulder the responsibility of being a target group representative. Their illness may make it difficult for them to participate. They may not have the energy required, or may find it difficult to concentrate. Their own situation and state of health may make it difficult for them to play a sufficiently driving role, a factor that is also taken up in Chapter 7.

A matter of concern regarding the financial situation of the target-group representatives was whether their entitlement to sickness benefit or unemployment benefit would be questioned due to their involvement in the partnership. Would they be considered too healthy to receive sickness benefit? This was a dilemma at the start of the project and the importance of the participants getting the go-ahead from the relevant authorities and of having their participation recorded in their rehabilitation plans was underlined.

Previous experience of meetings and knowledge of meeting procedures – for example an awareness of meeting routines and knowing how to request the floor – may be elements of individual competence that facilitate the participation of target-group representatives. Several of the representatives have said that their lack of experience was a problem initially, and that the language used at the meetings was also an obstacle. The study by Wistus (Chapter 9) also reveals that individual experience of how work is conducted in meetings makes life easier for the representatives.

8.8 The organisational level

At the organisational level, my focus here is mainly on an organisation that does not exist, namely that for the target group. There is no specific organisation for the target group, there is no tradition of including the target group as a partner, and in the studied partnership the target group consists of several sub-groups.

The target group did not establish any form of organisation for itself. The lack of such an organisation for the target group also meant that there was no natural context in which to train new development-partnership representatives in, for example, meeting techniques, or to identify and discuss the issues that the target group wanted to pursue in the partnership concerning, for example, changes in the regulatory systems.

There was no previous tradition in the county of including the target group as a partner, and the organisational representatives consequently had no experience of this. The only existing experience of this type is that the Social Insurance Office has reference groups with various client organisations, while the County Labour Board sometimes conducts focus-group interviews with different target groups.

The fact that the target group consisted of several sub-groups means that the target-group representatives had to consider several different perspectives. In the development partnership studied, people on the long-term sicklist predominated, both as participants in the activities and as representatives at development partnership meetings.

8.8.1 *The social level*

At the social level, factors such as benefit and payment levels, regulations and supervision affect the situation of the target-group representatives. Political decisions may change the conditions governing all of these three factors and have an influence at all three levels. This may relate, for example, to a change in the direction of labour-market policy that also changes the preconditions for participating in projects. The authorities involved may also adopt new working methods regarding, for example, supervisions and follow-up.

Decisions on the regulations governing sickness and unemployment benefit may affect the situation of target-group representatives. Several of those who participated in the activities arranged by the development partnership studied pointed out that they felt that 'big brother was watching them' in that public officials were careful to point out that such participation should not comprise more than five hours per week. The result was that some participants were fearful about having their names recorded on attendance lists, which in turn led to problems for the project's co-funding.

8.9 Discussion

How were the ideas about the participation of the target group translated in the local context in the partnership studied? The partnership documents state that the target-group representatives should play a governing role, by means of their participation in various governing functions, and also share their experience.

When the project started it seemed that the forms and content of the role of target-group representative was not entirely clear, as is indicated by the change in designation (beneficiary, expert and participant). When the target-group representatives were recruited to the development partnership, there was a greater focus on including them on the basis of their experience rather than on their governing role in the project. 'The Participants' item on the agenda also indicates that the focus was more on sharing and presenting experience than on encouraging active participation on the other items. If conveying experience was the main function of the participation of the target group, then 'The Participants' item fulfilled this function and there was 'no need' for the target-group representatives to concern themselves with other issues such as the financial status of the project.

Financial issues acted as obligatory passage points for the project on two occasions. The first concerned the financial situation of the target-group representatives, which was important to their participation and to the start-up of the project. The second concerned the financial crisis in the project which had to be resolved for the project to survive. On this occasion, the target-group representatives were not allowed to take part in the discussion with the funders. On the first occasion, the experience of the target group was of great importance to the start-up of the project. On the second occasion, however, the experience and views of the target group were not considered to be as important.

The target group was represented in the development partnership and in various working groups. It took responsibility by participating in meetings and by helping to select the activities run by the project. However, the target group did not participate as much in the management of the project itself. The question here is whether it was not allowed to take responsibility, or whether it did not want to? Factors such as the members' state of health and the lack of an organisation of their own may have been important here. If a target group is to assume more responsibility in the running of a project it is, in my view, important that it also takes responsibility for the orientation of the activities, the achievement of targets and the financial situation. This demands more of the representatives than that they simply represent themselves and their own situation. They need to be more well-informed of the objectives and aims of the project in order to be able to take on more responsibility.

In my view, therefore, the ideas about the participation of the target group were, in this partnership, translated more in terms of conveying experience than in terms of shouldering responsibility for the governance of the project.

I feel that one of the greatest difficulties associated with the participation of the target group as a partner is the state of health of the target-group representatives (above all in the case of those on the long-term sicklist), as it can be difficult to play a driving role if one is not feeling well. This requires the understanding of the other members of the partnership. Another difficulty that clearly emerges in my study is the lack of an organisation for the target group itself. It can be difficult to hold a group accountable, or demand that it should shoulder certain responsibilities, when it has no organisation of its own. Without such an organisation, there is also no natural forum for training new target-group representatives and no structure to back-up individual representatives. In the partnership studied, however, the target group did hold preparatory meetings that provided a form of back-up for the presentation of the group's views at future development partnership meetings.

The lack of an organisation for the target group itself is also taken up in Chapters 7 and 9. In my view, such an organisation would offer the target-group representatives the opportunity to grow and develop. People who feel well are able to shoulder a greater responsibility, and in their own organisation the members of the target group would be able to get training in democratic processes by, for example, electing their representatives to the development partnership. A target-group organisation could be compared to a trade union which, among other things, canvasses the views of its members and promotes issues of importance to them.

In the partnership studied, I do not see the target group as an equal partner in relation to the organisations. On the other hand, there are differences between the organisational representatives in terms, for example, of taking responsibility and the level of involvement in decision-making. However, the target group representatives were respected and listened to by the other members of the partnership when it came to their experience of being sicklisted and unemployed. The fact that the target-group representatives conveyed their experience to the organisational representatives may lead to insights and changes in the long term.

The question remains whether a target group should be included as a partner in a partnership or not. My answer at the moment is that I believe it is good to involve the target group as it comprises the people who will be affected by the measures taken and the solutions found in a project. However, I am not entirely sure whether the target group should be included as a partner – with all the obligations and responsibilities this entails – or be represented in some other way. I do believe, however, that it is important to discuss and clarify the role that the representatives of a target group should play in a partnership in order for their participation to be effective – for the target group as well as for the partnership concerned.

References

Blomquist, C (1996) *I marknadens namn. Mångtydiga reformer i svenska kommuner.* Stockholm: Nerenius & Santérus Förlag

Callon, M (1986) 'Some elements of a sociology of translation: Domestication of the scallops and the fishermen of St Brieuc's Bay'. In Law, J (ed.) *Power, Action, and Belief: A New Sociology of Knowledge?* London: Routledge & Kegan Paul

Czarniawska, B & Joerges, B (1996) 'Travels of Ideas'. In Czarniawska, B & Sevón, G (eds.) *Translating organizational change.* Berlin: de Gruyter

Erlingsdóttir, G (1999) *Förförande idéer – kvalitetssäkring i hälso- och sjukvården.* Lund University: Ekonomihögskolan

EC (European Commission) (2003) *Guidelines for successful public-private partnerships.* Bruxelles: European Commission

EQUAL (2000) *Gemenskapsinitiativprogram för EQUAL 2000–2006, SVERIGE*

Fernler K (1996) *Mångfald eller likriktning. Effekter av en avreglering.* Stockholm: Nerenius & Santérus Förlag

Hacking, I (1999) *Social konstruktion av vad?* Stockholm: Thales

Hwang, H & Suarez, D (2005) 'Lost and Found in the Translation of Strategic Plans and Websites'. In Czarniawska, B & Sevón, G (eds.) *Global ideas. How Ideas, Objects and Practices Travel in the global Economy.* Malmö: Liber

Johansson, R (2002) *Nyinstitutionalismen inom organisationsanalysen.* Lund: Studentlitteratur

Kristensson Uggla, B (2002) *Slaget om verkligheten.* Brutus Östlings Bokförlag Symposion AB

Latour, B (1986) 'The Powers of Association'. In Law J (ed.) *Power, Action, and Belief: A New Sociology of Knowledge?* London: Routledge & Kegan Paul

– (1987) *Science in action.* Milton Keynes: Open University Press

9. Birds of a feather flock together – On representation and equal relationships in partnerships

9.1 Introduction

Traditional hierarchical forms of organisation for development work have been questioned and criticised because of democratic shortcomings. There is above all criticism of a lack of thorough grounding at different levels and far too narrow a representation, which means that many players who are directly affected by problems are not represented. Partnership has been launched and described as an answer to this criticism and as a form of organisation that permits exactly this broad representation and equal relationships between players from different contexts and levels (see the EQUAL Programme document entitled 'Integrating partnerships in ESF programmes 2007–2013', Geddes & Benington 2001). The strategy in partnerships is to work through representation ('top down') and to involve those players who are closest to the problem ('bottom up') in order to permit co-operation between players who in traditional organisational forms find themselves at different levels and thus rarely meet (see Chapter 1). It is thus hoped that partnership will constitute a vitalising complement to prevailing democratic processes. A central concept in the talk about democratic vitalisation is also that co-operation in partnerships is a more effective way of directing and organising community planning and community development. Broad representation in network-like, non-hierarchical organisational forms should give rise to more effective problem-solving in that the players involved in the co-operation design quicker, more flexible and needs-oriented solutions, so-called *good governance* (Integrating partnerships in ESF programmes 2007–2013).

But how is partnership conducted in practice? Does organisation in a partnership involve a potential vitalisation of democratic processes? The purpose of this chapter is, on the basis of studies of Swedish development partnerships within the EU programme EQUAL, to analyse how democratic values are expressed in the practice of partnership.

Stott and Caplan show in Chapter 3 how many of the concepts that are used to describe and talk about partnership are linked to democracy. Examples of central concepts that comprise democratic values are broad representation, involvement, equality, empowerment and transparency. This chapter is limited to dealing with two central democratic concepts – representation and equal relationships. The following questions are in focus:

- What does representation look like in the development partnerships in terms of the partners' gender, age, background and organizational affinity?
- How do partners, co-ordinators and participants perceive relationships within the partnerships?

These questions are used to describe representation and equal relations in the partnerships studied and also to conduct a general discussion on the subject of partnership as a possible complement to or renewal of traditional democratic processes.

9.2 Methods and materials

The empirical material that serves as the basis for this chapter has been taken from a study of development partnership within the Swedish EQUAL Programme over the period 2004–2007. The work has been conducted using an interactive research approach with the aim of creating knowledge that is both theoretically and practically interesting (see Aagaard Nielsen & Svensson 2006). In more concrete terms, this means that the work has been conducted in a research and development project in close co-operation between researchers, co-ordinators and partners from different development partnerships.

In this chapter, use is made of both quantitative material (in the form of a questionnaire) and qualitative material (in the form of semi-structured interviews). The questionnaire material is based on an investigation performed with the aim of creating a broad picture of the partners' and co-ordinators' experience of partnership as a form of organisation. The investigation was targeted at 420 partners and co-ordinators in the 43 development partnerships that were active within the EQUAL Programme in Sweden at the time of the investigation, i.e. spring 2005. 245 responses from 29 development partnerships were received, which means that the total response rate was 58 per cent.

In order to deepen and modulate the picture provided by the questionnaire, qualitative interviews were used to study the experience of participants, partners and co-ordinators of working in partnership. The interview material consists of a total of 35 interviews.[1] The interview printouts have been processed thematically, where the selection for example is based on an endeavour to indicate patterns in the material, as well as breaks with such patterns. The conclusions and preliminary analyses have, as part of the interactive research approach, also been discussed together with a working group consisting of ten co-ordinators from development partnerships within the project NTG Partnership.

9.3 A background to the EQUAL Programme Development Partnerships

The EQUAL Programme is an EU programme that is administered and financed by the European Social Fund. The programme runs over the period 2001–2007. The purpose of the EQUAL Programme is, through innovative solutions, to combat discrimination and exclusion on the labour market. Development partnership is a compulsory form of organisation in order to be granted funds within the programme.

Within the EQUAL Programme, a development partnership is a form of organisation that is based on co-operation between various players from the private, public and voluntary sectors. Development partnerships must be broad and include many different players with the aim of creating a firm grounding and legitimacy for the results of the development work. The activities shall be founded on local needs and initiatives from the target groups themselves (Community Initiative Programme for EQUAL 2000–2006 SWEDEN).

---

[1] Of these 35 interviews, 16 were conducted over the phone. Included in the interviews are 10 co-ordinators, 5 sub-project managers, 18 partners and 6 participants who represent discriminated or vulnerable groups, but who were not involved as partners in the partnerships. 10 different partnerships are represented in the interview material. The interviews were semi-structured.

It is envisaged that the co-operation between the partners in development partnerships will result in innovative solutions. Innovation in this context means new approaches and methods, new fields of competence and employment opportunities, as well as changes in the political and institutional structures surrounding the labour market and working life. Underlying principles of the programme are that the co-operation shall take place through consensus and equal relationships between partners. The work is performed on the basis of a jointly defined problem or development area and is based on a formal agreement and a joint action plan with a strategy and with funds in order to work on the common problem or development area. (Community Initiative Programme for EQUAL 2000–2006 SWEDEN).

In the programme declaration for the Swedish EQUAL Programme, broad representation and equal relationships appear as underlying principles for how the work in the development partnerships is to take place. Furthermore, there is a clear ambition to unite 'top down' and 'bottom up' strategies in that development partnerships are expected to work with both empowerment and structural impact. Organisation in partnerships appears to require broad representation both horizontally and vertically, over several different sectors of society as well as on different levels (locally, regionally, nationally) in order to be able to unite empowerment with structural impact. Have these ambitions made their mark on representation? Have they provided opportunities for players from different backgrounds and from different levels to participate in the work of the partnerships on equal terms?

9.4 Partnerships and democracy – theoretical starting points

Stott and Caplan show in Chapter 3 how many of the concepts that have been used in order to describe and discuss partnership are linked to democracy. Examples of central concepts that comprise democratic values are broad representation, participation, equality, empowerment, inclusion and transparency.

Partnership has been described by various individuals, especially political science researchers, as a step in the development from government to governance – a development that has moved increasingly from traditional hierarchical State direction to direction through interaction with players in network-like collaboration organisations (Peter 2001, Rhodes 1997). From this perspective, partnership is discussed as a complement to traditional, representative, democratic processes and as something that may have the potential to vitalise democracy (see Chapter 13).

As the introduction to this chapter suggests, in the discussion of partnership there is also a connection between democratic values and efficiency. The idea is that partnership through democratic values such as broad representation and more equal relationships creates solutions that are better adapted to local requirements and more firmly founded; within the EU this is often referred to as a strategy for *good governance*. Democratic aspects thus have a bearing on the perspective of this book – partnership as a strategy for innovation and development work that is sustainable in the long term. A basic starting point for this chapter is that democracy in partnership is an interesting area of study, not only as a value in itself but also as a precondition for sustainable development work (especially if the development work concerns social exclusion and involves marginalised groups).

Theoretical definitions of partnership are often based on a common aim and a mutual exchange between each partner (see for example Nelson & Zadek 2000, Malmborg 2003). These definitions may give an impression that the individual will and agenda of each partner are compatible with those of the other partners, and that the relationships consist of an equitable win-win situation. Caplan & Stott discuss definitions of partnership in Chapter 3 and point out that these often present a simplified picture. Is it not conceivable that partnerships that work with complex social problems could involve situations in which each partner does not gain as much from the short-term changes that the work results in, although all partners in the long term have an interest in solving the problem?

Definitions of partnership are often simplified precisely by disregarding the fact that dependence and power relations may take different forms different in partnerships (see Chapter 3). I have specifically chosen to view partnership on the basis of Caplan & Stott's definition with the aim of enabling a description of relationships within partnerships that make power aspects and inequalities visible.

Earlier research suggests a discrepancy between the discourse of partnership as being characterised by democratic values and how democratic values have been expressed in partnerships in practice. Geddes and Benington (2001) have studied local partnerships within the EU and are of the opinion that equitable co-operation in partnerships is only possible if each participant is seen to contribute relevant resources to the work. The results obtained by Geddes and Benington show that partnership offers a potential for better development work, but also entails democratic challenges.

> Partnerships can improve collaboration and trust, and promote policy innovation and resource synergy, but they also frequently marginalise the excluded themselves, who remain largely the objects of policy, and may weaken the accountability of the policy processes, in terms of traditional representative democracy. (Geddes & Benington 2001, s. 7)

Stott and Caplan show in Chapter 3 how many of the concepts that are used to describe and discuss partnership are linked to democracy. Examples of central concepts that incorporate democratic values are broad representation, participation, equality, empowerment, inclusion and transparency.

Partnership has been described by various individuals, especially political science researchers, as a step in the development from government to governance – a development that has passed increasingly from traditional hierarchical government direction to direction through interaction with players in network-like collaboration organisations (Peter 2001, Rhodes 1997). From this perspective, partnership is discussed as a complement to traditional, representative, democratic processes and as something that may have the potential to vitalise democracy.

In the Swedish context, Hudson and Rönnblom (2003) show that there is a tension inherent in the partnership model between on the one hand a desire to include all the players concerned and on the other a tradition and principle of acting through consensus. A focus on consensus runs the risk of concealing conflicts and differing interests. Partnerships risk being based on those perspectives that are represented by the largest number or the strongest players, rather than on a breadth of perspective. This is interesting in relation to the EQUAL Programme, because broad representation and consensus are both underlying principles for the organisation and the work of the partnerships. Hudson and Rönnblom propose as an alternative Young's deliberative model of democracy as a possible model for including a greater breadth of perspective in partnership work. In brief, deliberative democracy can be described as an attempt to strengthen the influence of citizens by active efforts to bring about inclusion – inclusion in terms of broader representation and in terms of an approach that increases the opportunities for citizens to exert influence over decision-making by creating the preconditions for communication, reflection and discussion[2].

---

2   The theory of deliberative democracy is based on Habermas' communicative action and discursive democracy (see Habermas, 1996). One criticism of this theory is that it focuses too strongly on consensus as being the goal for democratic processes. Young's (2000) deliberative democracy model relates, however, specifically to work against social inequality and deals with the problem by stating that consensus can conceal different perspectives and interests. In this model consensus is a desirable goal, but not a basic starting point or

In this chapter – as do Hudson and Rönnblom – I use Young's deliberative view of democracy in order to discuss partnership and democracy. In my opinion, the deliberative democracy model is of particular interest in studies of influence on the part of traditionally marginalised groups and in non-traditional and non-hierarchical organisational forms that are believed to function as facilitators of development work simply by serving as a complement to ordinary organisations.

According to Young (2000), one of the challenges of creating democratic processes that are characterised by equality is the effort to include everyone whose interests are affected by the decisions. In today's democracies there is a connection between social and economic exclusion and political exclusion. Formal political systems appear to strengthen inequality rather than challenge it. Therefore, in order to combat inequality, new alternatives are needed for democratic processes.

Young presents a deliberative democracy model which aims at promoting equality and increasing inclusion in democratic processes. Democracy is seen from this perspective as a method and process for solving collective problems. The model is based on the principle that democracy is created through communication. The democratic process is based on problems, and collective discussion is one way of solving problems and of managing conflicts between different needs and interests. In this model, it becomes possible and important to deal with conflicts as a constructive element of problem solving. Practical consideration comes into focus when the basis for the decision-making is not to find a solution which the majority support but rather to find the solution which those involved together consider to be backed by the strongest arguments and reasons.[3] A process of democracy on these lines is characterised by normative values such as inclusion, equality, reasoning and transparency (Young 2000).

In my opinion, the thoughts on renewal of democratic processes expressed in discussions about partnership has common points of contact with a deliberative view of democracy. A partnership can be regarded as a potential arena for gathering everyone who is affected by a problem and, through collaboration between these players, together finding effective solutions to this problem. As several theoreticians point out (see Dewey 1933, Schön

---

an absolute prerequisite. Young also feels, unlike Habermas, that deliberative models can be used within and as a complement to representative systems of democracy.

3   Consequently, representation is of central importance in this model of democracy since those who are represented are those who assess the various alternatives. As with other models of democracy, this aspect provides scope for different interpretations and opens the door to questions concerning *who* has the power to formulate and assess the suitability in different alternatives.

1983, Engeström 1999), problem-solving is closely linked to action – to identifying problems and developing new solutions and approaches that are tested in practice. Collaboration in partnership incorporates action, not least when proposed solutions are tested (e.g. new methods for practice, training, influencing attitudes). Therefore, the democratic process in partnerships cannot only be understood as discussion, but also as practical action in which the players concerned jointly test and learn from different solutions in order to find new (innovative) solutions. Thinking about and learning from the concrete actions serves as a basis for decisions. Studying how this takes place will therefore be important when studying democracy in partnerships.

Representation is treated in this chapter empirically on the basis of quantitative values – which individuals and organisations have participated as partners in partnerships? Representation is discussed on both an individual and an organisation level. Representation (Pitkin 1967) is a question of relations between those who represent and those who are represented – how is something absent made present, and to what extent is this possible? In this case representation is studied in a simplified form and in terms of who has been present, but analyses and discussions indicate the need to reflect on conditions for, and the content of, presence and representation in partnerships. This relationship is discussed in the chapter in relation to the question of equal relationships.

Included in the definition of equal relationships is participation, the possibility to be listened to in a partnership and to influence the decisions made in connection with partnership activities. The focus is on what the interviewees say about how they perceived and experienced these possibilities. Consequently, perceptions and experience of representation and equal relationships are studied, as well as what the representation actually looked like – in terms of which individuals and organisations were represented as partners in the partnerships.

9.5 Experience from development partnerships in the EQUAL Programme

The following section presents the empirical results of the study. First, a presentation is given of representation in the development partnerships and this is followed by equal relationships with a focus on influence and the possibility of being listened to in the partnership.

9.5.1 Representation

Representation is described in the study on both an organisational level and an individual level. The partners are organisations, but in order to understand the relationships, collaboration and work in development partnerships, I am of the opinion that it is also important to consider which individuals represent the organisations in partnerships.

One interesting aspect of representation in development partnerships is that it has two directions. Those individuals who work in the partnership represent their organisation in the development partnership and the development partnership in their organisation. In other words, the partners represent both their own organisation as well as the development partnership. So which organisations are represented in the partnerships?

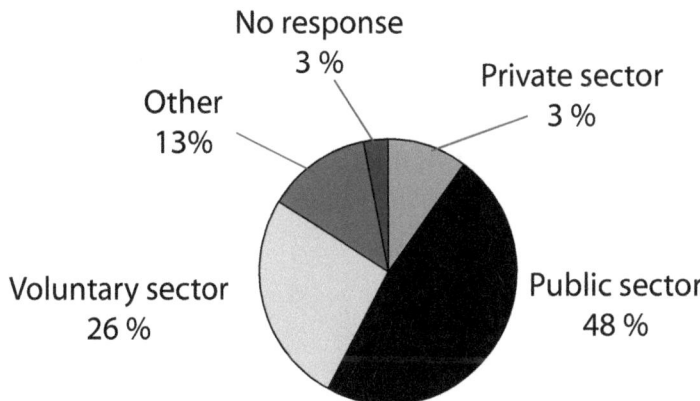

Figure 1. Representation of different organisations in partnerships.

Figure 1 shows that 48 per cent of the partners come from organisations within the public sector, 26 per cent are from the voluntary sector and 10 per cent represent the private sector. The public sector is thus well represented.

In order to gain an impression of those individuals who represent the organisations as partners in development partnerships, questions were asked in the questionnaire about age, gender country of birth and level of education. The gender distribution in the partnerships is even: 49 per cent are men and 50 per cent are women. The age distribution shows that 2 per cent of the partners and co-ordinators are between 20 and 29, 56 per cent are between 30 and 55, and 42 per cent are between 55 and 79. Young people are represented to a very limited extent in the development partnerships.

The level of education among the partners is generally speaking high. 77 per cent of those who responded to the questionnaire have studied at a university or institute of higher education for more than 2–3 years[4]. One of the questions asked concerned the country in which the respondent was born. To the question: 'Where were you born?' 88 per cent answered Sweden, 4 per cent another Nordic country, 3 per cent another European country and 5 per cent that they were born in a country outside Europe. The results correspond to the normal distribution for the country in general.

To summarise, it can be concluded that the development partnerships have an even gender distribution but otherwise consist of a relatively homogenous group – well-educated, Swedish-born men and women with a relatively high average age who to a large extent represent the public sector. What then is the situation regarding the representation of groups or individuals with experience of discrimination and exclusion?

Most of the partners in the development partnerships are professional players from the public sector. Those groups and individuals who are directly affected by problems of exclusion and discrimination on the labour market are only represented in the development partnerships to a limited extent. The absence of such participants is explained by two of the development partnerships by the fact that a demand that only organisations are allowed to be partners makes it difficult for groups that are not organised to participate as partners in a partnership.

In several cases, the question of the representation of discriminated groups in development partnerships appears to be a foreign concept – they are not defined as players who are expected to be involved in the work. Discriminated groups are seen members of sub-projects that are run by the development partnerships rather than as representatives in a development partnership.

Certain co-ordinators would like to see greater representation from discriminated groups and forms of work that facilitate their participation, but they have experienced resistance from other partners in the partnership. In certain cases, regulations and practice (for example secrecy laws) in the organisations that are included in the partnership create obstacles that obstruct the representation of discriminated and excluded groups in partnerships.

---

[4] This can be compared with the general educational level in Sweden, where 20 per cent of the population aged between 25 and 64 have at least a three-year institute of higher education or university education (Statistisk årsbok Sverige 2007/Statistical Yearbook of Sweden 2007 p. 568)

9.5.2 Equal relationships

Several of the questions in the questionnaire concerned involvement in different parts of the work of the partnership and the possibility to make one's voice heard in the development partnership, that is on the one hand being able to advance opinions and on the other that these opinions are taken into account and influence the decisions made by the partnership. In face-to-face interviews as well as in the interviews conducted over the phone, most of the partners and co-ordinators stated that they had experienced ample opportunities for participation in various aspects of the work carried out by partnerships and had the opportunity to be heard within the partnership. In some cases, the ability to make one's voice heard and to exert influence are regarded as being areas of individual knowledge and competence rather than things that are dependent on working methods and relations within the partnership. Experience of work in meetings is part of this knowledge and is said to be an important precondition for being able to advance issues and for being heard.

> Yes, I think that everyone has been heard. Each meeting has an agenda that we follow. If you don't understand how this kind of meeting works you have to take the initiative to find out for yourself. You have to take your own responsibility for this sort of thing. (...) For those people who feel they have not been heard, I can only say that you must be prepared for what you want to take up. If the meetings are formal, you have to know how meeting techniques work. That's the way things are. (Partnership g, Partner 1, Telephone interview 051011)

Language appears to be another condition that governs the ability to be heard and exert influence in a partnership. Different ways of speaking are valued to differing extents, and affect who has been heard in the development partnerships.

> I think everyone has been heard. It has felt good. (...) Women have a different language than men. What women do and say is less valuable than what men do and say. Until that attitude changes, nothing will change. (Partnership f, Partner 1, Telephone interview 051010)

In the above quotation, the importance of language is related to gender. It is easier for men to make themselves heard at a meeting because their way of talking and acting is valued higher than women's. Gender also appears to be important in connection with the position the individual holds in his home organisation. In the above quotation, the chances of being heard are a matter of individual preconditions in terms of knowledge, experience and behaviour. In other interviews organisational preconditions for being heard appear, such as forms of work and roles in the partnership. In these answers, language and a person's way of speaking are regarded as being closely related to organisational conditions rather than individual. In the quotation below, a co-ordinator describes how the gender, position, venue for the meeting and the prevailing culture within the organisation that is hosting the meeting have interacted and influenced the form and content of the meeting and the chances of being heard.

> Yes, things have changed over the course of time. First of all we had meetings at the Ministry of Defence, and there the culture was more formal. That was during my first year. It resulted in a more male-dominated way of talking. The men, and above all the bosses, were the ones who spoke. It is a tradition there. But then we stopped having our meetings there. It just happened that way. The meetings were held in different places after that. Things became more relaxed and there was a different atmosphere. We talked more about the softer issues after that. It was difficult to initiate assessment discussions to start with. The meetings were fairly undemocratic and structured at the beginning. (Partnership f, Co-ordinator, Telephone interview 051010)

In this example, the physical venue, the premises of one of the partner organisations, was important to the form and structure of the meetings and the work done. The culture in this partner organisation set its stamp on the meetings, which meant that structured and undemocratic meeting forms favoured the chances for men and managers to make themselves heard. The physical venue for the meetings and the culture that was represented there set frameworks, which meant that position and gender influenced the subjects, that came up on the agenda. Once the premises for the meetings were changed, both the form and the content of the meetings changed as well as the chances to make oneself heard.

A pattern appears in the material in which most people are pleased with the climate in the partnership (in terms of openness, trust and non-competitive relationships) and feel as though they have been heard. At the same time, there is also a pattern of factors that has affected the chances of being heard and of exerting influence on the partnership. Gender, meeting techniques, language and position interact with the meeting forms of the partnerships as preconditions that govern the possibility of the partners to make their voices heard in the partnerships.

Earlier, it was noted that discriminated groups were largely unrepresented in the development partnerships. In one of the partnerships that we studied, participants from an excluded group were represented at some of the partnership meetings, although not as formal partners. In this development partnership, the participants have been active in a project together with the project manager and in the partnership that has had the overall responsibility for this project. The participants have been heard in the partnership in that the partners have listened to their experience, but the participants do not feel as though they have been involved in and been able to influence strategic decisions in the partnership. One example of this is the fact that the participants have had certain opportunities to influence things in the rehabilitation project, for example the type of activities that are to be included in the project, although they do not feel that they have been able to influence the strategic issues addressed in the development partnership.

> I do not know what has been said in the other groups that I was not in, but I do not feel that we have had the opportunity to have any influence. The way I see things is that we have had the chance to decide what colour the curtains should be, at that level. OK, we have tested various activities, such as relaxation and chi-gong, but when it comes to the really heavy issues that the co-ordinator and the ... (pause) we have been fairly powerless in those areas. (Partnership 1, Focus group interview participant, 050405)

The development partnership is perceived partly as an organisation alongside the project, as an organisation in which the participants do not have a given place.

> ... I think they should have understood this business of partnership a little earlier. I had no feeling that they co-operated. It felt more as though we were in this project and that they had their meetings alongside. It felt as though it had nothing to do with us, but that it was some sort of partnership that they would create. But we were already this little group and had no part in it. (Partnership 1, Focus group interview participant, 050405)

The above quotation shows a distance between the participants and the development partnership. The participants see themselves as being part of a project that the development partnership runs, rather than as being actively involved in jointly conducting the development work. One participant talks about a meeting with the development partnership:

> Researcher: When you were at a meeting with the partnership, how did you experience the atmosphere at the meeting?
>
> Participant 1: I felt really small, really small.
>
> Researcher: Why?
>
> 1: These are difficult things (laughter) partly because these giants were my former employers, the labour exchange, the social insurance office. They are people in

organisations that you never see. They are somewhere out there, people who you only hear the names of. They are on a higher level than us, that we don't usually meet. I had met one of them through my work, but the others – I had only seen their names in the papers. We weren't as strong as them. It was horrible.
(Partnership I, Participant, Interview 050405)

In this quotation, structures and positions outside the development partnership are relevant in order to understand the participant's sense of feeling small in the meeting with the partnership. The partners in the development partnership are people who are on a different level to the participants when it comes to power and influence – people who are visible publicly in the media and who are seen by the participants as having a strong position with a lot of influence.

Gender, meeting techniques, language, position and roles are some of the factors that influence the chances for participation and influence in the development partnerships, preconditions that favour certain partners and disfavour others.

9.6 Partnership – challenger or custodian of prevailing democratic processes?

The empirical results show a conflict between the ambition of the programme to create heterogeneous partnerships and the actual homogeneous composition of partnerships. Representation also appears in the partnerships to interact with the possibilities for equal relationships. Work forms are characterised by those players that are represented, in this case largely the public sector. The homogeneous representation creates work forms that on the one hand favour the majority who recognise them, and on the other hand disfavour those who are not accustomed to the work forms concerned. The material in this chapter shows that the relationships between partnerships and discriminated and marginalised groups are characterised by the fact that the development partnerships are content to canvass the opinions of the discriminated groups' opinions but do not really regard them as relevant and equal partners. This is interesting in relation to Geddes and Benington (2001) who are of the opinion that a precondition for equal co-operation is precisely that each partner in the partnership is identified as a player with something relevant to contribute. Based on the current representation in development partnerships, the relations appear to be characterised more by a traditional relationship between professional players from the public sector and discriminated and marginalised groups in which the individuals become objects for change rather than a resource for identifying and solving problems at a community level.

The results show that the ambition to unite 'top down' and 'bottom up' strategies is not being realised in the partnerships' representation or in terms of equal relationships. The representation consists of traditional players who are already well established in ordinary systems for handling working life and labour market issues. The partnerships are largely regarded as equal with good opportunities for partners to be heard. However, these opportunities would appear to be conditional on a series of preconditions such as position in the partner organisation, gender, language and meeting techniques.

Based on the results of this chapter, there appear to be tensions and dilemmas in the ambition to combine 'top down' and 'bottom up' strategies or, in the terms of the programme document, structural impact and empowerment. If a partnership is to bring about changes at the structural and social levels, is it then not the case that representation is required from well-established players who have the mandate to make these changes? The homogeneous representation can be regarded as a natural consequence of the aims of the partnerships, although such an explanation disregards the 'bottom up' perspective. It is therefore a dilemma that a strategy that really unites the 'bottom up' and 'top down' strategies requires representation from (and equal relationships between) those who have the mandate to change *and* those who have the experience and the knowledge of being discriminated and marginalised.

In the discourse of partnership, there is also a connection between democratic values in partnerships and the effects of the work of partnerships. Organising in the form of a partnership is assumed to be more effective for running development work than traditional forms of organisation. The results presented in this chapter indicate an important issue for further study, namely the interaction between representation and the problem definitions and solutions that the partnerships test to solve problems relating to discrimination and exclusion on the labour market. Do homogeneous and traditional forms of representation risk creating problem definitions and solutions that reinforce traditional relationships and reproduce prevailing structures rather than innovative solutions that challenge prevailing structures and vitalise democratic processes?

One way of understanding the potential of partnership to vitalise the democratic process, inspired by Young's deliberative democracy model, is to set problem definition in focus as the basic starting point for the work. The question of how and by whom the problem is defined is of central importance in understanding how the work and possible solutions will be structured. In somewhat simple terms, traditional problem definition processes lead to traditional players, roles and solutions. What is needed in order to break this circle? How can critical questions be asked in order to inspire partnerships to adopt new problem definitions, attitudes to relevant players, work forms and solutions?

Hudson and Rönnblom (2003) show that a focus on consensus risks concealing different perspectives, interests and conflicts. The question is whether a focus on consensus can explain the homogeneous representation in the partnerships studied. Where is the scope in partnerships for different perspectives and interests? If partnerships are to be able to vitalise democratic processes there is a need for working forms and representation that are not based on consensus, but which instead focus on and highlight differences and conflicts in problem definitions and proposed solutions. Such processes demand and justify broader representation, new forms of work that make equal relationships possible and processes in which consensus is not a starting point that is simply taken for granted but rather a possible goal.

A partnership is formed around a common problem, and so problem solving is already in focus. In Young's deliberative model (2000), communication and reasoning already focus on problem definitions and solutions. Being able to drive processes and development work where solutions are based on how suitable they are, rather than on the solutions that most of those involve prefer may seem to be obvious. However, the problem appears to be that problem definitions and power relationships (which become of interest in discussions on assessing the suitability of solutions) are not always visible and something that we are aware of.

Organisational forms can set external frameworks for formally enabling broad representation and equal relationships, but to really be a potential renewer of democratic processes knowledge is required on driving processes that question and challenge traditional problem definitions, work forms and potential solutions. One challenge in connection with partnerships is therefore to find problem areas and development input that are sufficiently well defined for partners (and any external funders) to spend their time and money on, but which are at the same time open and flexible for processes that support critical reflection, discussion and permit conflicts.

In the intentions and the programme documents, partnership constitutes a potential vitalising of democratic processes, but in the practice of partnership there are problems that reveal tensions and dilemmas between several underlying principles in the concept of partnership. Tensions between 'top down' and 'bottom up' strategies, tensions between the ambition to work innovatively and to challenge prevailing structures (system impact) and to act in consensus. A homogeneous and traditional representation favours consensus, but does consensus favour innovation and the vitalisation of democratic processes in terms of challenging prevailing structures? The position of the partnerships viewed from an organisational perspective leads us to the question of how partnership can function in the borderland between ordinary structures (with representatives from the organisations that work there) but at the same time provide scope for solutions and approaches that it is not possible to test within an ordinary framework? The position of the partnerships in an individual perspective leads us to the question of how individuals can meet on equal terms despite the fact that in ordinary structures they find themselves in different relationships of power and dependency to each other (e.g. politicians, managers and white-collar workers in the public sector, employers – employees, clients – and officials from the employment office, social services and social insurance agencies)?

The discourse of partnerships may indicate democratic renewal similar to the ideas of deliberative democracy and governance though the empirical results show that partnerships appear as non-hierarchical organisations with the potential for broad representation and equal relationships, but partnerships are in fact reproducing hierarchies and power relations similar to those of traditional hierarchical government and prevailing democratic processes.

This is a problem – not only because the talk about and ambitions of partnership are not put into practice – but also because partnerships are not subject to the same demands in terms of transparency and responsibility that organisations within the system of representative democracy have. These conflicting circumstances indicate the need for further studies on how representation, power relationships and hierarchies are created in non-hierarchical, collaboration-based organisations for development work, especially since these organisations are motivated and legitimised as alternatives to ordinary forms of organisation and democratic processes (see also Chapter 13).

9.7   A glimpse into the future – practical conclusions

The results of my study show that democracy in partnerships does not come about by itself – simply by referring to our way of organising ourselves in partnerships as being non-hierarchical, inclusive and equal. Democracy in partnerships may be of importance in several ways, both for the legitimacy of the partnership as well as for its capacity to work innovatively and create solutions to the common problem it has focused on. The results may be disappointing for someone who had hoped that partnership would prove to be a form of democratic renewal. In order to modulate this picture, a presentation is given of some of the practical conclusions reached in the study, not as finished proposals for solutions but as possible starting points for continued discussion.

An attempt to translate the view of deliberative democracy into practical partnership work involves challenging established practices and ways of thinking. This requires an approach, knowledge and methods that enable dialogue, critical reflection, learning and process-oriented evaluations of the solutions that are tested.

Partnership work requires thorough work on problem analysis and openness in order to reformulate and find new definitions of the common problems of partnerships. Representation in partnerships also requires an open attempt and desire to challenge traditional roles – who is an expert and who is the subject of change? In partnerships, it is organisations that are the formal partners. This is a problem, because most marginalised groups are rarely organised. There may also be differences in problem definitions and approaches that create unequal relations in partnership work. How do the organisations work within the private, voluntary and public sectors? How can these different cultures, goals and approaches meet within the framework of one and the same partnership?

In order to allow working forms that work inclusively, awareness is needed of how meeting forms, the division of work and language affect the possibilities of different partners to take part and make themselves heard. Active efforts to design working forms that all partners feel comfortable with and which permit a process with sufficient trust and commitment to dare to enter into conflict and disclose differences in ways of thinking and practices are of central importance. Process management, external support and process-oriented evaluation can serve as aids in creating a process of this type.

Clarity is also needed concerning what is required from partners in terms of commitment and the implementation of a partnership's results. A partnership can be regarded as a free area outside ordinary structures, which provides its potential for renewal. However, in order for the solutions to be sustainable, the results should be implemented in ordinary structures. This makes heavy demands on the partners involved, particularly those who represent local authorities which are often directed from a national level. Here, openness and preparedness are required for the changes at the community level that the work of the partnership may indicate as being necessary. If there is no connection with ordinary structures, partnerships will lack the potential for actually influencing and renewing democratic processes.

The results indicate that the formal organisation in partnerships does not in itself challenge prevailing democratic processes and ways of conducting development work. But if we regard democracy as a process and power relationships as relationships that are actively created and recreated in collaboration between individuals and organisations, this paves the way for change. In this way it will be possible to disclose how inequalities are (re)produced in an apparently non-hierarchical organisation and based on this knowledge raise the awareness of power relationships and inequality in development work.

References

Aagaard Nielsen, K & Svensson, L (2006) *Action and Interactive Research – Beyond Practice and Theory*. Maastricht: Shaker Publishing

Dewey, J (1933/1998) *How we think. A restatement of the relation of reflective thinking to the educative process*. Boston: Houghton Mifflin

Engeström, Y (1999) 'Innovative learning in work teams: Analyzing cycles of knowledge creation in practice'. In *Perspectives on activity theory*. Engeström, Y, Miettinen, R & Punamäki, R-L (eds.) New York: Cambridge University Press

Geddes, M & Benington, J (2001) (eds.) *Local Partnerships and Social Exclusion in the European Union – New forms of local social governance?* London: Routledge

Gemenskapsinitiativprogram för EQUAL 2000–2006 SVERIGE (EU-initiative programme for EQUAL 2000–2006 Sweden / *my translation*)

Habermas, J (1996) *Between facts and norms: contributions to a discourse theory of law and democracy*. London: Polity Press

Hudson, C & Rönnblom, M (2003) 'Uteslutande partnerskap?' In Brynielsson, H & Jerneck, M (eds.) *På jakt efter en ny regional samhällsordning!* (Excluding Partnerships? in *On the lookout for a new regional social order!* /*my translation*) Stockholm: Svenska kommunförbundet

Integrating Partnerships in ESF Programmes 2007-2013. A framework for programming. Report by an ad hoc working group of Member States on partnership. EQUAL 2006.

Malmborg, F (2003) Conditions for Regional Public-Private Partnerships for Sustainable Development – Swedish Perspectives in *European Environment*, Vol. 13, No. 3, pp. 133–149.

Nelson, J & Zadek, S (2000) *Partnership Alchemy – New Social Partnerships in Europe*. Köpenhamn: Copenhagen Centre

Peter, J (2001) *Local governance in Western Europe*. London: SAGE

Pitkin, H (1967) *The Concept of Representation*. Berkeley: University of California Press

Rhodes, R A W (1997) *Understanding governance: Policy networks, Governance, Reflexivity and Accountability*. Milton Keynes: Open University Press

Schön, D A (1983) *The Reflective Practitioner: How professionals think in action*. New York: Basic Books

Statistisk årsbok Sverige 2007 (Statistical Yearbook of Sweden 2007, Official Statistics of Sweden / *my translation*) Sveriges Officiella statistik: Statistiska Centralbyrån

Young, I M (2000) *Inclusion and democracy*. New York: Oxford University Press

10. Inclusion of immigrants – effects of different kinds of partnerships

10.1 Introduction

The phenomenon of partnership is spreading, and is thus becoming increasingly important for different groups. Policy-makers as well as researchers claim that partnership as a form of organisations favours social inclusion, which justifies an investigation into the similarities and differences between two different types of partnership with the goal of including immigrants.

In Chapter 1, the difference between holistic or focused partnership is discussed. Partnerships with a holistic approach are described as including 'everything' and as working simultaneously on many different levels and towards different goals. The term focused partnerships means that they are directed towards one goal or outcome. My question is whether it is possible to see any difference in the inclusion of immigrants depending on the type of partnership involved. By inclusion, I mean in this context both the degree of inclusion of immigrants in the actual partnership work as well as the result of the partnership's work in the form of the inclusion of immigrants in society.

The development partnerships within the Swedish EQUAL initiative can be characterised as focused partnerships of the type described in Chapter 1. When it comes to the importance of EQUAL for inclusion, I base my conclusions on other people's research and evaluations. Regional growth partnerships in Sweden are a good match with the description of 'holistic' partnerships. I have studied these myself, and intend to discuss them in more detail.[1]

In practice, it is difficult to draw a clear boundary between holistic and focused partnerships. It is difficult enough to define partnership in itself. As Ken Caplan and Leda Stott conclude in Chapter 3, the term partnership is used for a variety of different phenomena. In one Swedish government survey, it is stated that partnership has become such a widely used term that it says nothing about the phenomenon that it is supposed to describe. The survey therefore proposes that the term be relinquished in favour of a more descriptive alternative (SOU 2003:123). In my opinion, however, this is not the answer. It is rather the case, as several of the participating authors of this book point out, that more empirical studies and theory development are needed in order for the term to become useable. This is particularly important in matters relating to inclusion and exclusion.

In this chapter, I intend to analyse how partnership work can influence the inclusion of marginalised groups into society. I will do this by comparing two different types of partnership, both of which have the overriding goal of supporting this type of development. I will be looking in particular at the integration of immigrants.[2] My reasoning applies primarily to these two types of partnership, but certain conclusions could also apply to partnership in general.

---

[1] The results of my studies have been presented in a number of reports and chapters of books in Swedish. In all, 57 interviews and two questionnaires have been conducted, as well as ongoing observations. All 21 proposals for regional growth agreements, growth programmes, basic input and finished programmes, as well as statutes, bills and government proposals within the area have been analysed. More information will be published on this subject in a coming paper.

[2] In many countries, a distinction is made between ethnic minorities and immigrants. In Sweden, these terms tend to be intermixed. In matters of policy, reference is often made either to immigrants or to people with a foreign background. The latter category refers to immigrants and people born in Sweden, both of whose parents are or were immigrants. When using the term 'immigrant', I refer mostly to the latter wider concept. For more information, see Statistics Sweden http://www.scb.se/Grupp/Metod/_Dokument/X11OP0203.pdf or for a very thorough survey of Swedish immigrant statistics, go to http://www.mkc.botkyrka.se/ and choose publications from the year 2006, and the publication *Pocket facts – statistics on integration*, published by the no longer active Integration Board. Almost every fifth person living in Sweden today was born abroad or has parents both of whom were born abroad.

10.2 The EQUAL programme's development partnerships and the inclusion of immigrants

The overriding goal of the EQUAL programme is to combat discrimination and promote the inclusion of marginalised groups[3], one of these groups being immigrants. A development partnership is defined as being composed of partners who co-operate on the basis of a *'well-defined problem – or development area, a formal agreement and a joint action plan'* (Wistus[4] 2006) in order to bring about *'concrete development efforts'* (Andersson et al. 2006a) which give rise to long-term changes in the partners' operations. A partnership on these lines shall – unlike a network – be composed solely of those players who enable the specific tasks of the partnership to be performed (Andersson et al. 2006a).

A development partnership is set up when one of the players has identified a condition and reformulated it into an important question or an alternative solution. On the basis of this, partners are sought in order to apply for funds from EQUAL to start a partnership. EQUAL's development partnerships have produced solutions that entail innovations in terms of inclusion. But various evaluations also point to the difficulties involved in living up to the inclusion objectives set. One reason given for this is that the development partnerships frequently lacked central players such as companies and business organisations. Even among those players who became partners, the senior management layer was missing. Inclusion has not been perceived as an important issue by all the potential players. The dissemination effects were limited, as well as long-term anchoring. The development partnerships within EQUAL have only had a short time to function (on average two years) and not enough resources to institutionalise the results.

EQUAL's development partnerships have often failed to live up to the goals of inclusion. Immigrants have had a limited influence on the partnership work and the development partnerships have not succeeded to any great extent in changing social structures. Development partnerships have often been more reminiscent of short-term projects and have frequently worked outside the regular operations of the partners (Andersson et al 2006b, Bernard Brunhes International 2004).

---

3   EQUAL is presented in greater detail elsewhere in this book (see Chapter 1).
4   From a presentation by Sofia Wistus, Linköping University, 2006-10-12.

10.3 The regional growth partnerships

The regional growth partnerships are partnerships whose main task it is to instigate sub-partnerships, development coalitions, alliances, networks, joint action groups or projects in a certain predetermined direction within a broadly-defined framework. The purpose is to try to influence or even force companies and organisations to enter into coalitions and dynamic networks. I call this type of partnership a system-manipulating partnership in order to distinguish it from the more focused development partnership.

The Swedish regional growth partnerships, whose operations during the period 2000 to 2007 I have studied, are examples of a top-down initiative for the purpose of steering the emergence of innovation systems for growth. The ambition is both to strengthen the relations between different players within an innovation system and to steer the direction of these relations. The principal objective is economic growth in the form of increased profit and more job opportunities, but there are also goals for sustainable development. Three areas are put forward as being particularly important in this respect: sustainable environment, gender equality and the integration of immigrants.[5] It is the attempts to implement the latter area that is the really radical innovation. The members of the regional growth partnerships should include relevant government authorities and municipal and regional organisations, as well as representatives from companies and interest groups. The experience of immigrants, women and young people should be represented. It has also been the case that people have taken part as individuals.

In the instructions for growth partnerships, a number of reasons are given for why they should work for the 'integration of immigrants'. An innovation system will be less effective if groups are excluded since it will not assimilate potential ideas, skills and expertise, which is assumed to influence innovations and development in a negative way (Lundvall 2003). Since the proportion of immigrants in Sweden is relatively large, their exclusion from the innovation system means, according to this assumption, a significant risk of innovations failing to materialise. There is also a legitimacy aspect. If regional innovation systems are perceived as excluding, they will not be sustainable. Linked to this aspect is a discussion of fairness and democracy. Since immigrants are regional citizens it is undemocratic if they cannot be involved in influencing how the results of their work are used. They have contributed to the economy of the regions

---

5   The 'integration of immigrants' is either clearly defined as a goal or it is the predominant interpretation of the meaning of the term social sustainability.

and should be entitled to receive resources in order to be able to take part in the creation of growth. There are in other words several arguments for an inclusion of immigrants in the regional growth partnerships.

Finally, it can be concluded that irrespective of the basis for an assumption of this type, the Swedish state has maintained normatively that the inclusion of immigrants is of decisive importance to the regional innovation systems for growth and necessary for increased growth. This conviction is reflected in the instructions for the regional growth partnerships.

10.3.1 The regional growth partnerships and the inclusion of immigrants

The inclusion goals for the growth partnerships impose demands for a number of radical changes since immigrant men and women are largely lacking within the regional partnerships. Barely five per cent of those who participated in growth partnerships had a foreign background. For the population as a whole, some 20 per cent have a foreign background. It is not merely as individuals that immigrants are lacking in a growth context, but also in the form of new perspectives and ideas. In various policy goals and programmes for the regional growth partnerships, it is presupposed that these shall include an immigrant perspective in all analyses, decisions, measures and evaluations, and that an immigrant perspective shall be represented in decision-making processes. My research shows that there are certain measures that can be linked to the integration goal, but in no case has an integration perspective *'permeated'* the activities. This conclusion is supported by both external and internal evaluations, such as self evaluation in the partnerships.[6]

In my studies, the term immigrant was found to be linked with a discourse on problems, resource requirements and cultural clashes, which meant that both proposals as well as players who represented an integration perspective were marginalised. Immigrants were not regarded as bearers of resources that could solve common problems, which the researcher Geddes (2000) regards as being a precondition for partnerships that try to combine growth with solving social problems. Regional growth partnerships did not have inclusion as a basic principle for their actions.

How could partnerships disregard these objectives for inclusion when they were approved unanimously in a common programme? It transpired that some partners in regional growth partnerships did not feel that

---

[6] This does not mean that nothing is happening. In the same way as several EQUAL partnerships can indicate progress, it can be shown during recent years that successful work has been carried out within the regional growth programmes. But these successes are limited and are far from the goal that the integration perspective should permeate all activities.

they had adopted and accepted the entire programme. Not everyone was involved in the regional growth partnerships voluntarily. The government organisations were ordered to take part, but used the opportunity to minimise their involvement by referring to various conflicting goals.[7] Several of the government authorities enjoyed extensive independence. Other partners too participated for a variety of reasons, which is something that Caplan and Stott (see Chapter 3) claim applies in the case of many partnerships. Some partners took part in order to make sure that they could defend their position in relation to other players. Others were involved in order to be able to conduct lobbying activities for their own issues.

The broad holistic approach gave the partners in the regional growth partnerships major opportunities to define what they wanted to collaborate on based on their own organisational logics (Hjern & Porter 1981). This type of system-manipulating partnership led to an organisational form which in certain respects bore a resemblance to a network with its looser connections (Ahrne 1997), at the same time as it was in other respects more structured. Instead of a holistic partnership, we can talk about a fragmentised partnership practice, especially if a comparison is made with the more focused approach in the ideal description of development partnerships. The conclusion is that partnerships may contain components that are reminiscent of a development partnership, whereas other parts are similar to a network. Considine (2006) is of the opinion that many partnership studies are based on a network approach. On the other hand, most of the researchers in this book regard partnership as being more organisational in character than networks.[8] As I see it, there are certain trends in the research towards increasingly regarding partnerships as hybrid organisations. Thacher (2004) talks about partnerships as being 'inchoate organisations', or organisations in the making.

Those partners who drove the core issues in the regional growth partnerships were well organised, based on previous networks (Clegg & McNulty 2002), and had ample resources. Other issues, such as the inclusion of immigrants were put forward of looser issue networks and temporary projects in which players with strong resources were either lacking or passive. Why then did the government fail to force the partners to abide by the commitments they had made in the partnership programme, including the goal of inclusion? In practice, enforcement was impossible.

---

7   The exception was the County Administrative Boards which were often more of a driving force on the issue of immigrant inclusion.

8   Ahrne (1997) distinguishes between organisations with clear limits, participant control, resource control and networks.

One reason was that the dependency of the state on different regional players taking part in the regional growth partnerships was greater than the need of the different regional actors to participate. A broad participation by the business community was necessary based on the theories of regional innovation systems. With the exception of the state organisations, the government could not order participation.[9] As a consequence, in several regions the largest Swedish employer organisation, the Confederation of Swedish Enterprise (*Svenskt Näringsliv*), chose to refrain from participating in the work of the regional growth partnerships and private companies were largely conspicuous by their absence.

Caplan and Stott are of the opinion (see Chapter 3) that partnerships exist because the partners see the co-operation as being something that creates resources for the participants, or that not participating could lead to negative consequences for a player. But the regional growth partnerships had little chance of attracting potential partners with money or other benefits since only limited resources were made available for development efforts. Nor were they able to threaten negative consequences as a result of non-involvement. The only course open to them was to appeal to local patriotism and refer to various advantages of co-operation in the long term. Altogether, this meant that the leaders of the regional growth partnerships were unable to require players to 'purchase' the entire package in order to become members of the partnerships. They were instead forced to accept the partners taking part on the basis of their own priorities and driving forces.

A large proportion of the organisations that took part in the regional partnerships – such as corporate organisations, labour market organisations and non-profit making associations – were themselves collaboration organisations without decision-making rights for their members. This meant that if a partner of a growth partnership made a decision, it did not necessarily lead to it being followed by the member organisations. At each intermediate stage, the question of the importance of immigrant inclusion to economic growth and the operations concerned had to be translated and renegotiated once again. In each new translation and negotiation, the predominant attitude to immigrants as being a problem that required extensive resources once again affected the result.

In practice, the same situation also applied within many of the partnership organisations that were not collaboration organisations since there was only limited scope for controlling different levels.

---

9   In practice it is also very difficult to force an involved participation on the part of a state organisation if the authority concerned does not see any reason to be involved.

In order to analyse this problem, use can be made of Kingdon's agenda concept (Kingdon 1995). According to this approach, each organisation has an agenda for what really needs to be done. The space available on this agenda is often limited and the requests numerous. This means that it is only in exceptional circumstances, and when a number of factors interact, that it is possible to take up new problems on the agenda. In the regional growth partnerships there were a number of key individuals whose task it was to influence the agendas of the participating organisations. But when it came to the integration issues, the key individuals in question had insufficient support, knowledge and resources in terms of money but most of all time. The time these individuals had to convince other players was always very limited. It was also felt that driving inclusion issues too hard could serve to dissuade members, clients and customers from co-operating since it was felt they could not see the connection between economic growth and inclusion. The limited space on each organisation's agenda meant that inclusion issues were often marginalised.

10.4 A comparison between two types of partnership

10.4.1 Similarities

There are a number of similarities between development partnerships in EQUAL and the regional growth partnerships. Both have the inclusion of immigrants as a goal and want to reduce discrimination and exclusion. In both types of partnership there was an insight into the importance of linking together economic processes in society with this type of inclusion policy. Both types of partnership were development-oriented. Another factor that unites them is the limited success in establishing and spreading an inclusion-oriented approach. They have not succeeded in getting marginalised groups to take part to any great extent.

In Chapters 1 and 2, the question of whether partnership represents a 'double strategy' for change, which includes both a strong representation 'from the top' and a participation 'from below', is raised. But either the strong representation from the top or the participation from below was lacking. Even where managements participated, their involvement was weaker with regard to inclusion issues.

Caplan and Stott (Chapter 3) point out that it is important to analyse resources and power in a partnership. The more material and symbolic resources a partner has, the more power and influence he has. In the case of both development partnerships and growth partnerships there were major differences in resources between different groups. For the most part, there were no organisations that represented the interests of immigrants. If there was such an organisation, it often suffered from a lack of money, personnel, equipment, space, contacts and other items that Caplan and Stott point out as being power resources. This was particularly evident when it came to regional growth partnerships. Immigrant organisations often lack a regional level. They may be strong locally and nationally, but rarely at the regional level (Reichel 2004).

In Chapter 2, there is a discussion on the difference between projects and partnerships. My research results indicate that inclusion within both types of partnership takes place more commonly in the form of a project than in the form of collaboration within a partnership.

10.4.2 *Differences*

Both types of partnership had inclusion as a goal. In the case of the development partnerships in EQUAL, this was a general goal and the structural changes the means. In the case of the regional growth partnerships, the situation was in practice the reverse. Economy and growth were the overriding goals and inclusion the means.

One difference was that EQUAL had a strong empowerment perspective formulated as follows:

> Empowerment is primarily a question of a change in the power balance between those who have power and the vulnerable groups and individuals who lack or have very little power. It is partly a matter of strengthening vulnerable groups and individuals so that they can accept greater responsibility for and increase control over their lives, and partly of changing the social, economic and political system to give excluded and vulnerable groups and individuals the chance to act generally in society and specifically within the labour market and working life. (Joint Initiative for EQUAL 2000–2006, ESF-council, Sweden, p. 76.)

The instructions for the regional growth partnerships prescribe that authorities and partnership players shall change their operations so that it becomes possible for immigrants to participate and exert influence. There is, however, an important distinction here compared with an explicit empowerment goal. Within the regional growth partnerships, there was no talk of building up the resources and competence of marginalised groups.

One important question is whether the development partnerships in EQUAL drive development *for* discriminated groups or if these groups are *included* as active players and contribute their knowledge and experience of what, where and when discrimination, marginalisation and exclusion are created. The answer to this question requires more research in the case of the development partnerships within EQUAL. In the case of the regional growth partnerships, the question can be answered with certainty: they largely drive development *for* discriminated groups rather than *with* them.

Caplan and Stott (Chapter 3) present a model for analysing influence in partnerships on the following levels:

- Control – initiates or leads particular steps or activities
- Influence – participates directly in decision-making, has a vote
- Consulted – involved in discussion, able to express opinions and give feedback
- Informed – receives information.

In most of the regional growth partnerships, there was no representation that could receive the information. Where there was, it was on the Informed and Consulted levels.

EQUAL's development partnerships normally came into being as a result of local initiatives. The regional growth partnerships were centrally initiated. They emphasise the local and regional involvement, but at the same time have a more controlling role in that they can be traced back to the government's desire to form partnerships that work in a certain predetermined way, and with predefined questions.

There were strong demands for structural changes in EQUAL's development partnerships and this is to a certain extent partly implicit in the regional growth partnerships. But there, structural changes were seen primarily as being necessary if they led to increased growth.

One of the demands for partnership is a desire among the partners to themselves be changed (see Chapter 2). Another demand is for the involvement to be voluntary. In the case of the state players in the regional growth partnerships, however, participation was ordered and took place without any great desire on their part to allow the organisation concerned to be changed.

Another difference between EQUAL's development partnerships and the regional growth partnerships was the size of the partnerships and their extent. In general, the regional growth partnerships were considerably more extensive even though there were EQUAL partnerships with just as many partners. The networks of the regional growth partnerships comprised more players and organisational levels.

10.5 Conclusions and discussion

In the introduction to this book, the question was posed as to whether partnerships are effective when it comes to implementing changes and creating innovations. As far as implementing inclusive practices for immigrants is concerned, for both types of partnership studied the answer is no. Neither EQUAL's development partnerships nor the regional growth partnerships have succeeded to any great extent with the inclusion of immigrants.

Consequently, the partnership form is not in itself a guarantee for the success of an inclusive practice. The active participation of players or organisations that could represent the perspective of immigrants was lacking. In most cases, the inclusion of immigrants was primarily driven by officials working for regional associations or county administrative boards. If we want an integration perspective or some other non-prioritised perspective to characterise an innovation system, the more active management of those responsible is required.

The regional growth partnerships were relatively powerless. They could not order compliance, had limited resources with which to attract the participants and could not threaten anyone with negative consequences. What remained were, above all, various forms of indirect control such as influence, knowledge creation, persuasion, etc. for which often only limited resources were available in the form of personnel, funds and knowledge. Nevertheless, it is still possible to see certain positive results of these efforts.

The reason for linking together inclusion with growth processes was to avoid immigrants being regarded as a burden or as individuals who did not contribute resources to regional growth.[10] There was also the view that the marginalisation of immigrants would have a negative impact on growth. However, the partnerships have not succeeded in getting the financial players to change their attitudes to immigrants as far as their operations are concerned. This appears to be the reason why both development and growth partnerships have had limited success with their inclusion goals.

---

10   An interesting question is whether it may be the case that even if immigrants are regarded as being economic resources for growth, immigrant organisations are not regarded as organisations that control these resources. Different authorities – for example within the education and labour market sectors – may be assumed to be of greater importance. Therefore, these are included but not the immigrants.

The strategies for achieving inclusion have above all been the following:

- Disseminating knowledge and marketing to various players to emphasise the importance of the integration of immigrants to economic growth.
- Introducing regulations and ordinances on representation to create a different practice.
- Setting conditions for access to resources from different public funds.

Within all these areas there is still much to be done. This means there are still many opportunities for improvement. Another strategy could be, as with the UN and the EU, to actively promote the development of non-governmental organisations in order to support new perspectives. Caplan and Stott (Chapter 3) and Scopetta (Chapter 12) are of the opinion that such organisations are important in order to create greater equality in the power relations within partnerships. Subordinate groups must have access to contacts, networks, expertise, knowledge, equipment premises and financial resources, etc. Immigrant organisations at present lack access to most of these resources. In order to strengthen the chances for participation on more equal terms, they may require support in a number of respects. Researchers have also shown that such support may lead to empowerment for immigrants (Marques & Rui Santos 2004) even though it may also lead to representation problems (Holmén 2002).

The solution to the problem is not increased linear control and measures from above. Research shows that it is difficult to direct self-organising systems that are supposed to solve complex questions. Sometimes it may be necessary to introduce new players. The fact that exclusion exists must be recognised as a basic fact. The interesting thing now is to conduct research on how this exclusion takes place and how we can develop methods for strengthening the power resources of immigrants in different partnerships.

A lack of regional support resources may also be important in the case of development partnerships (see Chapter 12). At present, arenas in which development partnerships can work or in which learning and reflection can take place are largely lacking. A successful example of inclusion and dissemination effects within an EQUAL project shows that here success was partly achieved through co-operation with a regional growth partnership.[11] There

11 NEEM stands for 'Networks for Entrepreneurs from Ethnic Minorities'. For information on NEEM in English, reference is made to http://www.neem.se/inenglish.asp. NEEM stems from the EQUAL project 'Diversity in Entrepreneurship', see http://www.d3city.

are further examples of regional growth partnerships in which development partnerships from EQUAL are mentioned.[12]

The introductory question of the dilemma between focused or holistic partnerships cannot be solved simply. The answer is: It all depends! The choice of a focused or holistic approach depends on the purpose and the preconditions. In most cases both choices are necessary – namely maintaining a focus on the development work but at the same time looking at the whole context.

The question of inclusion and partnership is becoming increasingly important. A new structure fund period is beginning, and inclusion goals will be a natural part of various national, regional and local initiatives. If the partnership phenomenon continues to grow in importance and immigrants continue to be excluded from large parts of the decision-making context, their voices will be excluded from the system dialogue. They will be shut out of or discriminated against in the structures in which the future will be determined. The risk of a continued and greater exclusion is significant.

Another conclusion underlines the importance of conceptual development and continued research. More empirical research is needed, but also more theoretical research. One element of conceptual development could be to describe partnerships on the basis of their purpose, function, and context. The research will probably not show pure forms of partnership. Most partnerships contain different organisational forms – such as networks and projects. A broad system-manipulating partnership will probably always consist of a hybrid between partnership and network. It is therefore important to develop concepts that can be used to describe partnership processes in these intermediate forms for collaboration.

---

org/English.asp. NEEM is involved in conducting the project PITEM with funding from NUTEK and Growth Objective 3. For information on PITEM, see http://www.balticfem.se/en/.

12 For example, the development partnership 'Diversity Faces' in Östergötland and '*Mångfald i Västernorrland*' (Diversity in Västernorrland).

References

Ahrne, G (1997) *Social Organizations, Interaction inside, outside and between organizations*. London: Sage

Andersson, M, Svensson, L, Wistus, S & Åberg, C (2006a) (eds.) *On the art of developing partnership*. Stockholm: The National Institute for Working Life

Bernard, Brunhes International (2004) EU-*wide evaluation of the community initiative EQUAL 2000–2006. Mid-term report*. Brussels: European Commission DG Employment and social affairs

Clegg, S & McNulty, K (2002) 'Partnership working in delivering social inclusion: organizational and gender dynamics'. *Journal of Education Policy*, Vol. 17, Issue 5, pp. 587–601

Considine, M (2006). *Partnerships and Collaborative Advantage: Some Reflections on new forms of Network Governance*. Centre for Public Policy, University of Melbourne, conference background paper

Geddes, M (2000) 'Tackling Social Exclusion in the European Union? The Limits to the New Orthodoxy of Local Partnership'. *International Journal of Urban and Regional Research*, Vol. 24, Issue 4, pp. 782–800

Holmén, H (2002) *Networking and Problems of Representation*. ICER, Linköping University

Hjern, B & Porter, D (1981) 'Implementation structures: A New Unit of Administrative Analysis'. *Organization Studies*, Vol. 2, No. 3, pp. 211–227

Isaksson Iliev, K, Wistus, S & Andersson, M (2006b) *Utvecklingspartnerskap som organiseringsform för hållbar utveckling – en enkätundersökning av utvecklingspartnerskapen i svenska EQUAL 2001–2006*. Lindesberg: APeL

Joint Initiative for EQUAL, 2000–2006, ESF-council, Sweden, p. 76

Kingdon, J (1995) *Agendas, alternatives and public policies*. New York: Harper Collins College Publisher

Lundvall, B-Å (2003) *Innovation Systems between Policy and Research*, paper at Innovation Pressure Conference, Tampere

Marques, M & Santos, R (2004) 'Top-Down and Bottom-Up Reconsidered: The Dynamics of Immigrant Participation in Local Civil Society'. In Penninx, R (ed.) *Citizenship in European Cities: Immigrants, Local Politics, and Integration Policies*. Aldershot: Ashgate

NTG Partnerskap (2007) *Partnerskap som organisations- och arbetsform. Beskrivning av utökade aktiviteter inom NTG Partnerskap*. Lindesberg: APeL.

Reichel, I (2004) *Ethnic Organizations and Social Inclusion in a Swedish Context*, paper at the Conference on the Integration of Immigrants from Turkey in Belgium, Denmark, France and Sweden, Bogazici University, March 26–27 2004

SOU 2003:123 *Utvecklingskraft för hållbar välfärd: delbetänkande av Ansvarskommittén*. Stockholm: Edita Norstedts

Thacher, D (2004) 'Interorganizational Partnerships as Inchoate Hierarchies: A Case Study of the Community Security Initiative'. *Administration and Society*, Vol. 36, No. 1, pp. 91–127

11. Who is allowed to contribute to sustainable development by participating in partnerships?

11.1 Introduction

This chapter attempts to answer the question of whether the partnerships have taken gender equality aspects into account in their work with the growth agreements. The issue of democracy is fundamental here. The issue of sustainable development, which presupposes a holistic approach, is also discussed in this context.

An attempt to integrate the gender equality dimension (mainstreaming) into a growth programme by running a gender equality project is described. In the analysis of this attempt, the question of the system versus the individual is discussed.

11.2 Regional work for growth

In order to improve the preconditions for growth, the Swedish government introduced what were first called growth agreements (2000) and subsequently growth programmes (2004). These agreements were the government's tools for facilitating the participation of various actors in their own regions, and were seen as a strategic element of a new industrial and commercial policy. The regional partnerships were intended to contribute to broad public participation with the main aim of creating local and regional mobilisation. The task of the regional players was to jointly decide which activities should be given priority at the local and regional levels. The agreements were to be seen as a learning process for those involved. The growth programmes represent a further development of the former growth agreements and involve national authorities and a wide circle of collaborating actors in the county – partnership (Westberg 2006)[1]. The aims of the programmes include creating dynamic and developing companies, increasing employment for both women and men and increasing the level of competence and education. In the evaluations conducted of the structural funds and the growth agreements that aimed to promote regional and local development it can be noted that the horizontal aspects, including gender equality, have practically become a non-issue.[2]

Initially, the government stressed that growth should take place on the basis of a market-economy approach, i.e. the assumption that commercial success leads to growth. Subsequently, the government increasingly stressed that growth should lead to a sustainable society and clarified ahead of the launch of the regional growth programmes what it meant by sustainable growth: 'Sustainable growth is growth that leads to sustainable development ... The programmes should thus contribute to offering present and future generations of women and men sound economic, social and ecological conditions ... It is in this context also important that social and environmental factors are seen as driving forces and opportunities for sustainable growth' (Ministry of Industry 2002 p. 3)[3]. Gender equality in connection with the growth agreements and the growth programmes thus entails that both women and men should be involved in conducting analyses and in drawing up growth strategies, as well as in implementing concrete measures. The objective of achieving broad public participation in order to pave the way for a dynamic process, in connection with the emergence of new actors and the formation of new constellations, presupposes the participation of women. Questions that it seems relevant to ask are therefore: Are women allowed to participate, and if so on what terms? Are they able to participate as equal actors and not simply on the basis of their role as representatives of the category 'women'?

---

1   According to the Government Offices, the national policy for regional development should co-operate as effectively as possible with the EUs structural and regional policies. The objective of the structural funds is to strengthen economic and social cohesion between the Member States of the EU and combat major regional and social differences between the countries (Ministry of Industry and Trade 1998).
2   The term horizontal aspects, also referred to as sustainability aspects, relates to gender equality, the environment and integration.
3   In Westberg 2006, quoted from Ministry of Industry 2002, p. 3.

11.3 Are old patterns being broken down?

A regional policy marked by gender equality and a sensitivity to the situation of women should be based on a holistic view of economic development. According to Henderson (in Horelli & Roininen 1999), the holistic view is based on a layered approach with the market economy at the top, followed by the public economy, then the social economy and finally the ecological economy. This view demonstrates that the economy does not consist of the market economy alone. The discussion conducted leads to an equality perspective that comprises a gender equality element. This can be understood to mean that both gender equality and equality are objectives for a regional policy that aims to promote the development of ecological, social, cultural and economic capital and its distribution between the women and men in the region.

11.3.1 Trust and social capital

It is increasingly emphasised that conditions and relations in the local community that create trust, confidence and social networks are decisive in determining whether people are prepared to take risks, for example by starting their own companies or driving development processes, and are important growth factors. According to one of the most quoted researchers in this field (Putnam 1996), social capital should be understood as norms regarding trust and networks of mutuality between the members of the community. Trust in civil society is thus an important part of the social capital. Swedish researchers have also addressed the importance of social capital. According to them, social capital is created, among other things, by credible political institutions treating all citizens equally and fairly, but they also stress the importance of location in the form of a strong identity and well-developed social networks, both of which are often generated by the work and activities of clubs, societies and associations (Holmberg & Weibull 2000, Johannisson & Madsén 1997, Westberg 2005).

One researcher (Uslaner 2000) claims that trust in society, institutions and individuals is more dependent on socialisation processes. According to him, children already acquire a basic view of the people around them that then has an impact on the type of trust they develop as individuals in later life – particularized or generalized trust. It is important to point out, however, that socialisation processes continue throughout our lives and are based in part on individuals who are important to us and their expectations (Westberg-Wohlgemut 1996). Generalized trust means that people not only trust people they know but also often people that are completely unknown to them. They have a positive view of the community around them and of the future and their own possibilities to improve society. Particularized trust means that people only trust their families and those closest to them. These people often belong to organisations that accept those who are like them but judge outsiders. They often have a pessimistic view of the future and of their own ability to improve society. Particularized trust can lead to conflicts, as the world is viewed on the basis of the values of one's own group and a suspicion of those who do not belong to it.

What is required to really integrate the gender equality dimension (mainstreaming) into growth agreements/programmes? In order to seek answers to this question, statistical material from the first two years of the growth agreements and the first year of the growth programmes has been processed (Ds 2001:15, Ds 2002:34, Nutek 2005). Some 40 interviews conducted in 2002 with all of the gender equality experts at the County Administrative Boards and the heads of the regional resource centres for women have also been reviewed (Hård 2005), as well as a number of questionnaires from the co-ordinators of the growth agreements and others.

11.3.2 *Representation in the partnerships*

In most of the partnerships, the distribution between women and men was unequal. The groups that traditionally represented their organisations also acted as representatives in the partnerships. The managers, who were usually men, became ordinary members. When the first partnerships were formed, there was no awareness of the significance of horizontal demands and this led, among other things, to the establishment of partnerships that contained only men. Those responsible for the composition of the partnerships felt that it was up to the organisations that were asked to take part to choose their own representatives, and if these happened to be men then this was not seen as a problem or an issue of any importance.

Following demands from gender equality experts and other actors for a more even gender distribution the number of women was increased in several of the partnerships, or women were linked to the partnerships in some other way. In some of the partnerships, women were given access when the time came to replace one of the previous members. In some counties, it was actively decided that representation in the partnership should consist of 50 per cent women and 50 per cent men. In practice, however, there was no major change in the representation of women. There was an in-built conflict in the question of who should be a member of the partnership: the person (often a man) who performed the decision-making function in the organisation, or the person (often a woman) who could perhaps contribute new ideas but who would have to go back to the organisation to get support and approval for these ideas. The decision was usually made in favour of the decision-maker with financial influence.

The degree of openness varied between the partnerships. Several counties arranged consultation processes and invited stakeholder to engage in a dialogue, while others were very formal and closed. Many of the partnerships were linked to working groups that prepared or drafted the content of what would become the various programme areas in the growth agreements. The members of these working groups often belonged to the same networks. If the group was based on a wider group of men, then they very often selected other men. A conscious choice of who should be represented in the groups was seldom made. Despite this, women were more often included in the working groups than in the partnerships.

My research results thus show that trust in the other actors in a partnership and the degree of openness to allowing access to new partners have a lot to do with who has the leading positions and the power to decide (see Chapter 2).

11.4 Is it possible to create partnerships marked by equality and gender equality?

Is it possible for a regional partnership for growth to succeed where society in general has so far failed, that is in creating a gender-equal society? In the study, the view emerges that the representatives in the partnerships see the task of representing their organisations as a question of power and of guarding their own preserves, instead of regarding the broadening of the partnership with new actors as a means of promoting development and of gaining access to new innovative ideas. The opportunities presented by including new actors would increase the attractiveness of the regions so that people living in the county would remain and other people would move there (see also Chapter 10 and Chapter 2). The idea of partnerships developing regional growth agreements that offer opportunities for new thinking is counteracted by making the usual decision-makers members of the partnership and 'plugging up' the system. The perception is that it is difficult to gain access to the inner circle. However, there is also awareness among those interviewed that it takes time to break up structures and organisations. When the work on the growth agreements began, competition arose in some counties between the work relating to the growth agreements and that relating to the European Social Funds. This was in direct contradiction to the intentions of the government, i.e. that the growth agreements should co-operate with the EU Social and Regional Funds as effectively as possible. In some cases, however, the partnership for the regional growth agreement was the same as that for the Social and/or Regional Funds and the work on the growth agreements was then of great help to the work with the funds. The idea of the partnerships was received positively because responsibility for drawing up basic material and data for a budget process relating to regional development was felt to lie with the partnerships instead of with the authorities. Funding was, however, a major problem. The financial situation of the counties varied widely, partly because funds were not tied to the agreements. In addition, many counties did not have access to regional structural funds that could provide greater flexibility.

Many interviewees wanted to see firmer directives from the government on the even distribution of the genders in partnerships. The view was put forward that it is sustainable development and not market-economy development that is crucial. Gender equality and other aspects that affect the potential for sustainable growth should be seen in the same way as infrastructure and education as 'fuel for growth' and should act as positive driving forces right from the start to stimulate sustainable regional development. As there was a strong emphasis on market-economy growth in the early directives for the growth agreements, the partnerships and business and industry in the regions found it difficult to see how gender equality in itself could contribute to growth. However, the later emphasis on sustainability made it more possible to see the benefits of gender equality as it was then possible, at least in theory, to link gender equality to (sustainable) growth.

The possibility for women to participate and exert influence was limited, however, by the mechanisms inherent in the hierarchical structure of society. This was also reflected in the view prevailing within the inner circles of the partnerships on what it is that promotes growth. The male norm in the homosocial networks was reinforced by a market-economy interpretation of growth based on a technical-economic rationality. This is also confirmed by Hedlund's example (Chapter 13) where she notes that 'the focus is on the growth of industry and commerce' and that the areas of priority are 'innovative environments, entrepreneurship and accessibility'. The technical-economic rationality sees people as a means to an end. The responsibility rationality, on the other hand, sees people as an end in themselves. These two 'rationalities' are often seen as being related to a specific gender[4], but more importantly they should be seen as being socially constructed. They are based on the gender division of work in modern society and arise as a result of various socialisation processes, gender labelling and immanent learning (Ve 1990, 1998, Gunnarsson 1994, Westberg-Wohlgemut 1996, Westberg 1998). The concept of technical-economic rationality is in many contexts perceived to be super ordinate to responsibility rationality. A prevailing technical-economic rationality's apparent gender-neutral orientation does not identify gender equality as a resource other than when it is demonstrated that a win-win situation is possible.

Gender equality is still perceived as something on the periphery, an empty show, even though a majority claim that they know what gender equality entails. One of the consequences of this is that the number of women and men itself becomes a norm, a factor that is easily integrated into the prevailing male norm on gender equality. If a partnership is able to present a representation of women and men that approaches 50-50, then the demand for gender equality is considered to have been met. This reasoning totally ignores factors such as power, homosocial networks and who has the prime right of interpretation. Even though the government has clearly stated that sustainable growth also means that gender equality should be taken seriously and seen as a driving force for such growth, the possibilities are limited by the sluggish structures in existing local and regional power centres where the actors continue to choose to work with each other. Hudson and Rönnblom (2003) say that gender equality seems to be perceived as being the same thing as women, and that women are mainly seen as biological beings that have special characteristics. In order for the participation of women to make a breakthrough, it is therefore necessary to link this to a win-win situation. This means that no one loses if mainstreaming is adopted, but rather that everyone wins.

Blom (1997) discusses how men, through homosocial networks consisting of men and marked by male values, learn to act on the basis of common 'male' norms. The analysis performed by Blom can be compared to the analysis and discussion conducted in connection with generalized and particularized trust, and which may entail that a measure of particularized trust is created within the homosocial networks. We attach the most importance to, and the trust the most, those who are most like us. Those who deviate in some way are excluded. As the regional partnerships consist of a majority of men, the homosocial structure and particularized trust may

---

4 Technical-economic rationality is more often associated with men and responsibility rationality is more often associated with women.

reinforce and preserve the male norms in the formulation of the growth agreements/programmes. The homosocial structure and particularized trust may also result in the composition of the partnerships becoming far too homogenous and in the results becoming a mutual confirmation of old ideas rather than reflection and innovative ideas for growth. The chapter by Wistus (Chapter 9) also points out that partnerships have a tendency to become too homogenous and that those who represent the powers that be are not especially motivated to lose their privileges (see also Hedlund, Chapter 13).

The experience described above and previous experience from European Social and Regional Fund programmes shows that gender equality is an area that cannot easily be addressed simply by writing in programme documents that gender equality must be taken into account both horizontally and vertically, or that sustainable growth comprises the social dimensions, including gender equality. An increased understanding of what sustainable growth entails, and the adoption of a holistic view that shows that it is not only market-economy thinking that counts, will also increase the realisation of the value of broad public participation, even though there is still a long way to go.

11.5 Mainstreaming regional growth programmes

In an attempt to change the view of gender equality as 'an empty show' in the documentation for a growth programme, an overall gender equality project was set up adapted to the needs of the County of Stockholm. The aim was to develop, co-ordinate, and disseminate the gender equality project within the county and to work with strategic gender equality issues in co-operation with other actors in order to develop a strategic plan for mainstreaming during the implementation phase of the regional growth programme with funding within the framework of the European Social Fund's Growth Objective 3 programme. The overall project platform ('*Sthlm Jämt*') used a strategy in which the experience gained and the lessons learned previously formed a critical mass of gender equality projects that the regional actors within the county would find it difficult to ignore. A strategy was formulated on the basis of this platform. This partly involved bringing different gender equality issues together within the platform in order to create synergies, and partly co-ordinating various projects and initiatives and activating funds for the projects and linking them to the platform for joint dissemination measures. The idea was that the co-ordination of projects and initiatives would increase the chances of the gender equality work leading to structural impact and of gender equality making a tangible breakthrough in the local and regional development work. Those responsible for the implementation of the project Sthlm Jämt formed a working group in which each member was responsible for one of the activities in the project. The working group defined the platform itself as a number of ongoing and potential gender equality initiatives that were gathered together to form a critical mass from which experience was gained and disseminated. This description made it clear that the platform was an ongoing process. The platform for Sthlm Jämt mainly 'lived' through the working group and the individuals in the organisations that formed the steering group for Sthlm Jämt and the reference group for the adoption of mainstreaming in the regional growth programme[5].

The research and development approach used was action-oriented. The processes underway to mainstream the programme areas and action programmes of the regional development programme[6] were followed. The task was to document and reflect on these processes and, as far as possible, provide feedback to the actors within the platform. The concrete plans for research, follow-up and evaluation, were partly intended to connect to a method for qualitative process evaluation. This method is based on documenting and discussing as much as possible. Sthlm Jämt's project managers were therefore asked to collect documentation (on discussions, seminars etc.) and to keep a diary of events and to reflect on these events. The researchers attended meetings and interviewed key individuals. Discussions and interviews were complemented by a targeted questionnaire and the results of this questionnaire were fed back to the project. The members of the working group for Sthlm Jämt, a steering group for the platform Sthlm Jämt and the co-ordinator for the regional growth programme were first interviewed at the start of the evaluation and then a second time during a later phase of the project period. Further interviews were conducted with representatives of the working group. Key individuals in the programme areas were interviewed in 2005 and 2006.

Within the framework of the project, actors within the county were offered training and support in methods for the mainstreaming of operations, projects and programmes. The aim was that actors in the county

---

5   The project also had a steering group consisting of the closest stakeholders, the County Administrative Board, the region's European Social Fund, the Regional Association of Local Authorities and the co-ordinator of the regional growth programme. A reference group was formed consisting, among others, of representatives of the various programme areas in the growth programme.

6   A regional development programme that aimed to draw up a strategy for the long-term sustainable development of the region (www.nutek.se – regional development).

would be trained in methods for mainstreaming their operations; including action programmes and projects in the regional growth programme and projects falling under Growth Objective 3. Gender equality and the discrepancy between society's rhetoric and practice at the workplace were largely seen as a knowledge area and a knowledge issue. The training measures were seen as one means of achieving the goal – greater gender equality in the Stockholm region. Once mainstreaming has been chosen as a strategy for society's gender-equality policy then it becomes natural to start development work with the process-based operational control of gender-equality policy at the local and regional levels. Mainstreaming is a strategic method for working towards the achievement of the gender-equality objectives set and includes highlighting prevailing conditions and circumstances for women and men. All issues affecting individuals should be examined from a gender-equality perspective and a special analysis of what the consequences of changes may be for women and men respectively should be conducted (www.naring.regeringen.se).

Mainstreaming is therefore not just a question of training, which was the main strategy adopted by Sthlm Jämt. Initially, the people responsible for the various areas (project managers) and the process manager for Sthlm Jämt's platform also attempted to interest the contacts for the various programme areas in a seminar on gender equality.

11.6 Controlling complex processes

Sthlm Jämt invested major resources to ensure that gender equality should not just be an issue that was paid lip service in the growth programme for the County of Stockholm but a case of real mainstreaming taking place in practice. This ambition, in combination with considerable financial resources,[7] should provide a good potential for sustainable growth marked by mainstreaming. More long-term and sustainable development should comprise active ownership[8]. How well did Sthlm Jämt succeed in achieving its aims?

---

7   From 2004 to 2006 inclusive, the entire Sthlm Jämt project had a turnover of SEK 180 million.

8   For a more detailed description see Svensson et al. 2005, 2007 and Chapter 1 and Chapter 14 of this book.

11.7 Active ownership

Drafting groups were linked to the various areas in the regional growth programme. These groups consisted, among others, of representatives of the partnership or people belonging to the organisations that made up the partnership. Gender equality projects within the framework of the Sthlm Jämt platform and linked to programme areas that had an active owner managed to mainstream their activities, i.e. in programme areas where Sthlm Jämt initiated projects and others took over ownership. This was a complete success in one area but only a partial success in another where there was disagreement about who initiated the project and who was the owner. The drafting groups for the other programme areas were not even passive owners of the projects that the Sthlm Jämt platform managed to organise. Instead, the projects remained external to the drafting groups but had a content that could be related to the programme areas concerned. These areas are described briefly below.

Protracted discussions on the role of one of the drafting groups and its link to the regional growth programme detracted from the effectiveness of the work. In 2004, Sthlm Jämt failed in an attempt to gain understanding for the importance of mainstreaming in the programme area concerned and felt that it was more or less excluded from further contact. Despite the fact that Sthlm Jämt repeatedly pointed out this lack of understanding and support, the revised action programme for this area contains statements on gender equality. Under the heading *Strategies for sustainable development* both gender equality and mainstreaming are mentioned as factors that add value to various activities in the programme. The action programme also says that statistics must be gender-divided and that the way decisions affect women and men must be taken into account. This drafting group thus included gender-equality issues in its action programme on its own initiative and this cannot be seen as a result of Sthlm Jämt's work. In another of the areas of the regional development programme, Sthlm Jämt did not have the impact it would have liked, probably because the programme area lacked a group of its own. In yet another area, the gender-equality work conducted by Sthlm Jämt was not considered to be important to the area concerned. In 2005, however, Sthlm Jämt began on its own initiative and with the assistance of several people connected with the development programme work, a survey relating to this programme area. Finally, one of the areas was already from the start a so-called sidecar to the regional development programme and Sthlm Jämt did not manage to influence this area either.

Despite the fact that several of the actors that made up the project's steering group and reference group were members of the partnership and of both the County Governor's group and the steering group for the regional development programme, they did not manage to gain support and understanding for the ideas and ambitions of Sthlm Jämt in these power centres. Thus, those working with the Sthlm Jämt platform did not manage to reach several of the drafting groups for the programme areas even though the preconditions for doing so were apparently good. Instead, compensatory projects were set up which, although they lay within the framework of the programme areas, became new sidetracks for the issue of gender equality. Considerable time and resources were invested in these sidetracks. An important success factor could however be identified in the work conducted by Sthlm Jämt which in part can be traced to the good contacts with the power centres of the partnership. In connection with the preparatory work with the structural funds, Sthlm Jämt redirected a project from the regional growth programme to the structural funds. This gave Sthlm Jämt an important role in the drawing up of the regional structural fund programme in the County of Stockholm. Three public officials – all women with close links to Sthlm Jämt – put together a proposal for the regional structural fund programme that was entirely based on Sthlm Jämt's platform idea. The model that Sthlm Jämt represented acted as a model for other areas. This proposal was then circulated for comment and meetings with a wide range of participants were arranged. The idea of organising platforms in the various areas was received positively and was included in the final proposal for Stockholm's regional structural fund programme. Sustainability factors such as gender equality, integration and the environment are well integrated in the document.

In her article on the preparatory work for the structural fund programmes, Hedlund (see Chapter 13) says that the partnership behind the structural programme was organised on the basis of principles of gender equality in participation and open discussions *outwards* and male-dominated, bureaucratic elite control *inwards*. In the cases I have described, the officials that formulated the programme were women with a conscious gender-equality perspective. Fears were, however, expressed by people in leading positions (men) that gender equality was no longer on the agenda in the region. At the County Administrative Board, for example, it was felt that gender equality had been an issue of priority and that it took up too much of the general discussion in the period that Sthlm Jämt was underway. The Board now wanted to prioritise other issues and include gender equality under the heading of diversity. Concern was expressed that if gender equality becomes one of many diversity issues then there is a risk that it will disappear from the agenda altogether. The women who wrote the draft for the structural fund programme are not in positions where they can influence the internal process once it starts. Previous experience indicates that is not enough for documents to be worded positively – it is the implementation that is important. It is therefore difficult to be clear about whether sustainability aspects will be prioritised in practice. There is reason to believe, however, that the male-dominated, bureaucratic elite will have the prime right of interpretation in the ongoing work to launch the structural fund programme in the County of Stockholm.

11.8 Results at the system and individual levels

Did Sthlm Jämt succeed in improving the preconditions for a tangible breakthrough for the gender equality dimension in local and regional development work? There is no clear answer to this. Succeeding in mainstreaming the work of the regional development programme and increasing awareness among the actors in the programme, would that be considered enough? Succeeding in increasing awareness of gender equality locally and regionally through the projects started on the basis of Sthlm Jämt's platform, would that be considered enough? That Sthlm Jämt, as a result of its platform in which many actors had the opportunity to meet, provided a greater potential for synergies between different gender quality issues – would that be considered enough? Is it required that Sthlm Jämt should have achieved good results in all of its prioritised areas? Where do the boundaries for a successful result lie? Where do the boundaries for a successful project lie? Is there a minimum level? The unique features of Sthlm Jämt are that it had good financial resources, a broad approach and acted through the platform. In the platform, the various activities crossed paths and experience was exchanged. In many ways, the platform functioned as a learning platform and many reassessments took place there that led to changes in direction when the direction being followed proved to be unfruitful. Some feel that a minimum level for a successful result is achieved if projects within the platform began to see the world through 'gender equality eyes', that the issue is now on the agenda at all, that changes have taken place at the individual level. Others feel that structural changes must take place before a result can be considered successful. Changing values is a slow process at both the individual and collective levels. There is interplay between the society we live in and our values. As we grow up, society forms our values, but we also form society in line with our values. It is therefore not possible to increase gender equality in a society simply by changing values at the individual level.

At the individual level, the assessment is that Sthlm Jämt was successful.

We believe that Sthlm Jämt succeeded in opening the eyes of many of the inhabitants of the county so that they are now aware of their own values and the basic values of others. They have also been strengthened in their efforts to change traditional gender roles and attitudes. It can also be noted that Sthlm Jämt succeeded in introducing the issue of gender equality in certain areas of the regional growth programme. Whereas previously practically nothing was said on this issue in the overall programme and the programmes for the various areas, it is now mentioned in several areas. In addition, Sthlm Jämt has helped to make sure that the gender-equality dimension is mentioned in the documents for the new regional structural fund programme in the County of Stockholm.

In terms of making an impact in the field of gender equality in the county in general, apart from the programme activities carried out that are not directly connected to the regional growth programme, a lot of effort was put into writing a gender equality strategy. In the work on this strategy many different players took part in focus groups, and both the mainstreaming reference group and the steering group for Sthlm Jämt discussed and presented their views on the content. As mentioned above, the steering and reference groups contain representatives of the power centres in the growth partnership. What remains to be done is to ensure that the wording that now exists in the two documents is also taken on board by the owners who will now take up the baton.

In the case of the regional structural fund programme, there will be a partnership for the entire programme in which the majority of the representatives will be politicians. This partnership will recommend the areas that should be prioritised in the structural fund programme launched during the year. In the case of the strategy for gender equality, there are hopes that the County Council, the County Administrative Board and the Association of Local Authorities in the County of Stockholm will adopt it and make it their own. In both cases, therefore, it is the politicians that will play a decisive role in determining whether the wording on gender equality is put into practice.

11.9 Conclusions and discussion

In this chapter, three of the four dilemmas taken up in the first chapter have been addressed. In the first project described, the dilemmas concerning the holistic view and the issue of democracy are discussed. As the aim was to see if and how the gender equality dimension was integrated into the old growth agreements, this automatically becomes a question of democracy. If gender equality was simply the same as there being more women in the partnerships, then it could be said that the democratisation trend in terms of the representation of women and men was positive. I have noted, however, that increased representation does not necessarily mean increased influence. There are examples of several different ways of excluding women from the decision-making processes, examples that Pincus (2003) describes as 'passive resistance' and Hedlund (1996) as 'obliging resistance' (see also Chapter 13).

The holistic view is closely linked to not simply viewing growth as market-economy growth alone but as sustainable growth, i.e. something that provides the potential for sound economic, social and ecological conditions. Despite the fact that women define growth on the basis of a holistic perspective, it is the technical-economic rationality of men that gains precedence, i.e. the market-economy orientation often excludes social and ecological conditions. The lack of a holistic view works in conjunction with the lack of democratic influence on the part of those groups that remain outside the partnership or those who are members of the partnership but have no power or right of interpretation. The exclusion mechanisms that exist in the case of immigrants (see Chapter 10) also apply to women. The broad holistic approach gave the partners in the regional growth partnerships a lot of leeway to define for themselves, on the basis of the logics of their own organisations, what they wanted to collaborate on. This meant that women were often not included, even though the gender equality discourse means in theory that women are included to a greater extent than immigrants. As many groups were excluded from the partnership, and as it was the same people as usual that made the decisions on funding and investments, it cannot be said that the partnership met the democratic criteria. In the Sthlm Jämt example, it can be noted that – despite ample funding and the support of several decision-makers – mainstreaming within the framework of the regional growth programme was only successful in a few cases. In the future, however, there may be a greater potential for democratisation in the regional structural funds as a majority of the partnership representatives will be politicians and the members of the partnership will have the task of proposing the areas that should be prioritised. This will give the partnership more power and a greater capacity to resist internal bureaucratic influence. However, mainstreaming must always be promoted from both a bottom-up and top-down perspective (cf. Chapters 1 and 2).

The results confirm the view of Portes and Landholt (1996) that the social capital can have negative effects in that common norms in groups and organisations may have an inhibiting effect on individuals in the group and an excluding effect in relation to others. The evaluation of the growth programmes conducted by the Swedish Agency for Economic and Regional Growth (Nutek) in 2004 noted that the partnerships for the various growth programmes felt that 'the sustainability aspects were better integrated in the programme documents than in the actual implementation while the programme managers felt the opposite'... 'Approximately 50 per cent of the partnerships felt that the environmental and gender equality dimensions were integrated rather well or very well in the programmes, which also applies to the programme managers in implementation'. Nutek concluded that mainstreaming was more pronounced in the growth programmes than in the growth agreements, but that a lot remained to be done before the growth programmes were completely mainstreamed. In general, the women were somewhat less positive about how well mainstreaming had been achieved. Nutek drew its conclusions on the basis of responses from the partnerships and programme managers that relate to written texts and not to implementation processes and activities. The social capital, as defined by Putnam (1996), has its limitations in the sense that the underlying homosocial norms make it difficult for groups other than those who are more 'similar' to exert influence. On the other hand, opportunities for sustainable growth can be opened up if general trust is interpreted as an element of the social capital on the basis of a responsibility-rationality approach.

Can regional partnerships, which are a component of regional industrial policy and the EU structural funds, as well as forums in which representatives of many different institutions /organisations are included (for example political bodies, trade unions and, to some extent, employer organisations) play the role of 'acting' partnerships for sustainable growth? If they are to be able to assume this role they must become and be regarded as a complement to representative democracy and not as legally-independent, decision-making bodies with a limited degree of representativity. The truth of the underlying assumption that partnership is a successful form for development work that aims to promote sustainable growth remains largely unproven.

References

Blom, Agneta P (1997) 'Strukturers betydelse för framgång – diskussion utifrån en studie av kvinnliga och manliga förvaltningschefer i landstingen'. In Nyberg, A & Sundin, E (eds.) *Ledare makt och kön* SOU 1997:135. Stockholm: Fritzes

Ds 2001:15 *Rapport om tillväxtavtalen. Första året.* Näringsdepartementet. Stockholm: Fritzes offentliga publikationer

Ds 2002:34 *Rapport om tillväxtavtalen. Andra året.* Näringsdepartementet. Stockholm: Fritzes offentliga publikationer

Gunnarsson, Ewa (1994) *Att våga väga jämnt! Om kvalifikationer och kvinnliga förhållningssätt i ett tekniskt industriarbete.* Diss. 1994:157 Luleå: Luleå tekniska högskola, institutionen för arbetsvetenskap

Hedlund, Gun (1996) *'Det handlar om prioriteringar': kvinnors villkor och intressen i lokal politik.* Diss. Högskolan i Örebro

Horelli, Liisa & Roininen, Janne (1999). *Ex-ante evaluering ur jämställdhetsperspektiv av Sveriges tillväxtavtal.* Arbetsrapport tillväxtavtal. Helsingfors: Tekniska Högskolan

Holmberg, Sören & Weibull, Lennart (2000) 'Det nya samhället'. In Holmberg, S & Weibull, L (eds.) *Det nya samhället. SOM-undersökning 1999.* SOM-rapport nr 24. Göteborg University SOM-institutet

Hudson, Christine & Rönnblom, Malin (2003). *Regional growth partnerships in Sweden - breaking down hierarchies or building new barriers for women's participation?* Paper presented at ECPR Workshop 23. Edinburgh 28 March– 2 April 2003

Hård, Ursula (2005) 'Presentation av Länsexperter i jämställdhet och ResursCentra för kvinnor, samt några centrala begrepp'. In: Westberg H (red.) *Regionala tillväxtavtal – en fråga om att bryta gamla mönster?: kvinnors och mäns delaktighet i arbetet med tillväxtavtalen.* Arbetsliv i omvandling 2005:8. Stockholm: Arbetslivsinstitutet

Johannisson, Bengt & Madsen, Torsten et al. (1997) *I entrepenörskapets tecken. En studie av skolning i förnyelse.* Ds 1997:3, pp. 192, 194. Stockholm: Fritzes

Nutek (2005) *På väg mot hållbar tillväxt?: regionala tillväxtprogrammen.* Stockholm: Verket för näringslivsutveckling

Pincus, Ingrid (2003) *The Politics of Gender Equality Policy.* Örebro Studies in Political Science 5

Portes, Alejandro & Landholt, Patricia (1996) *The downside of social capital.* The American Prospect online, 26, May–June 1996

Putnam, Robert (1996) *Den fungerande demokratin. Medborgarandans rötter i Italien* Stockholm: SNS Förlag

Svensson, Lennart, Åberg, Carina, Andersson, Mats, & Paulson, Jonas (2005). Att leda projekt och utvecklingsprocesser. Visanu (a co-operation between IS/ Nutek. Vinnova). Rapport 2005:18. Stockholm: Vinnova

Svensson, Lennart, Aronsson, Gunnar, Randle, Hanne & Eklund, Jörgen (2007) *Hållbart arbetsliv. Projekt som gästspel eller strategi i hållbar utveckling.* Malmö: Glerups Utbildning AB

Uslaner, Eric (2000) *Trust and Consequences.* College Park: University of Maryland-College Park. http://www.bsos.umd.edu/gvpt/uslaner/communpsq.pdf

Ve, Hildur (1990) Women's experience – Women's rationality. Paper presented at the Conference: The construction of Sex/Gender: What is a Feminist Perspective? Lidingö, Sweden

— (1998) 'Education for Change: Action Research for Increased Gender Equality'. In Macinnon, Alison, Elgqvist-Salzman, Inga & Prentice, Alison (eds.) *Education into the 21st Century. Dangerous Terrain for Women?* London: Palmer press

Westberg-Wohlgemut, Hanna (1996) *Kvinnor och män märks. Könsmärkning*

av arbete – en dold lärandeprocess. Arbete och Hälsa 1996:1. Stockholm: Arbetslivsinstitutet och Stockholm University, pedagogiska institutionen
Westberg, Hanna (1998) 'Könsmärkning av arbeten'. In: Gunnarsson E, Andersson, S & Westberg, H (eds.) *Känsla och regelverk i balans.* Stockholm: Arbetslivsinstitutet och Folksam
— ed. (2005). Regionala tillväxtavtal – en fråga om att bryta gamla mönster. Arbetsliv i omvandling 2005:8. Stockholm: Arbetslivsinstitutet
— (2006) 'Brett medborgerligt deltagande är en grogrund för nya idéer'. In: Danilda, Inger (red.) *Vem får bidra till tillväxten?: om jämställdhet och integration i tillväxtprogram.* Stockholm: Arbetslivsinstitutet
www.naring.regeringen.se

12. Partnerships for sustainable change: the Austrian pacts and their contribution to sustainable change exemplified by the 'Green Paper for the Elderly'

This chapter aims to present the lessons learned from the Austrian employment partnerships, to discuss recent results in respect of the four practical dilemmas envisaged in the first chapter of the book and to debate whether partnerships are a strategy for sustainable change in the field of labour market policies.

The article consists of three parts: first, contributions of the Austrian partnerships to sustainable change will be discussed. Second, practical aspects of partnership work will be described, such as how the partnerships influence policy, exemplified by the 'Green Paper for the Elderly' developed within a multi-level collaboration of pacts. Furthermore, process findings such as the need for further clarification of partnerships' scope of opportunities are presented and, last but not least, the author concludes by analysing the results achieved so far, thereby questioning whether partnerships are a strategy for sustainable change and innovation.

12.1 Do partnerships organise sustainable change?

12.1.1 *The Austrian TEPs and their contributions to sustainable change*

What can be expected from partnerships? Are these new forms of governance capable of changing the system? Are the alliances key players in mobilising reforms?

In Austria, Territorial Employment Pacts[1] (TEPs) were set up because of the belief that the Austrian labour market and employment policy is confronted with particular challenges that cannot be met by just a few institutions on their own (e.g. concentration of unemployment to certain target groups, gender segregation on the labour market, shifts between industries, economic sectors and regions).

Consequently, partnerships were established, initiated from the top. The Austrian Federal Ministry for Economics and Labour welcomed the European Commission's (EC) pilot action 'Territorial Employment Pacts' and made funds available for all Austrian regions, which has resulted in the implementation of pacts in all nine Austrian Provinces since 1999. Additionally, some TEPs were set up at the sub-regional level. Due to this top-down approach, the partnerships carry out functions allocated from the top. The widespread regional partnerships aim to (1) identify the difficulties, ideas and objectives regions are facing with respect to employment policies; (2) mobilise all available resources in favour of an integrated strategy, based on the region's needs and entrenched in a formal commitment – the Territorial Employment Pact; (3) improve the co-ordination of job-creation measures and (4) implement measures to boost employment. Although directives from the top are limited (e.g. while funding is being provided for the partnership structure, the alliances autonomously decide on their content of work), the pacts are supervised from the national level. The national Co-ordination Unit of the TEPs serves as a neutral intermediary body, matching the demands from the partnerships and the needs from the top.

Realistic expectations of what partnerships can do primarily have to be related to their functions. Thus, the main tasks of TEPs are co-ordinating partners and their topics, developing joint work programmes (TEP programme) and implementing the measures according to the priorities of the TEPs. In Austria, the priorities vary from region to region. In 2006, the rural TEP Tyrol, for instance, placed emphasis on the regional co-ordination of offers for educational and vocational guidance, whilst TEP Vienna focused on programmes for the integration of specific target groups, such as youth (see table 1). However, implementing innovation, including civil society's concerns etc., are consequences of their work, as described in the following.

---

1   www.pakte.at

Table 1. Example of TEPs, their emphases and areas of action, as well as their main partners in 2006**

Examples of TEPs	Emphases and Areas of Action	Main Partners
Tyrol	• Regional co-ordination of offers for educational and vocational guidance; • Development of standards for employment projects; • Socio-economic enterprises; • Non-profit employment projects; • Career guidance of Municipalities, AMG Tyrol	Province, AMS, BSB, WK, AK, ÖGB, IV,** Chamber of Agricultural Labour, Provincial Chamber of Agriculture, Tyrolean educational institute 'Grillhof', Association Association of cities and towns
Vienna	• JASG measures (measures for the target group youth); • Implacement and outplacement foundations; • Programmes for entrants and re-entrants into the job market; • Programmes for counselling and promoting working people and for integrative vocational training; • Vienna – Bratislava Interregional Employment Strategy	City of Vienna, AMS, Vienna Employment Promotion Fund (waff), BSB – Provincial Office Vienna, interest group representatives of employers and employees (provincial working group)

* Co-ordination Unit of the TEPs, 2006
** Abbreviations: AMS_Public Employment Service, BSB_Federal Office of Social Affairs, WK_Economic Chamber, AK_Chamber of Labour, ÖGB_Federation of Trade Unions, IV_Federation of Industry

The Austrian TEPs are part of the 'Austrian labour market system'. Metaphorically speaking, they construct their 'house' on this foundation, thereby 'opening the doors between the rooms', i.e. establishing links between the institutions that have already been in existence for many years, such as the Public Employment Service, the Federal Provinces, the Offices of Social Affairs etc. The Austrian pacts are defined as contracted regional partnerships to better link employment policy with other policies in order to improve the employment situation at the regional and local levels. In co-operating as partners, their specific aims are:

- to increase effectiveness and efficiency in the use of resources
- to improve the quality of support given to certain target groups
- to secure and create jobs
- to obtain funding for the regions

The TEPs attempt to improve the system they are part of. More precisely, the partnerships work within the existing policy framework, tailoring programmes to the specific needs of the regions. The Austrian partnerships were set up among the relevant institutions in labour market policy to agree upon and implement joint programmes for promoting employment. They neither take over the roles of each partner nor compete with the institutions; instead they harmonise and complement the work done by the institutions. They balance interests, elaborate links and use synergies between the institutions in order to find joint solutions. By working together, the partnerships fill gaps that are left open by institutions that work individually. These gaps exist for many reasons: changes in our economies and societies, political developments (e.g. rising unemployment rate of older workers as a result of early retirements), as well as the increase in complex situations made partnerships valuable. Furthermore, individual institutions often show resistance to reform due to a lack of motivation, possibilities or competence and, often, do not adequately adapt to new challenges but get trapped in institutional deadlocks.

While partnerships follow the rules of the system they also, step by step, push ideas forward, implement innovative projects and practice new ways of collaboration, communication and culture. Coordinated and integrated approaches are taken by the partnerships in their various circumstances and settings: they communicate across all levels – from the local to the regional to the national and the international level - and do so (often) apart from ordinary hierarchies. All partnerships networked by the OECD LEED Forum on Partnerships and Local Governance[2] are cross-sectoral (i.e. combining economic sectors horizontally) and are characterised by multi-level cooperation. However, in order to better solve problems at the local and the regional level, the alliances have to follow a thin line: while crossing cultural and institutional borders in their daily work, partnerships have to be cautious in order not to lose partners due to cultural differences, communication gaps, etc. However, they manage to change the behaviour of individuals and institutions, transform (national) policies in a way to better meet the needs of the territory and, consequently, make policies more attractive to citizens. Due to the increased involvement of local and regional actors, responsibilities are taken and shared. Thus, solutions tend to become more sustainable.

Due to their huge potential, partnerships are in fashion. Nowadays, programmes call for the formation of alliances due to directives set up by the EC and the EU member states. Thus, many initiatives build on the

[2] see http://www.oecd.org/cfe/leed/forum/partnerships

idea of partnerships. A closer examination reveals that collaboration in the form of a partnership, i.e. with partners that cooperate bilaterally, is widespread. On the more advanced level, partnerships characterised by contracting between various partners, a holistic approach, the development of a long-term strategy etc. – just to highlight some characteristics (see also chapter 3) – are also much more common in comparison to the projects and programmes of the past. Many of those depending on a single fund, such as EQUAL development partnerships, will hardly continue after the end of the fund. Even if their long-term impact has to be questioned, they contribute to sustainable change in terms of practising new ways of collaboration, communication and culture while they exist.

12.1.2 *Recent results in respect of the four practical dilemmas*

By questioning whether the system approach of partnerships excludes the individual perspective as indicated in the first practical dilemma, it has to be mentioned that all the partnerships examined represent a formalistic model, simply because they contract with various partners (see above). The system perspective (characterised by professionalised work, rules of procedure etc.) is, therefore, present in all partnerships, albeit to a varying extent. However, within the same partnership organisation loose forms of cooperation are also practiced requiring informal, voluntary activities and procedures (individual perspective). In the majority of partnerships surveyed, both perspectives, the system perspective on the one hand and the individual perspective on the other, are in place. The Austrian experience shows that, at best, the advantages of both approaches are integrated in the work of partnerships.

With reference to the second dilemma (Does the holistic approach of partnerships minimise the outcome due to a lack of focus?) the experience is as follows: Though partnerships practice a holistic approach, they normally set annual priorities in order to keep a clear yearly focus. Since outcomes are important in any case (also in non-complex, ordinary approaches), much effort needs to be made, which includes not losing sight of the outcome. However, the real challenge met is measuring the outcome, especially the added value of alliances: as partnerships work intensely on projects – the level at which the majority of funds are allocated – they frequently report on project results. But their achievements are much more than the sum of these results. Since many factors influence the final outcomes, indicators still have to be developed that support determining the overall achievements as well as the indirect influences of the alliances. Thus, a way needs to be found to prove the added value in a more holistic way, thereby including cooperation as the focal point for any work at the project level.

In respect of the third dilemma, the Austrian TEPs play a minor role in relation to democracy. Given that mainly financiers, social partners and other (mostly) official organisations are part of the decision-making committees, already strong actors are reinforced. In order to become a member of one of the partnerships' boards, a clarification process takes place. Generally, individuals and NGOs do not have decision-making rights at the TEP programme level due to target conflicts[3]. In all other boards, such as working groups and platforms, NGOs are important partners to drive the partnership forward, albeit the level of influence varies from partnership to partnership. In Austria, many more actors (NGOs, gender mainstreaming experts, Offices of Social Affairs, municipalities, etc.) joined the partnerships over time and became responsible for active labour market policy.

In this article, 'organising sustainable change' is understood as the sum of ways, methods and approaches by which new ways of collaboration, communication and culture are practised resulting in a change of behaviour of individuals and institutions in order to, finally, improve the (labour market) system. In this respect, the question 'Do partnerships organise sustainable change?' can be affirmed, although 'contributing to sustainable change' more precisely describes partnerships' efforts, especially with reference to the Austrian experience. None of the nine Austrian TEPs call for 'changing the system' in their objectives, but all of them aim to improve the regional labour markets. The evaluation of the Austrian TEPs[4] proved that the partnerships contributed to the improved effectiveness, efficiency and transparency of policies. Nevertheless, the alliances are not key-players in mobilising reforms, they (slowly) improve the system from the inside (as part of the system).

Now, 'how can they change the system if they follow the rules of the system and are part of the system?' (The fourth dilemma). The following part will describe the efforts made and the lessons learned by the Austrian partnerships in this respect, exemplified by a multi-level collaboration of the TEPs, the 'Green Paper for the Elderly'.

---

[3] The two functions, deciding on the support of projects on the one hand and implementing projects on the other are partly incompatible.

[4] TEP Evaluation (WIFO, Huber P (2003), Evaluierung Europäischer Sozialfonds 2000-2006 / Ziel 3 Österreich / Schwerpunkt 6: Territoriale Beschäftigungspakte, Wien)

12.2 Multi-level collaboration of TEPs: partnerships' scope of opportunities and limits

Two years ago, the TEPs decided to join forces to improve the labour market situation of the elderly, especially older workers and job-seekers. In 2005, Austria's employment rate for people aged 55–64 was 31.8 %. Austria was (and still is) far from reaching the Lisbon goal of a 50 % employment rate for older workers in 2010. In order to put older job seekers to work and keep older workers employed, the Austrian partnerships established a nation-wide development partnership, – TEP-EQUAL-Elderly[5]. This alliance was set up by all Austrian TEPs at the provincial level under the coordination of the ZSI[6], hosting the nation-wide Coordination Unit of TEPs (Kooo). Kooo supports the various projects conducted by the Austrian Employment Pacts and its partner institutions by means of information exchange, strategic co-ordination and joint activities. The development partnership applied for funding within the Austrian EQUAL Programme and since funding was approved operates as a 'meta-partnership' of all alliances in respect of the target group, i.e. the elderly.

This chapter describes the process of establishing the Austrian-wide partnership by providing information on the forms of collaboration practiced and answers the question: 'Why did the Austrian TEPs join forces?' The method used, recent results achieved and obstacles met will be presented. Finally, the lessons learned on the partnerships' scope of opportunities and limits (how far do they want and are allowed to go in order to exploit their full potential?) will be debated.

12.2.1 Collaboration between TEPs

Although each pact formally co-operates with its partners entrenched in the 'Pact Agreement', the Austrian TEPs mainly practised informal collaboration with each other. Despite formal cooperation between levels, such as the contractual obligations between provincial TEPs and their sub-regional structures (three Austrian Provinces, Styria, Vienna and Upper Austria perform their work together with their sub-regional structures), the formal collaboration of partnerships at the same level has been observed only rarely over the last ten years. Only some sub-regional TEPs at the same level contracted with each other, which was the case in the

---

5 www.elderly.at; TEP-EQUAL-Elderly is funded by the Federal Ministry of Economics and Labour and the European Social Fund (ESF).
6 ZSI-Centre for Social Innovation; www.zsi.at

Province of Styria. Actually, even cross-border co-operation between TEPs and their neighbouring counterparts were informal at the beginning.

Loose co-operation and networking was developed intensively between the partnerships and boosted through Kooo, which brings the partnerships together on a regular basis in order to support learning and facilitate information exchange on failures and best practices. All Austrian TEPs first joined forces in the form of a loose co-operation within the 'TEPGM-project' in 2002, inspired by the intention to jointly implement gender mainstreaming. Nevertheless, what was new (and innovative) to all those involved was a contracted co-operation between all Austrian provincial TEPs.

12.2.2 Why join forces?

In reference to TEP-EQUAL-Elderly, the formal co-operation was stimulated by the weak inclusion of older workers on the labour market. The partnerships considered working together to improve the labour market in order to support and learn from each other. The partnerships tested a new and innovative labour market instrument in three Federal Provinces, the so-called 'elderly plans', exchanged their experience on their pilots nationwide and developed an 'Elderly-tool box'[7] in order to mainstream their experience, the methods used and the results achieved.

The underlying motive for the collaboration all across Austria was to enhance power by co-operation ('the whole is greater than the sum of its parts'). It was considered that in order to increase the employability of older workers, consultation with all the relevant stakeholders was necessary. It was felt that a 'White Paper' would be the best method of serving the needs in order to, finally, improve the situation for the target group by jointly influencing policy at all levels.

Now, could the partnerships really influence policy with the enhanced power provided by collaboration? This is discussed below.

12.2.3 The 'Strategy for the Elderly' of the Green Paper

Initially, the partnerships created a joint vision for 2035, thereby collecting and merging ideas from all nine partnerships, each representing approximately eleven institutions at the regional level. In addition, NGOs, universities, companies, other stakeholders and private individuals (including older workers and job-seekers) were consulted in order to complement the vision.

---

7   see www.elderly.at (in German language only).

The partnerships also developed trends and scenarios for 2035 together with Austria's top scientists in various fields (labour market policy, social sciences, economy, futurology, demography, ergonomics etc.). Finally, the 'Strategy for the Elderly', published in the Green Paper, was created by linking labour market policy with the three most central policies, the economic, social and education policies. Figure 1 illustrates the process of establishing the White Paper.

Process

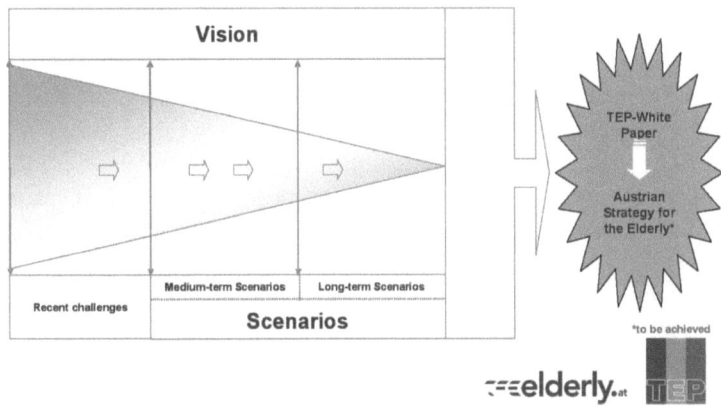

Figure 1. Process of establishing the White Paper

The strategy covers a wide range of policy interventions aiming at sustainable economic growth and social cohesion. The recommendations do not only link policies horizontally but require coordinated changes at the national, the regional and the local levels.

As shown in table 2, the policies linked are 'Labour market and economic policy', 'Labour market and social policy' and 'Labour market and education policy'. The vision and elements of the vision are connected to these policy pillars. Finally, challenges as well as general recommendations and potential TEP activities are described for each element of the vision.

To give an example, the vision of the pillar 'Labour market and economic policy' is an 'Intergenerational equitable Labour market' (A). The elements of this vision are the following: (A1) Intergenerational equitable employment opportunities in a flexible labour market; (A2) Full acceptance and use of strengths of older workers on the labour market; (A3)

Continuous life-long and intergenerational equitable HRD in enterprises; and (A4) Equal opportunities. As for A1, oversupply in the labour force along with a lack of workplaces (few intergenerational equitable workplaces) are the most important challenges encountered. In order to achieve the vision, the general recommendations given in the 'Strategy for the Elderly' include facilitating employment (reducing non-wage labour costs, minimising the wage principle giving privilege to older workers, specific arrangements for protection against dismissal) and investing in age-based workplaces. An example of a TEP activity related to this element of the vision is the implementation of pilots in the field of new forms of work (e.g. short-time work, qualified part-time work etc.).

In total, a set of 130 activities is provided, a large number of which can be implemented by the TEPs. Examples include the implementation of age-neutral funding practices, promoting intergenerational staffing policy at the regional level (road shows, competitions, internet bourse for exchange of best-practices, regional certification for age-based SMEs etc.), as well as better coordination of local and regional training offers (see Table 2). The strategy facilitates the setting-up of bundles of measures at the regional and local levels, all to be adapted to respective territorial conditions.

The method used was to establish a Green/White Paper. It was planned to publish a White Paper after consultation with all relevant stakeholders across all levels and sectors in Austria. The consultation demonstrated the great interest of all the actors involved. However, many obstacles had to be met, in particular during the consultation phase.

12.2.4 Lessons learned

In order to improve the situation of older workers on the labour market, the need for a consolidated and co-ordinated approach was confirmed by the actors. In addition, a common perception and consensus was achieved during consultation by the vast majority of TEPs regarding the main statements and topics covered within the Green Paper.

The joint work of researchers, practitioners and policy makers was perceived as added value by all involved. The cooperation facilitated a comprehensive and holistic picture of the situation of the elderly, expressed by the several experts from diverse professional backgrounds. This know-how pool served as a basis for all further project work.

The method facilitated broad consultation and the involvement of the

Table 2. The structure of the 'Strategy for the Elderly' published in the Green Paper*

Pillar	Vision	Elements of the Vision	Challenges	General Recommendations	Examples of TEP-Activities	TEP-Contributions on the co-operational level
LABOUR MARKET AND ECONOMIC POLICY	An Intergenerational Equitable Labour Market	A1 Intergenerational equitable employment opportunities in a flexible labour market	e.g. ☐ Oversupply in labour force along with lack of work places (few intergenerational equitable work places)	e.g. ☐ Facilitate employment (reduce non-wage labour costs, reduction of the wage principle privileging older workers, specific arrangements for protection against dismissal) and investment in age-based workplaces	e.g. ☐ Pilots in the field of new forms of work (e.g. short-time work, qualified part-time work, etc.)	e.g. ☐ Clarification of interests and development of joint regional perceptions
		A2 Full acceptance and use of strengths of older workers on the labour market	e.g. ☐ Predominant argument on the decrease of productivity of older workers	e.g. ☐ Launching a fundamental paradigm shift, a new understanding of the employment of older workers and transculturation in SMEs	e.g. ☐ Campaigns for raising awareness	
		A3 Continuous life-long and intergenerational equitable HRD in enterprises	e.g. ☐ Lack of intergenerational equitable HRD in enterprises	e.g. ☐ Promoting intergenerational staffing policy (use of tailor-made personnel development plans, on time retraining, innovative management methods, such as diversity management and active generation management)	e.g. ☐ Promoting intergenerational staffing policy at regional level (road shows, competitions, internet bourse for exchange of best-practices, regional certification for age-based SMEs, etc.)	
		A4 Equal opportunities	e.g. ☐ Discrimination of disadvantaged persons (e.g. older workers, women, migrants, etc.	e.g. ☐ Equal participation, no discrimination	e.g. ☐ Implementation of age-neutral funding practices	

* Please contact the author for the full version of the 'Strategy for the Elderly'

Table 2. The structure of the 'Strategy for the Elderly' published in the Green Paper*

Pillar	Vision	Elements of the Vision	Challenges	General Recommendations	Examples of TEP-Activities	TEP-Contributions on the co-operational level
Labour Market and Social Policy	B Socially Protected Ageing	B1 Sustainable social protection	e.g. □ Absence of smooth transition into retirement	e.g. □ Implementation of a comprehensive package (basic income, stop early retirements, introduce smooth transitions, etc.)	e.g. □ Pilots for alternative forms of work	
		B2 Guaranteed age care and health care services	e.g. □ Cost increases for the healthcare and care systems	e.g. □ Use of the labour market potential in the field of health-care and care services (information campaigns, training in healthcare and care services)	e.g. □ Initiation and promotion of regional eldercare and healthcare platforms	
Labour market and Education Policy	C Education and Vocational Training during all Phases of Life	C1 Conditions for life-long learning are in place	e.g. □ Decrease in vocational training of all age groups	e.g. □ Flexibility and modernisation of the education system (reorientation of the duration of training, combining education with continuous vocational training, promotion of sabbaticals)	e.g. □ Counselling/activation (career coaching, knowledge management training in SMEs)	
		C2 Inter-generational and age-based training offers	e.g. □ Few inter-generational equitable training offers	e.g. □ Creation of adequate intergenerational equitable training offers	e.g. □ Better coordination of local and regional training offers	

stakeholders.[8] Process facilitation turned out to be of extreme importance in order to involve the actors, steer the process and clarify the interests. One advantage of the method was that it increased awareness: as an intermediary result, the pacts integrated recommendations into their annual working programmes already during the consultation phase. Thus, the TEPs aligned and influenced policy even before launching the product.

Other lessons learned include the challenge of balancing interests nationwide: Due to the consultation with many stakeholders, the 'Strategy for the Elderly' combines statements from diverse interest groups. For instance, the Green Paper neither highlights the employers' nor the employees' points of views, instead it balances the interests of all involved without losing a clear focus (see the second dilemma).

During consultation, a clarification of the scope of opportunities of the partnerships was needed: which recommendations can be implemented by the partnerships on their own (without additional clarifications at the national level)? Where are their limits? And to what extent do they want to influence (national) policy? Though the strategy is mainly directed at the regions[9], some recommendations still require actions from (national) bodies not directly involved in the partnerships. These activities are listed in the general recommendations (see Table 2). In addition, the design and detailed description of some activities was left unclear in the Green Paper mainly because the responsibility lies with the politicians. The strategy, for instance, recommends the introduction of a basic income into the Austrian social security system, but does not describe its definite form.

Nevertheless, the TEPs intensively discussed their potential during consultation. Since partnerships vary in respect of their power (e.g. depending on the partnership setting, the individual partners on board etc.), there was no clear line to be found on how far to go together. Whilst some TEP partners acknowledged the Green Paper as an essential tool (and opportunity) to make progress on the issue not only at their territorial level but also at the national level, others did not want to push themselves into politically explosive debates. Even now, the scope of opportunities of what partnerships can do and want to do varies from region to region. In order to exploit the full potential of the partnerships, this clarification process will continue within each single partnership in the future.

Finally, difficulties occurred during consultation at the national level,

---

8 Consultations with relevant stakeholders were held at the local, regional and national levels via a tour to the TEPs and their partners (approx. 165 stakeholders at the regional and local levels were consulted during eleven consultations).

9 The aim is to implement the strategy and numerous measures by the TEPs by funding the recommended activities at the TEP level.

although almost all partners consulted at the regional level confirmed the necessity of transforming the Green Paper into a White Paper. It was recommended not to publish the White Paper due to basic objections: concerns in respect of the pact's power to implement some recommendations, the method used (e.g. Are partnerships allowed to publish a Green/White paper?) and the activity conducted in the context of EQUAL were expressed. The difficulties could indicate the inability of institutions to perform in unfamiliar circumstances and under uncommon procedures: on the one hand it was unusual for the national level to discuss (and negotiate) with bodies at the regional level which do not have a national counterpart (NB: there is no nation-wide TEP). On the other hand, by debating in parallel with national and regional bodies of the same institution (and as equal partners), the hierarchical order was not kept.

Although no White Paper was published, all involved underlined the necessity for further dialogues between the stakeholders. Consequently, a follow-up project was launched with the aim of assisting the partnerships to select the most important potential TEP activities out of the 130 recommended measures. After reducing the set of activities to the 10–20 most relevant TEP measures, the partnerships will clearly define the form of these activities. This follow-up project will only be targeted at the regional TEP actors, based on the section 'Examples of TEP-activities' of the 'Strategy for the Elderly'.

From the author's point of view, the attempt to broaden the partnerships' scope of opportunities failed as soon as national policy was addressed. Obviously, partnerships have to make both ends meet. Nevertheless, the example demonstrates that the method facilitates a consolidated strategy across many stakeholders and across regions. The partnerships empowered themselves by clarifying necessary matters, such as their specific scope of opportunities and limits. Furthermore, regional partners' parent institutions at the national level carefully observed the steps taken by the partnerships. The process also made it obvious that risks have to be taken by applying new approaches. However, while breaking barriers with this multi-level collaboration, the partnerships influenced policy and contributed to sustainable change.

12.3 Conclusions

Considering partnerships as bodies that change the system only step by step – as exemplified by the multi-level collaboration of the Austrian TEPs – are they worth the trouble?

An input/output ratio serves as a starting point in approaching this question: in Austria, € 200.000 are spent on funding the partnership structures per region annually. To support the development and implementation of TEPs, the costs, in particular of the operative structures of the pacts, are subsidised within the framework of the Austrian Operational Programme for Employment 2007–2013 (in 2000–2006 Objective 3 Programme), with co-funding being provided by the European Social Fund (ESF) and the Austrian Federal Ministry of Economics and Labour. The support structures are offered because examples have shown that a predetermined organisational structure is essential for activities to be effective. Positive results are much more easily achieved when full-time pact co-ordinators deal with the entire project.

Regarding the output it has to be mentioned that the Austrian TEPs coordinate € 700 million allocated to active labour market policy (data of 2006; the budget is provided by the partners of the partnerships for measures and target groups). The total TEP budget has increased dramatically since the beginning (2000: € 200 Million), demonstrating the rising acceptance and acknowledgment of the alliances' added values by the partners. Today, TEPs are important institutions in the Austrian labour market and employment policy. The partnerships have increased the involvement of actors in labour market and employment policy, successfully linked policy areas at the regional, sub-regional and local levels and – according to the TEP evaluation (Huber 2003) – contributed to a better coherence of objectives related to labour market and economic policies as well as to improved effectiveness, efficiency and transparency in labour market policy. The partnerships prove their added value by adapting measures to local circumstances and target groups, improving policy services through continuous and systematic procedures and securing financial support for the regions.

But do they exploit their full potential? As shown in Figure 2, the partnerships' scope of opportunities can range from a common denominator to a partnership with an expanded scope. The common denominator describes a partnership implementing measures which are agreed by each individual actor. The scope of opportunities in this case is narrow; the potential of the partnership, e.g. in influencing policy, low. Partnerships with an expanded scope inspire also institutions, policies, regions, etc. not directly targeted by the partnership. In this case, the partnership has an effect on, for example, the institutional policies of partners and/or actors next to the partnership (e.g. via the joint strategy), the long-term orientation of the region in policy fields not directly targeted from the partnership and so on.

When taking the joint TEP budget as an indicator for reflecting the overall potential of the Austrian TEPs (another indicator could be policies linked at the regional level) it must be said that they still do not exploit their full potential (e.g. not all of the partners' available budget is coordinated within the TEPs). But they are widening their scope of opportunities as demonstrated by the increase in the total TEP budget over the last few years (see above), as well as by the multi-level collaboration (see part 2.2. of this article).

Partnerships' Scope of Opportunities

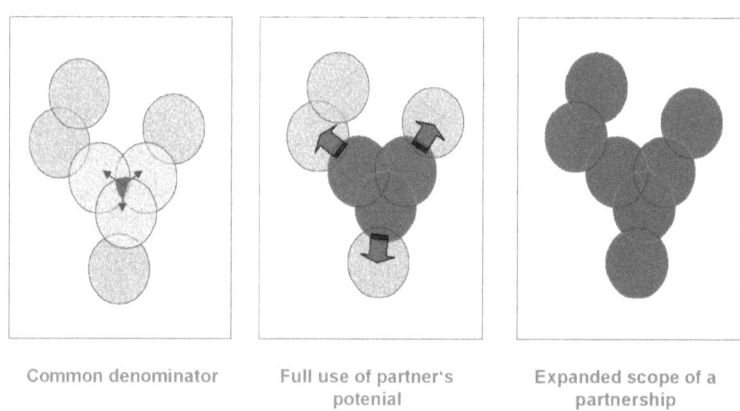

Common denominator   Full use of partner's potenial   Expanded scope of a partnership

Figure 2: Scope of opportunities

In widening their scope of opportunities, partnerships need to feature openness, flexibility and dynamics. Furthermore, the Austrian TEPs accept new challenges and respond to changes. They regularly demonstrate their readiness and willingness to learn from good practices and failures (e.g. in co-operating in the nation-wide Austrian TEP network offered by Koo0[10]). TEPs facilitate horizontal and vertical co-operation by working across institutional boundaries and administrative districts. TEPs adopt principles of good governance for their work, such as participation, openness, accountability, transparency, efficiency and coherence. Overall, the TEPs have made valuable contributions towards reaching the Lisbon goals.

To sum up, a great deal is being done with the small amount of money being provided by the Federal Ministry of Economics and Labour, offering benefits for many actors involved at the local, regional, national and

---

10   Annual average costs of Koo0 are approximately € 275.000.

international levels. The advantages of partnerships are not only recognised in Austria: directives set up by the EC and the member states – as discussed previously – are stimulating the foundation of partnerships all across Europe. Moreover, the OECD started its OECD LEED Forum on Partnerships and Local Governance[11] in autumn 2004 in order to seek ways to optimise the contribution of partnership structures on local governance and the effectiveness of policies.

More and more partnerships across the OECD member and non-member countries – from the EU and South-East Europe to North America and Asia Pacific – are now seeking to play a broader role, influencing the development of policy itself. Partnerships are thus endeavouring to become an integral part of both policy design and delivery, at all governance levels, as expressed in the 'Vienna Action Statement on Partnerships'. The Action Statement was agreed by participants of the 3rd Annual Meeting of the OECD LEED Forum on Partnerships and Local Governance on 1–2 March 2007 in Vienna, aiming to enhance governance by improving the dialogue and co-operation between policy makers, and between policy makers and other stakeholders, at the local, regional and national levels, in turn fostering economic development, social cohesion, environmental sustainability and quality of life.

In order to achieve multi-level and cross-sector collaboration, partnerships require a receptive culture among policy makers in regional, national and supra-national government institutions. The participants of the 3rd Forum Meeting in Vienna therefore invite governments and partnerships to work together with the aim of:

(1) Ensuring flexibility in policy implementation
(2) Establishing robust communication mechanisms through which partnerships can influence and comment upon policy developments which will impact upon their areas
(3) Better aligning policy objectives
(4) Establishing strong evaluation tools for measuring added value
(5) Building the capacities of local, regional and national stakeholders to work effectively in partnership through training and development
(6) Providing a secure financial base

Thus, many challenges still have to be met, some of which were described previously: developing adequate performance indicators to measure added

---

[11] Proposed by the Austrian Federal Ministry of Economy and Labour and the Austrian Coordination Unit of TEPs

values and debating the scope of opportunities and limits of the partnerships, especially in multi-level collaboration, are important steps to be taken in the future.

With reference to Austria, the partnerships, furthermore, should keep an eye on their quality of work, as expressed by Huber (2005): 'Against the background of limited resources of the TEPs, the issue of ensuring the quality of work should be addressed. It seems that it is necessary to clearly focus on what the TEPs feel responsible for'. Thus, the partnerships should (re)consider their functions and enhance their expertise in areas related to their functions in the future. The partnerships should pay attention to developing ambitious TEP programmes that support innovation and aim at sustainable solutions. Especially due to the limited resources and their implementation routines, there is a risk that they will scale down to the point where they only administer standard programmes. In this respect, the national Co-ordination Unit has an important task to fulfil. The Unit should constantly point out the weaknesses and act as a stimulation for innovation.

But, are we on the right track? Are partnerships a strategy for sustainable change and innovation? To date, partnerships are meeting the expectations. For many years now, partnerships have impressed us by finding solid ways to overcome obstacles: innovative strategies have been developed and new approaches introduced to deal with complex problems. Partnerships are on the way to breaking down institutional and organisational barriers, as well as hierarchical rules. Though they are not key-players in mobilising reforms, they have a huge potential for organising sustainable change. By joining forces together with policy makers – as called for in the Vienna Action Statement – partnerships will implement a strategy for sustainable change and innovation to an even greater extent. What needs to be done is to build capacity within the partnerships, but also to empower them so that they can leave their mark in organising sustainable change.

References

Huber, P (2005) WIFO – Austrian institute of Economic Research. Update of the TEP-evaluation (Aktualisierung der Halbzeitbewertung, Schwerpunkt 6, Evaluierung Europäischer Sozialfonds 2000–2006) Translated and shortened by the author

The author's expertise: The article is based on experience gained in three projects relating to partnerships at the ZSI – Centre for Social Innovation, Vienna: the 'Austrian TEP Co-ordination Unit', the 'OECD LEED Forum on Partnerships and Local Governance', and 'TEP_EQUAL_Elderly', a development partnership of all province-wide TEPs.

13. Partnership, gender and democracy

13.1 Introduction

Conceptually and in practice, partnership is closely linked to a new perspective concerning the role of the State and politics in modern society. Sustainable development, regional development, public health and urban renewal are examples of new policy areas. Traditional political decision-making and control are regarded as inadequate to handle such complex problems. A great number of different partnerships and networks can be identified where the State is one of many players. 'From government to governance' is a general statement that is often quoted in social science research. 'Government' represents a hierarchical chain of control with imperative decisions. 'Governance', on the other hand, designates authoritative decisions arrived at in 'negotiations'. The implementation of the decisions takes place in collaboration between different players. *Multi-level governance* is a term that depicts how local development in a small municipality can be intertwined with negotiations in Brussels on regional structural funds. Private-public partnerships and network politics raise questions about the impact on certain fundamental values in representative democracy. Social representativity and political accountability are, for example, areas in which problems have been addressed in social science research. Partnerships as ideal and practice exist within a number of policy areas at both the international and local levels. The spirit of partnership characterises the Rio Declaration, Agenda 21 and Habitat ll (Elander 1999, 2002), as well as the European Structural Funds and collaboration between Swedish municipalities. Many partnerships aim to create an ecologically, socially and economically sustainable society. Often there is a close link to the ideas of inclusive planning and deliberative democracy in which different groups, so-called 'stakeholders', meet. If a partnership includes the relevant players within a specific area and they meet as equals, then perhaps we can speak about 'deliberative' or 'discursive' democracy (Dryzek 1990).

From 42 up to 47 per cent of the elected representatives in public bodies at the local, regional and national levels in Sweden are women, which put Sweden in second place in the world in this respect. At the same time, the role of women in political leadership and the exercise of power is marked by the fact that this is a time of major political changes. Some changes in political systems mean that the EU now plays a governing role on certain issues. The Swedish municipalities have increasingly taken over responsibilities that were previously the preserve of the state. A structural transformation of political systems is also underway. Institutionalised relations between the political and public-administration spheres in terms of power and responsibilities are breaking up and becoming intermingled. One important question is in what way and on what terms women and men are participating in these changes? What interests are being promoted or institutionalised? It is reasonable to assume that the system changes are leading to changes in hierarchical levels, which in turn may have different results for women and men. Questions of interest from a gender perspective are: What operations are being organised in accordance with what principles? What power relations are being strengthened or undermined? What values are being institutionalised and in what set of spheres/social sectors is this taking place? (Jónasdóttir 1996). This book raises the question of whether partnership vitalises democracy or risks becoming an elite project. Another important question is the status of the critical potential in a consensus-oriented organisation and whether a partnership can change a system that it is already a part of. In this chapter, I will address these issues in a study of gender, politics and regional structural funds.

13.2 The 'woman-friendly state' meets New Public Management

The term 'the woman-friendly state' was introduced by Helga Hernes (1987 p. 11) in an analysis of what was specific about the Scandinavian welfare states in the 1980s. She believed that it was possible to speak about 'state feminism' in the sense of there being a political alliance between the state and women. This alliance related to women's citizenship, employment in the public sector and their role as clients or consumers of public care. In this chapter, I will examine citizenship in the sense of participation in the 'modern' partnerships of the 21st century. In contrast to much Anglo-Saxon feminist research, which points to the patriarchal nature of the state, Hernes pointed out that the relation between the state and women in Scandinavia has been positive and characterised by *closeness*. Conditions in the corporative system in which business and industry, the trade unions and agricultural organisations engaged in negotiations with the state were characterised by a relative *distance* between the public and the private. Raum (1999) points out that the state had some interest in handling tensions on the labour market in connection with collective bargaining and in regulating, for example, parts of the agricultural market. Actually *taking over* the tasks of the market was however seldom on the agenda. She emphasises, with the support of Scandinavian research, that the alliance between women and the state had a completely different focus. The mobilisation of women in the voluntary sector of civil society aimed to induce the state to *take over* responsibility for health care, child care and eldercare from the private sector. This regarded both the family and different types of voluntary organisation. The collective mobilisation of women is given as an explanation of why public institutions in which men predominate pursued 'woman-friendly' policies (Raum 1999 p. 42).[1] An important point is that this mobilisation, at both the local and national levels, also met resistance in the public sphere and that a hard struggle was often required to pursue the issues concerned (Karlsson 1996, Larsson 2004).

New Public Management is an overall term for new approaches to the governance and management of the public sector that achieved a major breakthrough in the 1980s and 1990s, above all in the UK, New Zealand and Australia (Montin 2007). An element of neo-liberal ideology can be traced in the toning down of social reforms and the emphasis on competition and efficiency. Individual rights and freedom of choice was mottos for the transformation and modernisation of the public sector. Most western European countries have been affected by the NPM philosophy, although there have been major variations between the different countries. The Thatcher and Reagan regimes appear to have been the most extreme. Even Sweden, with its reputation for a stable, social-democratic welfare state and well-developed and far-reaching local government autonomy, has experienced significant changes. The areas of politics and public manage-

---

[1] Birte Siim (1988) speaks about 'the complicated partnership' between the state and women that comprises both a public responsibility for reproduction and the control of women's lives.

ment changed at the national, regional and local levels. As a result the alliance between women and the welfare state was tangibly weakened during the 1990s. The economic values that superseded other values have had such a dramatic impact that certain researchers use the term *economism* (Hugemark 1994, Lundquist 1993). Some researchers feel that NPM has had an unusually strong breakthrough in Swedish politics (Bäck & Larsson 2006). Others believe that it is mainly on the level of 'talking and thinking' that ideals from this philosophy have become 'modern' (Montin 1993).

The NPM philosophy and its emphasis on efficiency and economic values introduced new yardsticks for public operations at all levels. The wave of organisational system changes can be described as a process in which a technically-economically limited rationality became predominant. Several researchers concluded that there was a risk that these changes would undermine the living conditions of women in particular (Sundin 1988). The changes in public operations can be regarded as a change in *gender coding* and part of a process towards a new *hegemonic masculinity* (Hedlund 1997, 2006).[2] These terms should be regarded as an attempt to describe the norms that tended to dominate in public organisation at different levels. A changed gender coding meant, quite simply, that many of the values and guidelines taken from the first wave of the NPM period were based on new patterns of thought constructed in a context (business and industry) where the knowledge of women or care issues played a subordinate role. The public sector that had been part of the alliance between women and the state now became a base for other alliances. One example is the attempt of masculine elites in the public sector to establish alliances with the private sector and to 'play at business' by becoming involved in networks and partnerships to generate growth. The narrow growth discourse can be seen as an expression of a hegemonic masculinity with a governing, desired practice exercised by men in power in the political, public management and economic fields (Lindgren 1999). This is exercised by a small group and recreated by a large group of fellow travellers who calibrate their actions in relation to the ideal notion that currently prevails. These processes say nothing about the sex of the various individual players. Some men being managers in the public sector in the 1990s had to give up their posts, voluntarily or otherwise, due to an inability to exercise management on the basis of new norms. On the other hand, a number of women managers function and feel very comfortable with the new norms.

---

2   Hegemonic masculinity is a concept developed by Robert Connell (1995) where he refers to Antonio Gramsci's theory on hegemony.

Those public operations are characterised by technical-economic rationality regarding objectives, performance, the follow-up of results, quality measurement and the production of services.

13.2.1 From NPM to governance and partnership

Governance, in the sense of political management and co-ordination rather than authoritative, top-down control, *government*, is being researched today from many different points of view. It is common that the term is defined as a change from a parliamentary chain of control to network control. Policy is then shaped, determined and implemented in interaction between different social players, of which the state is one. Ideas on new democratic processes, civil society, networks and the renewal of institutions can be seen as a reaction to the 'hard' period of New Public Management. (Newman 2001, Rhodes 2000). Janet Newman points out that it is important to note that it is an expression that 'lives' in the exchange between practitioners and researchers. It acts as a descriptive and normative term that prescribes the form that government should take. She feels, however, that it is possible to use the ideas underlying governance research as an analytical instrument. This can facilitate an understanding of the interaction between the state and civil society, governance and citizens and of the institutional complexity in the public sphere.

It is worth noting that established capital interests and powerful bureaucracies dominate many networks, according to Ingemar Elander (1999, 2002). Popularly-elected politicians and marginalised groups are in a weaker position. The trend towards an increasing number of partnerships raises questions regarding legitimacy and the accountability of the players involved. Partnerships can be studied from different perspectives, according to Elander. First, they can be viewed in terms of an increase in power for capital interests that gain a direct link to the democratic process. Secondly, they can be seen as a way of avoiding the decision-making processes of the political institutions. Thirdly, they may provide a new route for different groups of citizens. Fourthly, they may be seen as an expression of a cosmopolitan model for democracy in which political citizenship is global with a shared responsibility for our fellow human beings in other parts of the world or for unborn generations. The important thing is to study different partnerships on the basis of their specific conditions and circumstances, Elander concludes. The policy dissemination of the partnership concept has succeeded in Sweden note Ian Bache and Jan Olsson (2001) in a comparison between Swedish and British development trends. They believe that the EU has played an important role through its structural fund policy. Olsson observes in his Swedish sub-study that the method adopted for the creation of Swedish partnerships for regional development has been based on traditions that are typical of Swedish political culture. These traditions stem from a corporative system in which the private sector, the state/local government sector and powerful non-governmental organisations have collaborated. The exclusion of local and regional politicians that was evident in the 1990s in the British case was not repeated in Sweden. On the contrary, it was regarded as self-evident that municipal and county council commissioners with responsibility for commercial and industrial matters and regional development should be involved when structural fund programmes were hastily drawn up. On what basis these politicians participated and how democratic feedback was provided for is, however, less clear. The key players were officials at the County Administrative Boards, state authorities and ministries. Unfortunately Bache's and Olsson's study is not doing any empirical observations or conclusions on gender.

In Denmark, problems relating to the democratic aspects of network politics or governance have been increasingly examined. The risk that closed groups cannot be held accountable in the same way as in a more open system is pointed at by Eva Sørensen and Jacob Torfing (2005). Different methods and techniques for creating an open public dialogue may solve this problem. Identification with, and a respect for, democratic norms is fundamental. Listening to, and showing respect for, the arguments of one's opponents, even if there is open conflict on the issue concerned is also very important, as are different methods for including weaker or disadvantaged groups. This normative branch of governance research can be referred to as *fostering*, it relates to adult socialisation and a strong belief in the *good will* of various players based on the concept of a mutual win-win situation. In the Swedish research the democratic aspects have been treated differently in that a power perspective has also been integrated into the problematisation of exclusion and accountability (Elander 1999, Hudson & Rönnblom 2003, Mörth & Sahlin-Andersson 2006).

Linda Soneryd (2004) points out that a shift from representative democracy to deliberative democracy can be discerned. Political decisions seem to be regarded as legitimate if they are based on discussions with and arguments from those affected by the decisions concerned.

Deliberative democracy is highlighted as a positive value by several researchers as a means of preventing, in various ways, partnerships or networks becoming closed and exclusive elite projects. A deliberative discourse marked by respect for the opinions of others, an honest willingness to listen and understand and an ambition to achieve consensus can be regarded as an ideal to aim for. It is however important to distinguish deliberative democracy from participative democracy in which participation in itself is the primary factor (Englund 2004). In the discourse ideal of deliberative democracy, power is eliminated to the greatest possible extent and legitimacy is rationally based, according to Jouni Reinikainen and Magnus Reitberger (2004). An important component of a deliberative discourse or decision-making process relates to not only weighing up different wishes and desires but also transforming them. 'Democratic institutions should encourage discussion and limit interest-based politics and 'horse-trading' to a minimum' (ibid. p. 293). They refer to a study of research of the American jury system, which involves a variety of procedures to ensure an impartial, deliberative decision-making process. Lynn Sanders (1997) found that structural inequalities based on gender and ethnicity still creep into the work of a jury. Even when factors such as access to information, education and fluency and confidence in speaking are equalised, the fact remains that white men dominate in terms of the process itself and the content of the decisions made. One conclusion is that by creating an apparently impartial procedure for public deliberations, power can be masked and indirectly legitimised.

13.3 Power and gender

Interpreting processes in terms of gender and power relations is difficult but necessary, both politically and theoretically/methodologically according to political scientist Maud Eduards (2005). Her theoretical review and referral to extensive empirical research shows how, over the years and still today, there is a resistance to the claims of women for a presence in decision-making positions. A basic dilemma is that women are identified as representatives of 'the gender equality problem' and that they exist as individuals and as a group, while men as a category exist neither in mainstream research nor in the political debate. Instead we meet men in their capacity as gender-neutral politicians, officials and experts. The resistance to women's demands for a presence and for a change in the content of decisions in various fields can be summarised by saying that they are allowed to participate as long as participation takes place in accordance with the principles of gender neutrality and consensus. According to Eduards, when women organise themselves and act in autonomous networks in various ways, this is regarded both as a resource and a threat. Some demands and actions are permitted, while others are 'forbidden' and arouse fierce opposition. The most forbidden action is to openly discuss the advantages or responsibilities of men and to point to men as a category or group. The concept that lies at the core of the predominant norm is that men do not exist as a category, or that they are regarded as a meta-category above all others. [3] 'The result is that women can be described as subordinate without men being designated superordinate' (Jansson 2001 p. 96). As research on the history of gender, power and politics shows gender conflicts are not unusual and the conflict dimension itself consists of men's collective resistance to the actions of women. The forms this resistance takes may be subtle and hidden, or more open and public, but they testify that the idea of consensus is problematical from a gender-power perspective.

Conflicts are a self-evident element of a democracy, according to Chantal Mouffe (2000), who has introduced the term *agonism*. Agonism means that conflicts are not necessarily an expression of hostile antagonism and that they can be handled in a civilised way within a democracy. I wish to argue that the ideal of consensus as an organisational principle in networks and partnerships may constitute an obstacle to women acting as an interest group with collectively-based demands. It hinders an open, political discussion on fairness and unfairness or the distribution of resources where women and men as visible parties meet in a dialogue that can also comprise conflict. This leads to a situation in which 'the right kind of women' as individuals are welcome to participate in various contexts as representatives of the under-represented gender. There they can collaborate with other women, representatives of different minority groups and other gender-neutral players (men). But who and what they are supposed to represent remains an unresolved question, as Eduards concludes. Although in the public rhetoric there is a lot of talk about women's rights and women as a positive resource in various contexts.

In her study of New Labour in the UK, Janet Newman (2001) finds that it is necessary to theorise about power and control in the 'modern' state and about how notions of the *modern* society are created. She finds that 'feminism is yesterday's politics' (ibid. p.177). The reason for this is that feminism is perceived to be prone to conflict, based on interest groups and 'outmoded'. 'What is the problem?' becomes a central question on which agreement must be reached in networks and partnerships where the formulation of the problem can in itself become an expression of the exercise of power (Bacchi 1999). One problem formulation that appears to be modern in the grey zone between research and practice seems to have a recurring, common theme: *change*. I believe that it is possible to transfer Olsson's discussion of globalisation theses and globalisation myths to the

---

3   Lecture by Jorun Solheim in November 1999, quoted by Maud Eduards (2005 p. 157).

discussion of change (Olsson 2005).⁴ An important part of this discourse is the thesis that it is necessary to be flexible and ready to accept change. Elements of criticism or opposition may be perceived as reactionary and as an expression of stagnation (Hedlund 2006). This notion is in turn closely linked to modernity and a construct of the modern where 'labels' are attached to phenomena of various kinds. This may explain why a recurring impression when reading the predominant literature on governance is that the problems and issues pursued by organised representatives of women's interests simply do not fit in. Women's organisations are not weighty enough; they are far too ideological and may be seen as lacking sufficient capacity for self-reflection and adaptability (Hedlund 2007a).

13.3.1 The power struggle for money for the regions and the presence of women – a paradox?

In this chapter, I will present the results of a study concerning gender and local/regional development. The empirical basis consists of an investigation of the processes in a structural fund partnership in a Swedish region. The data-collection methods used include participatory observation, documentation studies and interviews with officials.[5] The activities investigated relate to the structural fund for sustainable growth, competitiveness and employment. The overriding decision-making levels, the European Commission and the Swedish government, identify women and men as target groups concerned in the so-called horizontal objectives, where there are clear expectations that gender equality and the needs of women will be incorporated into the policy areas.

Within the framework of the EU structural fund system, there has been a development over time in terms of the demands regarding organisation and the inclusion of different groups in the drawing up of programmes and the implementation of projects. The first period, 1995–1999, can be described as a masculine-dominated project run by public officials. The national ex ante evaluation noted that the work on the growth agreements was fraught with shortcomings regarding gender equality aspects (Horelli & Roininen 1999). A group of women activists involved in regional development work reacted and contacted Mona Sahlin, the declared feminist and Deputy Minister of Industry of the time. She stressed a political will

4   See also the discussion in Hedlund, Gun and Lennqvist-Lindén, Ann-Sofie (2004) *Governance – ett begrepp för genusforskningen?* Application to the Swedish Research Council.
5   References of empirical data in detail is presented in *Partnerskap, kön och demokrati* (Hedlund 2007 b). (Partnership, gender and democracy 2007. Report to Vinnova in Research Program: Applied gender research in strong research- and innovation environments).

to reinforce gender equality in the agreements. The minister's statement was subsequently criticised by the activists as this ambition failed. In an alternative evaluation of the growth agreements carried out by experts on gender and regional issues, the assessment was that the partnerships excluded women and that the plans to achieve gender equality in the regions were far too vague (Lindsten et al. 2001). According to another study, the officials of the County Administrative Boards, who played a central role in the work on the growth programmes, prevented the integration of a gender equality perspective into the wording of agreements. When describing their own role in the process, the County Administrative Boards' own gender equality experts said that they had been marginalised and that their expertise was not utilised (Westberg 2005). Nor were the active women at the various regional resource centres included in the work. The recommendation of the ex ante evaluation at the end of the 1990s that 'information and training' would solve the problem of the masculine-dominated partnerships can be regarded as an example of a legitimising evaluation.

The agreements between the government and the regions were replaced by so-called regional growth programmes. The aim was to co-ordinate efforts in different sectors in order to develop sustainable, local, labour-market regions. In a subsequent ex ante evaluation, it was noted that the work on these programmes was largely identical to the work carried out in earlier periods. In the period 2004–2007 too, commercial and industrial development, entrepreneurship, competence development and the infrastructure/living environment were the common themes of the efforts made. The gender equality perspective was still weak; perhaps even weaker than in the previous regional growth agreements. In the formulation of objectives, no region consistently took the situation of men and women as its starting point, even though gender equality was mentioned here and there. The partnerships involved in the work on the regional growth programmes in the period 2004–2007 were less broadly based and private companies and voluntary organisations were not as common as before. Local authorities and county councils, however, played a more prominent role. Gender equality existed in partnerships in only a few of the regions and the account given of how the process and the meetings were conducted was often all too brief. It is not possible to see clearly from the programme reports presented whether county experts on gender equality or regional resource centres for women participated. In several areas, it was felt that it was better to have small and effective partnerships in which funders and implementers dominated. Organisations with limited resources were regarded as being of little interest in this context. In its report, the Swedish

Institute for Growth Policy Studies (ITPS) notes that the programmes lost some of their legitimacy. The fact that State resources are no longer allocated to programmes raises the relevant question of why the programmes need to be approved at the government level at all. The power struggle between regions that aim to increase self-determination and flexibility and a State that aims to control regional development comes to light in various official documents.

The new national strategy for regional competitiveness and employment for the period 2007–2013 aims for a greater degree of co-ordination between the regional growth programmes and the EU structural funds. However, the EU regional structural fund programme Objective 2 for the period 2000–2006, was also criticised because the horizontal objectives (gender equality, integration and the environment) were not a sufficiently taken into account in the implementation of the programme.

13.3.2 *Power struggle between masculine elites and the presence of women politicians*

In the region studied, intensive work was conducted on the EU new regional structural fund programme in the late summer and autumn of 2006. A new aspect of this period was that the work was carried out in so-called 'greater regions'. It became apparent that work with the structural funds is a policy area that remains a stable masculine preserve. As in the 1990s, no real political control was evident during the initial work. This work was instead dominated by a masculine elite of officials from the four regional federations recently-formed by the 52 local authorities involved. In April, these officials set up a drafting group tasked with setting the desired course for the structural fund programme. The programme's objectives and strategy were approved by a small group of leading regional politicians from the four regions at a meeting in August. This meeting was attended by 29 men and 5 women. The hope was that by 'jumping the gun' the regions would be well prepared for the programme work. The struggle for power over regional industrial and commercial development had been underway for some time between various masculine regional, political and bureaucratic elites. 81 028 706 EUR (approximately SEK 730 million) was to be distributed between the 52 local authorities involved. The state civil servants maintained their dominant role. The adoption of a new national strategy by the government in June 2006 ended a vision of a local authority-governed region with power over the EU structural funds. The August meeting with the local authority players was held in a resigned atmosphere. It ended with the civil servants calling on the politicians to 'monitor' the objectives agreed on: accessibility, competence development, commercial and industrial development and attractiveness.

One County Administrative Board was given responsibility for collaborating with four other counties to create a partnership for a 'greater region programme'. The two open partnership meetings for the structural fund programme held in the autumn were attended by only a few directly-elected local authority and county council politicians. Commercial and industrial issues are by tradition a masculine gender-coded area of local politics and only three women council members from the 52 local authorities were among the 126 participants. Programme-governing partnerships with a focus on industrial development (Objective 2) appear to be a masculine preserve in political circles while project-implementing partnerships with a social or rural development focus (Objective 3 EQUAL, Leader +) seem to have a different gender coding with women politicians and public officials or project managers of both sexes.

13.4 Civil servants take over

As in the case of previous programme periods, the directives from the EU and the ministry were presented late and the work was marked by great haste. According to the government directives, the new 'greater region partnership' was to be based on previous partnerships. In one of the four counties there was an 'old' partnership made up of industrial and commercial organisations, trade unions, local authorities/county councils and State authorities at the local and regional levels. A few NGOs were represented, mainly long-established, traditional organisations with links to the corporative model, e.g. the County Agricultural Society. Other counties had less broadly-based partnerships consisting of a smaller group of bureaucratic and political elites. It was well-known that the former County Governor of the county with primary responsibility for the programme openly prioritised the representation of women in various publicly-appointed bodies. She regularly pointed out that civil servants must actively continue their search for suitable women. 'Look harder,' she often said. A special list of competent women in the region had been drawn up to be used as a pool of resources when the need arose and a routine had been established for this work[6].

---

6   This routine was also a result of the dissemination of experience from pilot projects for gender-equal partnerships, see Marianne Bull (2001, 2002)

The process behind the new partnership can be seen as an attempt by the State to control and co-ordinate the local and regional players. The ideals of trust, learning and a mutual win-win situation appeared to be a fiction to one of the civil servants involved. She reacted to the fact that the management at her workplace constantly 'talked politics' and seldom about the actual issues or real collaboration. Despite the lack of time available, the county with primary responsibility managed to send out invitations so that the percentage of men was not too excessive: 66 per cent at the first meeting and 60 per cent at the second. The lack of women politicians was compensated for by inviting women who were trade union representatives, local authority and State authority managers, civil servants from the County Administrative Boards and officials from local authority federations. The programme was briefly referred to relevant organisations and players for comment and their comments were submitted county by county. There were also a number of extra meetings where the aim was to present and gain backing for the proposal. A civil servant who attended many of the partnership meetings and who worked actively to reach both women and men was pleased about the fact that there was a real discussion of the proposal at these meetings in which women also made their voices heard.

> There was broad participation and the women were active. There was discussion about the use of resources and the priorities that should be set. What was perhaps a bit new was that environmental and energy issues came up and that some people commented on how the SWOT analysis was done. Otherwise it was 'traditional business and industry'.

A review of the lists of participants and of the invited organisations shows that public players and 'weighty' established organisations predominated. Business and industry were not particularly well represented and one of the major national industrial organisations declined to take part. Organisations for women or immigrants were not represented, although three individuals who represented alternative ideas relating to the social economy did take part. The concept of 'broad participation' differs depending on one's perspective and another of the interviewees saw something else.

> Personally, I think it was very unfortunate that the structural fund work was done so quickly, it was difficult to ask different people and to spend enough time on presenting the programme and getting support and understanding for it, which is a bit of a shame. Everything was done in such a rush. I felt all the time that because it concerned a greater region, not just a county, that individual groups, networks and organisations got lost, which made things more difficult.

The steering group for the drafting of the structural fund programme itself was made up only of civil servants. The meetings were attended by 9–12 men and 2–3 women. During the actual writing of the programme it proved difficult to counteract the dominant position of the men. The recently-appointed County Governor practised non-implementation of the EU and state policy on gender equality in a 'passive resistance' (Pincus 2003) despite some attempts to 'harp on about gender equality'. When all the working groups except one had been appointed, however, it became obvious that the predominance of the men would not be considered legitimate in future ex ante evaluations.

> Eventually they saw for themselves that, oh dear, there are a lot of men!

The head of the programme office, a woman, 'subsequently reacted and then ensured that the balance between the co-ordinators was fairly equal, with three women and four men'. Otherwise, the drafters of the programme consisted of 49 men and 13 women. The working groups on sustainable development and the enlargement of the region included most women. Areas such as analysis, innovation and entrepreneurship were the preserves of the men. The criticism levelled at the failure to use the gender equality experts as a resource in the regional development work led to 'a change for the better'. Gender equality experts from two different counties were involved in the programme work with varying degrees of success. Representatives of the masculine-coded growth discourse were not particularly receptive to expertise in the gender equality field. 'X thought that it was difficult to get anything through. It was not so easy, even though they feel that things went relatively well'. The interviewees however felt that the work on the structural fund programme itself is important because so much money is involved. This also means that it is very important who leads and participates in the writing of the programme.

> Yes, that is why the question of who writes the programme is so important. Now I am talking about EU funds and money from the structural funds, or regional development funds from the State. Here sit those who write the programme, here sits the partnership that decides on applications, and then the structural fund delegation, and then those who work with regional growth programmes. Who are the people sitting there? It's the same old faces and they make sure that those who normally get the money still get the money. That's the way it works.

The description of 'the same old faces' comprises a limited, predominantly masculine elite consisting of civil servants and a few politicians. The new partnership in the greater region with representatives was practically fictional when it came to the joint governance of objectives and indicators. The programme objectives adopted by the politicians at the meeting in August now acquired a different and narrower focus on economic growth. An official who represented the local-authority governed regions and who took part in the internal work saw no signs of deliberative discussions. He is not worried about appearing not to be 'modern' and takes the risk of being perceived as unwilling to accept change. He critically comments on the public players' constant 'flirting with apathetic representatives of business and industry'.

> Partnership is a pest, it doesn't work at all. It's some kind of imported idea (...) that doesn't fit the Swedish democratic system at all. Everyone of course praises the good co-operation between the partners, that's expected. I don't think you can buy industrial development. (...) The money from the structural funds should be used to promote the assignment of the public sector and to ensure that the basic conditions exist for effective and efficient commerce and industry.

The predominantly masculine steering group monitored the practical work on writing the programme and adopted certain standpoints in principle on the various proposals submitted in the course of the referral process. A number of views on the operative action programme were submitted, but 'the same old faces' made it very clear which perspective counts in the event of clashes between objectives. A referral body that felt that a discussion of the balance between economy, ecology and the social perspective was lacking was told: 'The economic dimension is primary and other dimensions are balanced in relation to this'.

13.5 Shift in objectives and indicators

The structural fund programme contains an ambitious structural description of the greater region and is arranged in accordance with the directives from the EU and the Ministry of Industry. There have also been some dialogues with the Swedish Institute for Growth Policy Studies (ITPS), which is an advisory and a supervisory authority. The focus is on the growth of commerce and industry, in particular with regard to small and medium-sized companies. The priority areas are innovative environments, entrepreneurship and accessibility. The shift away from the politically-accepted objectives of competence supply, industrial/commercial development and attractiveness can be seen as a reinforced masculine coding in relation to what the interviewees called 'traditional business and industry'. For the period 2007–2013, it is proposed that there should be fewer projects than previously. These should involve the participation of organisations with a lot of capital. The new greater region is expected to provide greater access to dynamic industrial and commercial interests. When read from a gender point of view, it becomes apparent that the programme is uneven. In certain sections, where the gender equality experts took part, it is clearly a lot of knowledge about, as well as references to, the gender equality discourse in the field. One example is the section on regional enlargement, which deals with the criticism levelled at this idea. The critics claim the difficulties associated with combining parenthood and work with extended commuting.[7] In other sections, a discussion of the situation of women and men is 'thrown in' here and there. This reflects the varying ability and desire of the programme authors involved to integrate the horizontal objectives. A gender equality expert pointed out that she tried to get various players to take personal responsibility for remembering that programmes and plans should take account of the situation of both women and men.

> You often have to go in and correct things afterwards, which is not much fun (laughter). (....) They often don't want to think for themselves, they want me to come in and put things right and say that this is wrong, you can't write this. I refuse to act as some kind of police. (...) I'm speaking now about civil servants at the County Administrative Boards.

Large parts of the operative programme appear to be gender blind regarding the link between objectives and selection criteria for future projects. The so-called horizontal objectives on gender equality and integration are expressed in quantitative terms without any well thought-out relation to implementation. The text is full of terms that are repeated in a mechanical way, forming almost a mantra for innovation and cluster policy. The genderless individuals that characterise the action programme spring from a masculine norm. This norm permeates, according to Katarina Persson and Ylva Saarinen (2003), the thinking on clusters, innovation potential, knowledge, growth sectors, and entrepreneurship.

> Well yes, there are certain sectors that predominate. When you talk about development it is enterprise, enterprise, enterprise and growth. They probably still see the public sector, where the women are, as a drain on resources. (...) In these growth areas, indicators like preschools and health are not included.

The women among the civil servants interviewed see sustainability policy as the battering ram that may lead to new thinking.

7   The criticism is that regional enlargement is a scientific term for analysis among social and economic geographers that has become a fashionable political term with the aim of constructing and creating greater regions for increased growth.

The broad concept of growth, via the concept of sustainable development, means that a new way of thinking is in the pipeline. But it's still too abstract; it's still the case that everything is a question of enterprise, and men and jobs.

Expertise was needed; sustainability was new and a little strange to many of those involved. Amendments and additions were made at the last minute. I believe that it is entirely possible to expand the concept of growth now. It is, if you like, on the agenda in a new way.

13.6 The women's networks and influence

There is an informal network for the women officials and civil servants who work with regional and industrial/commercial issues in the county councils and local authorities and at the County Administrative Boards. In 2003, a formal and high-profile network called *Kvinnolobbyn* (The Women's Lobby) was also formed in the county. This network is exclusive and consists of women in management positions. The network aims in various ways to act as a counterweight to the predominance of men in business and industry and in leading positions in society. The fact that the network is in the nature of an elite project is a deliberate strategy in order to match a number of elite networks for men. The network comprises 27 women who are politicians, entrepreneurs, researchers and senior officials in the county. It is also intended to extend contacts to the EU women's lobby. The objectives of the Women's Lobby are, among other things, that the gender perspective should be taken into account in the work on the regional growth programme. The expertise, experience and perspectives of women should be utilised. The language used in the Women's Lobby's programmes and operational accounts conveys a spirit of harmony and co-operation between men and women. The message is that women are an unutilised resource and that their efforts are not valued equally to those of men. A formal organisational structure of the network did not work very well and 2006 it was decided to work in a process-oriented way.

> Now we have a better chance to join groups that we are interested in and to talk about things that interest us even though we may not have all the factual background. (...) The new members that join groups can bring something new with them and lead us along new lines. The process can take a new direction and things are not at all fixed and ready in the way that I sometimes felt was the case in the four committees.

The official who introduced a new working method formerly worked for a popular movement. She reacted to the fact that group dynamics were not working well. Her view is that hierarchy and inflexible structures do not favour innovative solutions. A new idea that came up and was implemented in Women's Lobby was based on the realisation that a background in business or industry affords authority and respect. Masculine homosociality can be challenged if men are not met as a group. Thus meetings were arranged between individual men being local executives and managers and women who were entrepreneurs or managing directors for large companies. The meetings discussed support for enterprise among women in a constructive atmosphere.

> This provided gravity. It meant that we were meeting at the same level.

An informal network functions effectively among the woman being civil servants and the Women's Lobby. Despite the message in public that women should be seen as a resource and not a threat, the Women's Lobby meets opposition. The masculine elite did not seem interested in inviting the expertise represented in the network to take part in the structural fund work. The continued funding of the co-ordinator function was not prioritised in the internal budget process at the County Administrative Board. The chairperson of the Women's Lobby, a Member of Parliament, adopted a strategy of open, public protest in the media to force through a financial solution.

Descriptions of the triad business and industry, the public sector and civil society are often recurring elements of the documentation on private-public partnership. The strong emphasis on economic growth means that players and arguments from business and industry have a particular gravity. This fact was exploited strategically in the Women's Lobby's efforts to promote enterprise among women. One dilemma is, however, that women who are representatives of business and industry seldom involve themselves in open, public discussions of gender equality. Those women who try to influence regional development issues are well aware of this dilemma. Open alliances on gender equality issues are not always appropriate.

> It's too tough for them. They are sitting there (*in the partnerships, GH:s comment*) because of their business and industrial expertise. There is heavy opposition; the gender quota issue is a real hot potato in the business sector. They want to sit there because of their competence and this is why I think it is difficult to pursue this issue. XX, the Managing Director of (...) is good on these issues but she is not able to become a spearhead.

Neither women in business and industry or officials in bureaucratic, hierarchical state organisations are, according to the interviewed, able to openly push for the power and influence of women in various partnerships. The only elite group that has openly represented the issue of the presence of women in decision-making bodies is the women politicians. This issue has been highly politicised for the last 20 years.[8] However, the percentage of women politicians is declining in the indirectly-appointed executive committees. Thus men, as chair of executive committees in the cities, are more often than women included in the regional partnerships. This is a result of the idea that representatives with power to represent their different organisations shall be included. Being a minority group and expected to be 'modern' and willing to accept change puts the women politicians in leading positions in a special situation. They may find it difficult to openly challenge the norms of the masculine hegemony on economic growth, innovation systems and entrepreneurship. In this case-study, an open conflict in the public view on resources for the Women's Lobby was, on the other hand, entirely possible in accordance with norms of what is 'women's issues'.

13.7 An alternative discourse

It seems as though the women civil servants at the regional level that comprise an informal network with their regional and local alliances have had a certain amount of influence on the writing of the programme. They also influenced the invitation lists to the meetings and the composition of working groups and co-ordinators in the practical work. The civil servants interviewed refer to research, reports and players in a way that indicates they are well aware of the ongoing alternative discussion on growth, regional development and partnership. They see the nationally politically-adopted objectives on sustainable development, with the three dimensions economic, social and ecological development, as a possible means of making way for new, innovative ideas. Those ideas are not characterised by masculine norms regarding living conditions, work and enterprise. Through the activities of the Women's Lobby, they are trying to strengthen networks where an open and problematising discussion can be conducted. The discussion covers topics such as women's solo companies, combination companies and service companies. It also includes the risk of women, as the owners of small healthcare companies, losing out in the public pro-

---

8   Sweden lies in second place in an international comparison.

curement process. Large-scale operations, regional enlargement, technological development, cutting-edge companies, innovation systems and clusters are not unchallenged in this context. This challenge does not seem to reach the partnership's masculine elite.

13.8 Conclusions

Questions of interest from the gender point of view are: what activities are organised in accordance with what principles, what power relations are strengthened or undermined, what values are institutionalised and in what set of spheres/social sectors does this take place?

The partnership behind the structural fund programme was organised on the principle of gender equality in participation and open discussions *outwardly* and of predominantly masculine, bureaucratic elite governance *inwardly*. The women bureaucrats made an active effort to recruit women when this was possible and they received some help in this from previous signals from above (the EU and the government). The principle 'look harder' and the use of pre-prepared lists provided positive results and led to participation on the part of women at the open meetings. These mainly represented organisational and official elites, while business and industry were sparsely represented and immigrant and women's organisations not at all. A further organisational principle is that men's informal networks are legitimate, 'gender neutral' and self-evident, while the formal organisation of women in networks must be defended in an open offensive and these networks do not constitute a natural resource base for the programme work of the partnership.

The power relations that have been strengthened are the alliances between those in bureaucratic elites at the regional and national levels who won the struggle for power over the business and commercial programmes. The alliances that have been undermined are those between citizens and directly-elected local authority politicians. The percentage of women politicians included in the new informal networks is very low and does not correspond to the level of representation in the political sphere in general. The influence of women politicians over regional and local development is a power relation that has been weakened. The frameworks for the local scope for action are created in elite partnerships where women constitute a clear minority. This lack of influence is reflected in the shift in objectives for the structural fund programme. Ideas on safeguarding certain public undertakings were replaced by investments in entrepreneurship and innovation with a clear masculine-coding of the activities. This can be seen as a further weakening of the remaining alliance between women and the welfare state. Instead there is an advantage of the alliance between business and industry and the State. Women in business and industry do not constitute a power base for the alteration or renewal of the distribution of resources towards the inclusion of gender equality by way of social sustainability. They are 'under pressure' in their own sphere and cannot risk their own authority being undermined. Women in the bureaucracies are restricted by hierarchies and a strong masculine hegemony. They do exercise the influence they can in terms of both form and content. All three groups meet in one of the counties in a formal and high-profile network, the Women's Lobby. The category 'women politicians' is the only one that can engage in open, public struggles with the masculine, bureaucratic elite on some priorities. However they find it difficult to challenge the masculine hegemony on innovations, economic growth and entrepreneurship, which represent the 'modern'.

The values that have been institutionalised are those of economism with a one-sided application of the growth concept. Economic growth is interpreted in terms of jobs, average pay and new companies. The spheres/social sectors relevant to this study are the public sector in the form of various authorities and bureaucracies that live in constant hope that business and industry will become more involved. The business and industrial sector, on the other hand, seem to show little interest in participating in discussions on structural funds and regional development. Despite this fact the business sector is strongly prioritised in the wording of the programme and as a potential receiver of funds in various projects characterised by critical voices as 'purchased industrial development'. The organisation of the process of the partnerships of regional structural funds can be seen as a method of bypassing the democratic, political decision-making process in which powerful capital interests are the winners.

This book asks the important question of whether partnerships can entail a renewal or extension of democracy or whether they risk becoming elite projects. The answer on the basis of the results of this case study is that partnerships concerning regional structural funds are elite projects that weaken and undermine representative democracy and manipulate ideas on deliberative democracy. Two other important questions that run through the book are what role the critical potential can play in an organisation characterised by consensus, and whether a partnership can change a system that it is a part of. The results of this study indicate that power relations and dominating discourses creep into partnerships, which leads to the marginalisation of critical voices. The spirit of consensus conceals underlying conflicts and it is doubtful whether the adult socialisation that is required to bring about a change among men in power is possible. The EU is the system that ultimately controls the conditions that govern the work on the wording of programmes and operative implementation in structural fund partnerships. The hasty nature of the work, the close adaptation of the wording to decisions in the pipeline in Brussels and the complicated bureaucracy are recurring features of the system. The critical potential may possibly come into play through stronger and more formal alliances between women's organisations and networks from various camps and groups who represent the internationally and nationally-established concept of sustainability. Alliances that was weakened during the 'hard' period of New Public Management can be rebuilt providing that fixed resources are allocated for this purpose. It appears that the increasing prioritisation of sustainable development as a concept that applies to something more than 'environmental issues' may open the way to thinking about social development that includes the lives of women, children and different marginalized groups. United Nations Climate Reports 2007 may be of importance for the challenge of the narrow economic growth perspective within political and bureaucratic elites. Feminist movements, 'green' economists, international experts and dynamic consultants should mobilise to make social and ecological sustainability *modern*.

References

Bacchi, Carol Lee (1999) *Women, policy and politics: the construction of policy problems.* London: Sage

Bache, Ian & Olsson, Jan (2001) 'Legitimacy through Partnership? EU Policy Diffusion in Britain and Sweden'. *Scandinavian Political Studies.* Vol. 24, No. 3, pp. 215–236

Bull, Marianne (2001) *Västra Götaland på väg mot jämställda tillväxtavtal.* Göteborg: Västra Götalandsregionen

— (2002) *Tillväxt jämnt-metoder som underlättar integrering av ett jämställdhetsperspektiv på regionalpolitik.* Stockholm: Näringsdepartementet samt länsstyrelserna i Västra Götaland, Blekinge län och Jämtlands län

Bäck, Henry & Larsson, Torbjörn (2006) *Den svenska politiken. Struktur, processer och resultat.* Stockholm: Liber

Conell, Robert W (1995) *Masculinities.* Berkeley: University California Press

Dryzek, John S (1990) *Discursive democracy: politics, policy and political science.* Cambridge; New York: Cambridge University Press

Eduards, Maud (2005) *Förbjuden handling. Om kvinnors organisering och feministisk teori.* Malmö: Liber Ekonomi

Elander, Ingemar (1999) 'Partnerskap och demokrati: omaka par i nätverkspoliti-

kens tid.' In *Globalisering - Demokratiutredningens Forskarvolym IX*. SOU 1999:83, s. 327–364. Stockholm: Fritzes
— (2002) 'Partnerships and urban governance'. *International Social Science Journal*. Vol. 54, Issue 172, pp. 191–204
Englund, Tomas (2004) 'Deliberativa samtal i ljuset av deliberativ demokrati'. In Premfors, Rune & Roth Anders (red.) *Deliberativ demokrati*. Lund: Studentlitteratur
Hedlund, Gun (1997) 'Kön, makt, ekonomi och organisation'. In *Styrsystem och jämställdhet* SOU 1997:114
— (2006) 'Genus och det nya kommunala ledarskapet'. *Kommunal ekonomi och politik*. Vol. 10, No. 3, pp. 41–62
— (2007a) *Samverkan på (o)jämlika villkor. Utvärdering av processen vid fördelningen av statliga medel till Roks medlemsjourer 2006*. Stockholm: Riksorganisationen Sveriges kvinnojourer
— (2007b) *Partnerskap, kön och demokrati*. Projektrapport till Vinnovas forskningsprogram Tillämpad genusforskning inom starka forsknings- och innovationsmiljöer, November 2007
Hedlund, Gun & Lennqvist-Lindén, Ann-Sofie (2004) *Governance - ett begrepp för genusforskningen?* Ansökan till Vetenskapsrådet (unpublished).
Hernes, Helga (1987) *Welfare State and Women Power*. Oslo: Universitetsforlaget
Horelli, Liisa & Roininen, Janne (1999) *Ex-ante evaluering ur jämställdhetsperspektiv av Sveriges tillväxtavtal*. Helsinki: Tekniska högskolan (Picaset)
Hudson, Christine & Rönnblom, Malin (2003) 'Uteslutande partnerskap?' In Brynielsson, Håkan (red.) *På jakt efter en ny regional samhällsordning!* Svenska Kommunförbundet. Stockholm: Kommentus förlag
Hugemark, Agneta (1994) *Den fängslande marknaden. Ekonomiska experter om välfärdsstaten*. Lund: Arkiv förlag.
Jansson, Maria (2001) *Livet dubbla vedermödor*. Doc. diss., Statsvetenskapliga institutionen, Stockholm University
Jónasdóttir, Anna G (1996) Genusperspektiv på statsvetenskap. *Genusperspektiv på forskningen*. Ds 1996:26
Karlsson, Gunnel (1996) *Från broderskap till systerskap*. Lund: Arkiv avhandlingsserie 44. Diss. Göteborg University
Larsson, Katarina (2004) *Andrahandskontrakt i folkhemmet: närmiljö och kvinnors förändringsstrategier*. Örebro Studies in History. Diss. Örebro University
Lindgren, Gerd (1999) *Klass, kön och kirurgi - relationer bland vårdpersonal i organisationsförändringarnas spår*. Malmö: Liber
Lindsten, Simone et al. (2001) *Om regionalpolitiken blev jämställd - jämställdhetsperspektiv på regionalpolitik*. Stockholm: Näringsdepartementet samt Länstyrelserna i Västra Götaland, Blekinge län och Hallands län
Lundquist, Lennart (1993) *Ämbetsman eller direktör? Förvaltningschefens roll i demokratin*. Stockholm: Norstedts juridik
Mouffe, Chantal (2000) 'For an agonistic model of democracy'. In O'Sullivan Noel (ed.) *Political Theory in Transition*. London: Routledge
Montin, Stig (1993) *Swedish Local Politics in Transition. A matter of rationality and legitimacy*. Örebro Studies No. 8. Diss. Örebro University
— (2007) *Moderna kommuner*. 3rd ed. Stockholm: Liber

Mörth, Ulrika & Sahlin-Andersson, Kerstin (2006) (eds.) *Privatoffentliga partnerskap: styrning utan hierarkier och tvång?* Stockholm: SNS förlag

Newman, Janet (2001) *Modernising governance: new labour, policy and society*, London: Sage

Olsson, Jan (2005) (ed.). *Hållbar utveckling underifrån?: lokala politiska processer och etiska vägval.* Nora: Nya Doxa

Persson, Katarina & Saarinen, Ylva (2003) *Kluster som ett regionalpolitiskt redskap i ett könsperspektiv. Män som hjältar i manliga kluster* Emma Resurscentrum, (www.emma.se)

Pincus, Ingrid (2002) *The Politics of Gender Equality Policy.* Örebro Studies in Political Science 5. Diss. Örebro: Örebro University

Rhodes, R A W (2000) 'Governance and Public Administration'. In Pierre Jon (ed.) *Debating Governance. Authority, Steering and Democracy.* Oxford: Oxford University Press

Raum, Nina C (1999) 'Women in parliamentary politics: Historical lines of development'. In Berqvist, Christina et al. (eds.) *Equal Democracies? Gender and Politics in the Nordic Countries.* Oslo: Scandinavian University Press

Reinikainen, Jouni & Reitberger, Magnus (2004) 'Kritiken av deliberativ demokrati'. In Premfors, Rune & Roth, Anders (eds.) *Deliberativ demokrati.* Lund: Studentlitteratur

Sanders, Lynn (1997) 'Against deliberation'. *Political Theory.* Vol. 25, No. 3, pp. 347–376

Siim, Birte (1988) 'Towards a Feminist Rethinking of the Welfare State'. In Jones, Kathleen B & Jónasdóttir, Anna G (eds.) *The Political Interests of Gender. Developing Theory and Research with a Feminist Face.* London: Sage

Soneryd, Linda (2004) 'Miljökonflikter och deliberation'. In Premfors, Rune & Roth, Anders (eds.) *Deliberativ demokrati.* Lund: Studentlitteratur

Sundin, Elisabeth (1988) *Omåttliga önskningar och måttliga framsteg.* Stockholm: FRN-framtidsstudier

Sørensen, Eva & Torfing, Jacob (2005) *Netvaerksstyring: fra government til governance.* Frederiksberg: Roskilde Universitetsforlag

Westberg, Hanna (2005) *Regionala tillväxtavtal – en fråga om att bryta gamla mönster? Kvinnors och mäns delaktighet i arbetet med tillväxtavtalen.* Stockholm: Vetenskaplig skriftserie från Arbetslivsinstitutet, Arbetsliv i omvandling 2005:9

14. Some practical and theoretical conclusions

In this final chapter, we will try to answer the main question of the book:

Does partnership represent a new and better strategy to promote innovation and sustainable change? To be able to answer this question, we will once again address the four dilemmas put forward in the first chapter of the book.

The first part of this chapter will thus focus on the practical and strategic implications of the research findings presented. In the second part, the findings are related to existing theories and concepts. One analytical model will be presented.

14.1 The four dilemmas – a summary of the four dilemmas

These four dilemmas have been addressed in the different chapters of the book. When we now try to summarise the results of the research presented we do not expect to get any clear answers to these questions and dilemmas. A sustainable change cannot be organised by trying to find simple solutions to complicated problems. Instead, we think that the research presented can be valuable in gaining a deeper understanding of the pros and cons of the partnership organisation. The following questions can be useful: When can the partnership organisation be useful? What kind of problems can be addressed in this way? What are the conditions that must be met if the partnership organisation is to be used? What other strategies for change can be used in combination with the partnership model?

14.1.1 *How to combine an actor and system perspective*

The first dilemma is that between an *actor* perspective on the one hand and a *system* perspective on the other.

The book's introductory chapter presents the ambition to adopt a double strategy for the organisation of the partnerships and the EU programmes. The idea is to be able to combine a top-down and a bottom-up strategy for development. The concept of a double strategy is highlighted in several ways. At the overriding level, it is assumed for example that it will be possible to combine top-down oriented governance from the central level with bottom-up oriented participation and influence through the partnerships. At the regional level, it is assumed that the target group will be able to exert influence and participate actively in the work of the partnerships. It is also assumed that actor-related activities at the local and regional levels will in general be able to lead to results and effects that have a system impact.

To what extent has the ambition to establish a two-way organisational strategy been realised? If we first examine the organisation and interplay between the central and regional levels, we can see that the results reveal considerable difficulties in promoting bottom-up oriented influence from the regional level. In the case of the Objective 3 programme, for example, Nilsson (in Chapter 6) points to a bureaucratisation of the work over time. A new centralised organisation was introduced in the middle of the period (2002), which led to increased hierarchical and centralised steering and a decreasing interest and a lack of motivation among the regional partnership representatives. The regional partnerships had few contacts with the national steering committee and with the national office representatives. They felt they had no mandate to influence the programme or to resist all the new regulations that came 'from above' at short notice.

At the regional level, a similar pattern emerges to a certain extent. Several authors underline the difficulties involved in generating more bottom-up related influence on the part of the target groups in the partnerships (see Chapters 6, 9 and 10). In many cases, the target groups do not participate at all in the work of the partnerships. Wistus (Chapter 9) demonstrates that there may be resistance in the partnership organisation to including the target group more actively in the work. The results presented by Andersson (Chapter 10), indicate that the work of the partnerships is characterised by work *for* the target group rather than by work *with* the target group.

There are, however, examples that demonstrate the possibility to combine the two strategies for change. The Austrian model (Chapter 12) tries to solve the dilemma between a top-down and a bottom up approach by combining the formalistic partnership model with looser forms of co-operation inside and alongside the partnership organisation. Engaged individuals can be involved in things they find interesting without taking part in the decisions on a system level. The co-ordination of local activities is organised by the representatives in the partnership organisations.

The results also indicate that a more bottom-up approach is used in the local project activities carried out and that these activities can help to strengthen the target group. However, these individual- and group-related results seldom lead to changes at the system level. Larsson (in Chapter 7) shows for example that the programme was successful in accomplishing an empowerment process among a group of women, but not in changing the structures causing their problems. The women – who were on sick leave – increased their resources in different ways but this empowerment process was not followed by changes on a system level. The partnership organisation did not perform such a mediating role between the individual and system levels, which it was expected to do. There was a clear 'gap' between the local projects and the partnership work. One reason for this gap was the exclusion of the women (the target group) from the decision-making process in the partnership.

On the whole, the empirical data presented in this book indicates that it has been difficult to realise the double organisational strategy, in which top-down and bottom-up related organisational forms are integrated, in practice. This does not mean, however, that these organisational strategies have not been applied. Both organisational strategies have been applied continuously, but in different situations and at different levels. In effect, the results indicate that these strategies, instead of being integrated, have acted as separate, parallel starting points for the activities carried out. The possibility to use the partnerships as mediating links between different levels and actors has not been utilized. In general, it does not appear that there has been any discussion between different actors at different levels on how the practical work on realising the ambition of a double strategy should be conducted.

14.1.2 To be all-embracing and focused at the same time

The second dilemma is that between a *holistic* and an all-embracing *approach* on the one hand and a focus on a specific objective or outcome on the other hand. Will the ambition to include 'everything' in a large partnership lead to such a wide focus that nothing is accomplished?

Indeed, the results indicate that handling an all-embracing approach is a complicated process that can give rise to a variety of problems. In Chapter 6, Nilsson points to some complications associated with the open approach in the partnership organization in the Social Fund, where the partnership organisation works on many levels and with different objectives at the same time. The role of the regional partnerships was often unclear. The regional partnerships should give advice (to the national and regional officials), present regional plans which should direct the different projects, follow up and evaluate the work and cooperate with important actors in the regional and local arenas. The risk with such an ambitious agenda is that there will be a lack of focus and that some objectives will be neglected. A lack of focus will make the evaluation of the projects and the programme more difficult. In the partnerships that were studied, little reflective learning was taking place. The learning ambition in the programme was taken over by formal and administrative purposes. Despite all these complications and difficulties, there were also advantages with the wide and open approach. The partnership representatives at the regional level became part of new networks, which gave them an opportunity to learn and access to new information, and was helpful in establishing new contacts.

In the Austrian example (Chapter 12), an attempt was made to combine a holistic perspective on change with local initiatives. When using this double strategy, a formative and process-oriented evaluation is considered to be necessary. With the provision of continuous feed-back, the partnerships can see how local initiatives and projects can be a part of a wider and more comprehensive strategy for change. Local projects are evaluated by the use of different indicators and put in relation to priorities on a system level.

One case is presented in which this dilemma was successfully dealt with. The brewery project (Chapter 4) was successful because of a clear and measurable objective – a five step limit for the transportation of goods or no delivery would take place. But in order to carry out and follow such a simple rule a lot of preparation, negotiations, discussions and practical solutions had to be accomplished based on joint participation on the part of different occupational groups, external experts and the senior management in the breweries. A partnership-like organisation was a necessity in order to organise this complicated action-oriented change process. Imposing demands and restrictions on the buyers (the restaurants) was something quite new, especially from the sellers' point of view. To introduce demands on the customer meant an important cultural change in the relationship between the seller and buyer, which therefore had to be mandated by the senior management in all the breweries. The different stakeholders in the partnership could benefit in many ways from a better work environment for the drivers. The costs for organising the change process were short-term, but the benefits were long-term – reduced absenteeism due to illness, easier to recruit new personnel, higher job satisfaction etc.

To sum up, the research results indicate that there are both problems and opportunities associated with an open and all-embracing approach. On one hand, the results presented above indicate that a holistic all-embracing approach can lead to complications in terms of ambiguity concerning partnership goals, roles and responsibilities. But on the other hand, an open approach might be an important factor in creating potentials for new contacts, collaboration opportunities and learning. Furthermore, the results also indicate that a more focused approach (as in the brewery case) may have many advantages in terms of less ambiguity, clear goals and a realistic mission. An interesting question, however, is whether this partnership strategy would also function on other – less-specific and measurable – issues.

14.1.3 *What are the consequences for democracy?*

The third problem or dilemma concerns the role of partnerships in relation to democracy. Will the partnership organisation take over some of the responsibilities that traditionally belong to the democratic system? Will partnership vitalize the democratic process or will the recruitment process to the partnerships imply a strengthening of already strong actors and organisations?

Stott and Caplan show (in Chapter 3) how many of the terms and concepts used to describe and discuss partnership are associated with democracy. Examples of central terms that relate to democratic values are broad representation, participation, equality, empowerment, inclusion and transparency. Wistus (in Chapter 9) also links the concept of equality to democracy. She writes that the rhetoric about equality is seldom practiced in the daily work in the partnership organisation. The culture, the language, the form of the meetings, the location etc. all have meanings and connotations that make it more difficult for certain groups to take part in the decisions made and to discus on equal terms with the strong partners (see also Chapters 7 and 10). When it comes to the other aspect of equality

– representation – Wistus finds that women are well represented, but not young people or private employers. The representatives are well educated, of middle age, and represent traditional institutions. The target groups are very seldom represented. The author points to a democratic problem with the exclusion of the target groups from the partnerships.

The results presented by Wistus, and also Bogren (in Chapter 8), indicate that the partnership principle – i.e. that the participants in the partnership represent their respective organisations – may be a factor that obstructs the participation of the target groups in the work of the partnerships. In many cases, the target groups have no organisation of their own. Bogren points out that – apart from organisationally-related problems – there are problems at the social and individual levels that mean that the target groups can seldom participate in the partnerships on equal terms. Despite this, she underlines the importance of the target groups being represented in the partnerships.

Our research results also indicate that the democratic process can be hindered by problems such as power games and hidden decision-making processes within the partnerships. In Chapter 13, Hedlund shows for example that the initiation and development phase in the structural funds was dominated by male officials and experts. There was a hidden decision-making process that excluded women and other groups that did not have a strong position in regional and national organizations. The social ambitions in the structural funds were less pronounced because of the strong economic focus among these experts and bureaucrats.

In an ideal situation, a private and political partnership could vitalize the political democratic system by organizing social innovation more effectively and by coordinating joint efforts from strategic partners. Such a partnership could also offer an arena in which to practice deliberate democracy. The results in this book do not support these high hopes that the partnership organization will vitalize political democracy. Instead, the results indicate that informal discrimination and exclusion processes take place in the partnerships. The experts and regional officials attained a strong position in the partnerships – especially in the formulation of the problems and objectives in the initial phase. The target groups were seldom represented in the partnerships and when they did take part in the meetings they were in a subordinate position. Their influence was often limited to the lowest levels – being informed or consulted, but they were seldom able to exert real influence, and never control, over the activities (see Chapter 10). The individual preconditions of members of the target groups for participating in the work of the partnerships may also make co-operation on equal terms more difficult (see Chapter 8).

To summarize, the preconditions for a deliberative model for democracy were not present in the partnerships we studied because such a model is based on equal participation, practical reasoning, an open debate and well-grounded solutions. But, on the other hand, it is also important to acknowledge that the partnerships have initiated a lot of projects in which excluded and marginalized groups could take part and increase their resources (see Chapters 7 and 10).

14.1.4 Can a consensus orientation be combined with a conflict perspective?

The fourth dilemma – which is related to the third one – has to do with the critical potential of the partnership organisation. The EQUAL partnerships are assumed in the main to be based on a consensus-oriented approach. This is evident, for example, in the demands for unanimous decisions that are placed on the partnerships. At the same time, one of the main ambitions is to achieve system-related changes. Can these two starting points or ambitions be combined, and in what way are these starting points expressed in the work of the partnerships?

The results presented in this book indicate in general that the focus is on a consensus-oriented approach in the partnerships studied. However, the results presented in several of the chapters also indicate that there are conflicts and different interests in the partnerships that are not brought to the surface and discussed. One author that confirms the absence of a conflict perspective in the partnership organisation is Hedlund (in Chapter 13). She also points out that the dominance of the consensus paradigm makes it illegitimate to talk about differences of interest and power differences between men and women. Wistus (see Chapter 9) also points out that hidden interests were not made explicit or open for debate in the studied partnerships.

One reason for the focus on a consensus-oriented approach may be the composition of the partnerships. The over-representation of traditional institutions (government institutions) that often characterises the partnerships may lead to a situation in which preserving and consensus-oriented views and solutions are preferred (cf. Chapters 9 and 13).

Another reason why conflicts and different interests are not brought to the fore may be linked to the role of the partnerships. In the Objective 3 organisation, the partnerships have a primarily advisory role. Nilsson (in Chapter 6) argues that because of this advisory role the partnerships have little to decide on, which can explain the absence of disagreements or conflicts. The agreements made are seldom challenged since the partnerships' objectives and plans are not put into concrete action. In this situation, it is easy to put conflicting interests and power issues aside (cf. Chapter 9).

Larsson (in Chapter 7) stresses the need to analyse the power relations in the partnership organisation. These relations are often hidden for the participants and the target groups. A group of women who were on long-term sick leave were invited to attend the partnership meetings on several occasions, but they could not influence the decisions made. The women were in a subordinate position because they met the management representatives from the organisations they were dependent on. The women were afraid that any criticism would have private and personal consequences for them. Larsson discusses how resistance to such an unequal power situation can be organised in a collective way (see also Chapter 13). She suggests that the participants from the target groups should be recruited from other geographical areas to avoid confrontation with their 'bosses'. Another conclusion from her research is that the partnership organisation must give the target group a necessary autonomy to avoid a 'hostage situation'. If meetings with system representatives are organised, then the target group should be in the majority.

Målqvist and Parmsund (Chapter 4) describe a change process which was characterized by a close cooperation between the union, management and a research group. It is obvious that this cooperation is based on unequal terms. The representatives from the senior management in the breweries were dominant in the decision-making process. The union had to rely on the goodwill of the management, because it was not obliged to be involved in such a proactive strategy for a better work environment. The union representatives knew that a traditional intervention from the state authorities would not have been successful in accomplishing these changes and therefore accepted the unequal situation.

The Austrian model for partnership organisation (see Chapter 12) also seems to be genuinely consensus-oriented. It is based on a balance of interests between the participant organisations and institutions. The strategy presupposes a joint interest between the partners and an ambition to change the system 'from inside' and make it more effective by continuous improvements instead of radical changes that will challenge the structural relationships.

Overall, the results indicate that the partnerships studied are in general based on a strong consensus approach. This means that conflicts and differences in terms of interests and preferences are seldom brought to the surface. Both programme-related rules and regulations and the composition and roles of the partnerships seem to contribute to this situation. The question is what potential do consensus-based partnerships of this type have for creating structurally-related changes? Can a consensus-driven organisation really change a system that it is a part of? If the members in a partnership represent the existing power structure, will they not have a strong interest in the preservation of these unequal relationships?

14.1.5 Some implications for a sustainable strategy of change

Four dilemmas with the partnership organisation have been addressed. The research presented indicates that the partnership organisation can not deal with these dilemmas successfully. The strengths of the partnership organisation – co-operation between different organisations, a wide and an open system-approach, a broad representation, joint solutions in a spirit of consensus – are at the same time its weaknesses. The partnership organisation runs the risk of being too comprehensive, unfocused, uncritical, and discursively oriented and of excluding different groups from participation on equal terms. These risks with the partnership organisation will – if they are not carefully dealt with – make the whole idea of social innovation and sustainable change impossible. The same goes for the idea of a change process based on a deliberate democracy ideal.

In the introduction, we asked the following question: Is partnership an effective strategy for organising social innovation and sustainable change? Based on the discussion of the four dilemmas above our answer is negative. Partnership is not a comprehensive strategy in itself. But we cannot be sure, because the reasons for the deficiencies with the partnership organisation must be analysed more carefully. Are the limitations something implicit in the organisation itself or do they have to do with the way the partnership organisation has been initiated, carried out and implemented? Maybe partnership is an effective strategy for innovation and sustainable change, but it has not been handled in the right way?

On the other hand, we have seen some positive effects from the cases presented in the book, for example the brewery partnership. One outcome of the research presented in the book is obvious – using the partnership organisation as a strategy for innovation presupposes a well-developed change competence among the partners. The high change competence in the brewery partnership can to a large extent explain the success and sustainability in this case.

To answer the question about the usefulness of the partnership organisation we have to understand the mechanisms behind innovation and sustainable change. We need theories and analytic models to gain a deeper understanding of the research results presented here. The ambition behind the book was to address practical dilemmas in the partnership organisation by using different theoretical perspectives – organisational change, power and empowerment concepts, project theories, ideas from organisational learning, gender analysis, theories about governance and participation etc. We have used a pluralistic approach in the analysis of partnership, which is based on a pragmatic orientation among most of the authors. We think that the focus on urgent problems in local and regional development will make the theory more interesting also from a theoretical perspective. At the same time, new theoretical insights can be helpful in the practical work.

In the following section, we will present and try to apply an analytical model. We will then see if this model is helpful in analysing the partnership organization as a strategy for innovation and sustainable change.

14.2 An analytical model

How can the type of co-operation strategy that partnership represents be studied and analysed? In the figure below we have tentatively presented some basic elements in a model to analyze partnership organization in relation to sustainable change. We do not claim that the model is all-embracing, simply that it presents what is by necessity a rough picture of a complex co-operation process. However, it can hopefully act as an aid in analysing and discussing partnership co-operation in relation to efforts to promote sustainable change.

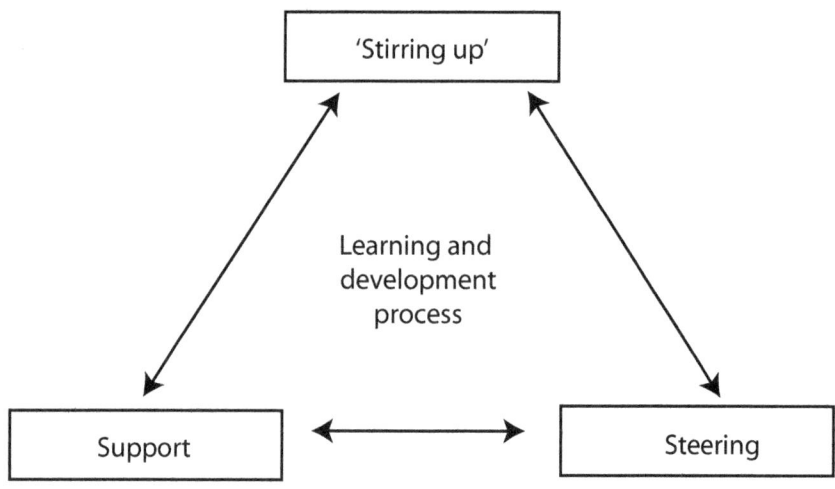

Figure 1. Three functions in an analytical model used to analyze sustainable change.

The model above is based on the three aspects, support, steering and stirring up. These aspects and the interplay between them can be assumed to be significant in an analysis of co-operation for sustainable development.

The first two functions are often presented as necessary elements in similar models for organizational and regional change. The support, which includes training, mentoring, networking, dialogue and participation etc. (Andersson et al. 2006) is a way of initiating and supporting change 'from below'. It is a way of increasing participation, involvement and motivation among the people concerned. The support element is especially important in the initiation phase. These elements are stressed in theories about organizational development (OD) and local change programmes. These theories stress the importance of participation, involvement, learning etc. and have been used in working life research in Scandinavia, the U.K. and the U.S.A. (Gustavsen 1996). In the case of the stirring up function, a critical reflection is found to be a necessity during the whole change process (Svensson et al. 2007). In stimulating such a critical reflection, interactive research can play a central role. Evaluation can be another way of 'stirring up', as can organising for a broad representation in the partnership. Stirring up entails introducing a bottom-up and from-the-outside-in perspective to the partnership that shakes up established working methods and promotes new thinking.

The steering function represents a function of control and co-ordination, which are important elements in a strategy for change that is directed at structures and systems. The role of the senior management and the politicians is seen as essential and is described in terms of an active ownership over the changes carried out. This active ownership presupposes the involvement of decision-makers at all levels – managers, politicians, executives, organisational representatives and so on throughout the development process (Svensson et al. 2007). This is a necessity in order to disseminate local changes and to be able to affect regulatory systems and structures. The need for the steering of developmental work is pronounced in economic, organisational and management theories and in the political sciences. In the partnership context, the problem of finding a balance between autonomy for individual partners and co-ordination for a joint result is highlighted (Mörth & Sahlin-Andersson 2006).

The sustainability of development work can be analysed as an interplay between the three elements or functions in the triangle, which is illustrated by the double-headed arrows in Figure 1. It is the interplay between support, steering and stirring up that provides a balance between the top-down and bottom-up approaches. Stirring up is aimed at both how support and steering are conducted. This can in the best case provide a basis for critical reflection and learning and contribute to the development of measures that are subsequently based on the experience gained – i.e. discussing targets and results and analysing the preconditions for co-operation.

How then can the results from the various chapters in the book be linked to the model presented above? In the case of support, the results in general indicate that the support from national authorities/agencies to the regional partnerships has varied. In the EQUAL partnerships, for example, there seems to have been more support and more contact between the regional partnerships and the central level than in the Objective 3 programme. The creation of more structured arenas for the dialogue between the central authorities/agencies and the regional partnerships was, however, unusual. The partnerships in the EQUAL programme have been supported by different activities – training, networking, counselling, guidance, mentorship etc – through the national thematic groups. These supportive activities have been important for the participation of the target groups in the different projects, but it is unclear how this support has contributed to co-operation in the partnerships and the quality of their work. The case study from Austria (Chapter 12) also provides an interesting example of a national and regional organization for support of the partnership organizations. Our results – and those of other research – demonstrate that there is a demand from the partnerships for such support, especially in connection with the initiation work (see Chapters 3 and 12).

In the case of the steering aspect, the results indicate that different steering strategies are used in different contexts. First, the results show that co-operation between the partnerships and the central authority/agency level is characterised by relatively strong financial and bureaucratic steering, especially in the Objective 3 programme. This steering is mainly top-down oriented, as the central authorities stipulate the conditions for partnership co-operation in various ways. In the Objective 3 programme, it also appears that central steering of the content of the work of the partnerships increased significantly during the latter part of the programme period. However, the bottom-up oriented steering relationship appears to have been weak. There were few channels for dialogue and discussion between the central authority/agency level and the regional partnerships in the Objective 3 organisation (see Chapter 6).

Secondly, the steering element seems to be less developed at the partnership level in the cases presented. There is a lack of active ownership in most of the partnerships, despite the representation of strong organizations and institutions (see Chapter 10). The actors representing these organizations – for example politicians and management in private companies – have seldom taken their role seriously. The representatives in the partnerships have seldom had the authority or mandate to make decisions on a structural level. Because of this passivity among the strong partners, the coordinators attained a strong position and often acted like traditional project managers. In the initiation phases, the experts and regional officials were able to use the passivity among the politicians to strengthen their own role. The weak steering mechanisms in the partnerships are obvious, especially in the Objective 3 programme. The fact that these partnerships mainly had an advisory function together with a strong 'top down' steering from the central authorities had negative effects on the involvement and interest of the partners. Hedlund (in Chapter 13) also focuses on the weak political steering of the regional partnerships in the structural funds. The brewery project is an exception to most of the cases because of the active ownership exercised by senior managers in the big companies, which made it much easier to steer the different activities. The Austrian example is also interesting from a steering perspective. It illustrates a combination of a top-down initiative and autonomy for the regional partnerships to decide over the activities and work forms. The Territorial Employment Pact is part of Austrian labour market policy. In this way, the regional partnerships get legitimacy and financial resources from the state.

Stirring up – the third function in the model – has seldom been used in a systematic way to learn from and reflect on how support and steering have worked. Although external evaluations were carried out – in the form of mid-point and final evaluations of the programmes at the national level – it does not appear that these evaluations have been used by the partnerships to develop their organisation or forms of work. Evaluation was also conducted quite late in the process. In the EQUAL programme, researchers have been involved throughout the programme period, but it seems that their research has often had an independent role and has not often been used as a support for the participants' own analysis of this form of co-operation.

How then can we summarise our results with regard to the three functions in the sustainability triangle? In the case of *steering* there has been relatively strong financial steering from the central level. In the Objective 3 programme, it seems that the steering of the content of the activities conducted at the regional level has increased over time. At the regional level, however, the results indicate that steering has been weak and that ownership has been passive in relation to the activities in the projects, as well as when it comes to taking responsibility for the results of these projects. At the project level, we can see a bottom-up related strategy for steering and co-ordination.

With regard to *support* there have been different activities, training courses, seminars, aids, networks, consultation and research efforts and so on. These support measures have often been aimed at project managers, sub-project managers and co-ordinators. The national thematic groups have arranged and run extensive activities that have been offered to the EQUAL partnerships. There have, on the other hand, been very few arenas for a dialogue between the central and regional levels in the organisation.

Stirring up is the element of the sustainability triangle that has been least well-developed. External evaluations, research, seminars and networking have taken place on a relatively large scale, but these measures have not been used in a systematic way to generate learning, reflection and dialogue regarding steering and support in the work of the partnerships.

14.3 Some research findings

In this section, we will present some other research and relate it to our findings and the model presented above. We will try to relate these research findings to the dilemmas presented above and the model for sustainable change.

14.3.1 *Managing a collaborative practice*

In several of the chapters of this book, the problems associated with steering and organising co-operation in partnerships are addressed. The complexity of this type of constellation for co-operation is highlighted in the literature on partnership (Huxham 1996, Huxham & Vangen 2000). Huxham and Vangen (2000) point out that complexity and a lack of clarity are two factors that can create difficulties in organising for co-operation in partnerships. This type of co-operation may involve complex hierarchies with several organisational levels (cf. Huxham & Vangen 2000, Gulati 1998, Osborn & Hagedoorn 1997). These problems are examined in the earlier chapters (see in particular the discussion concerning the holistic or focused approach). Andersson (see Chapter 10) discusses, for example, complexity and the difficulties concerning organizing and steering issues in partnerships that have a wide, all-embracing approach compared with more focused and action-oriented partnerships.

In traditional organisational theory, the importance of setting up clear and distinct objectives as a means of handling complexity and a lack of clarity in an organisational context is often underlined (cf. Morgan 1986, 1997, Thompson & McHugh 1995). The literature on partnership also highlights the importance of common visions and objectives (Brinkerhoff

2002, Malmborg 2003). Having a common vision is seen here as an important basis for a successful partnership. The lack of common objectives and values has been identified as a cause of the problems in private-public partnerships (Mörth & Sahlin-Andersson 2006). However, although the importance of common objectives is emphasised, the importance of the individual partners feeling that they can achieve their own objectives through the partnership is also underlined. It can often be difficult to agree on joint partnership objectives, especially in private-public partnerships where both the private and public sectors are represented (cf. Brinkerhoff 2002, Malmborg 2003). There are often different views and expectations concerning the partnership's objectives and aims (Huxham 1996, Spekman et al.1998). In this context, it is important that the individual organisations in the partnership see that their own expectations can be met by the work of the partnership. Otherwise there is a risk that they will regard the work as worthless and unimportant. Malmborg (2003) writes that it is important to set aside time in the initial phase of a partnership to clarify the objectives and expectations of the different partners in order to avoid misunderstandings later on. The results presented in this book also indicate that there are different interests and expectations among the partners in partnerships (cf. Chapters 9 and 13). However, it does not appear that these have been brought to the surface and discussed or used as a starting point for the work of the partnerships.

Partnership work, however, is not only affected by the partnership's internal organisation and steering. The context in which the partnership exists is also important from the point of view of steering and organisation. This applies not least to the partnerships studied in this book. The partnerships here work within the framework of a major EU programme that is organised at the national level. The partnerships are expected to work towards overall objectives that focus on competence development, gender equality, integration and so on. Management by objectives is a common principle for organising operations and is linked to concepts such as improving efficiency and rationalisation, as well as to decentralisation (Milsta 1994, Samuelsson 2005). Research has shown, however, that it in practice it can be difficult to steer development work using overall objectives, especially if these are defined too statically and narrowly (Engwall 2002).

The research presented in this book demonstrates the difficulties associated with exercising central steering primarily based on objectives stemming from a technical-economic rationality as, among other things, this ignores social objectives that form a part of sustainable development (see Chapter 11). However, it has also proved difficult to gain acceptance for a responsibility rationality in partnerships that comprises social and democratic values. It is much easier to get women included as representatives in a partnership than it is to change views, values and perspectives for a more gender-equal and sustainable society. Companies are less interested in taking part when the focus is not on the growth discourse (see Chapter 10), but as the programme requires their participation the funders and politicians reduce the demands governing their participation and obligations. Policy documents include passages on inclusion and social aims, but these do not govern the work. Often, they are not even taken seriously. This gives rise to a gap between rhetoric and practice in a partnership (see Chapter 11). In the studies presented here, it is evident that the EU's horizontal objectives (on gender equality, accessibility and integration) have not had any major impact on the activities, and hardly on representation in the partnerships either (see Chapters 7, 9, 10, 11, 12).

Mörth & Sahlin-Andersson (2006) address the problems associated with steering and organisation in a partnership context on the basis of the aspects of autonomy and co-ordination. They point out, for example, that there is a conflict between centralised and formal steering and organisational strategies on the one hand and decentralised and informal strategies on the other. It is, for instance, common that the desire for flexibility and cross-sector collaboration acts as a driving force for co-operation in a partnership. This desire creates the need for autonomy and more decentralised organisational principles. At the same time, it may be more difficult to combine such needs with demands for co-ordination, predictability and clarity regarding the powers and responsibilities that are often connected with more formal, centralised organisational principles. The problem here is one of a conflict between the demands and needs for autonomy and the demands and needs for co-ordination. This conflict is also evident in several of the contributions to this book. It is particularly visible in connection with the discussion of the dilemma concerning the possibility to combine the actor-related and the structurally-related perspectives. The examples presented in the book show that it has been difficult to combine the central level's demands for co-ordination and predictability with the partnerships' needs for autonomy (cf. Chapter 6). However, there are similar problems even within partnerships. For the partnerships to function effectively, some form of division of labour and certain rules for co-operation are required. However, the very idea of partnership is that the partners are independent and equal actors. In several of the examples presented in the book, co-ordination appears to be relatively weak. At the same time, the results indicate that the partners are not equal in the partnerships and that there are certain strong actors or partners (e.g. organisations in the public sector) who tend to take/get more space and receive a greater response for their interests than other actors.

To sum up, the balance between autonomy and coordination seems to be crucial when it comes to managing collaborative practice. Davies (2002) links this problem to innovation and sustainable change. She writes that partnerships for sustainable development require flexibility to allow innovative structures and relationships to flourish, but they also demand clear statements of objectives at the outset to avoid misunderstanding through the raising of false expectations.

14.3.2 *Supporting collaborative practice*

Earlier in this chapter we have noted that collaborative practice is often complex and ambiguous. Vangen and Huxham (2003) claim that such collaborations are difficult to manage and the likelihood of disappointing outputs is high. Handling such complexity places great demands on the partners involved in this type of collaborative relationship.

How then can we support the work of partnerships? Support can be provided both inside and outside the workplace. It can be based on peer or professionalized support. A network or a partnership organization can be used for learning and support among equals. Individual support can be handled by a mentor or a tutor. But the support function can also be organised by professional groups, like consultants or researchers.

With regard to support functions inside partnerships, the importance of commitment and adequate competence within the partnership is underlined (Brinkerhoff 2002, Malmborg 2003, Roberts 2000). Having the right competence in the partnership can prevent imbalance and role conflicts between different partners (Malmborg 2003). Several authors point out the importance of enthusiasts, agents for change and political actors who spend a lot of time working for the partnership, both inside the partnership itself and externally (Brinkerhoff 2002, Williams 2002, Pettigrew 2003). Brinkerhoff (2002) uses the terms champions in this context, i.e. a kind of entrepreneur or advocate who works to create legitimacy for the partnership both externally and internally. These champions are assumed to have knowledge and skills relating to communication, organisation and negotiation.

The research in the field also highlights leadership as a support function for the work in partnerships. Leadership may, for example, be important in creating cohesion and when initiating efforts to establish basic starting points for the work of the partnership (Andersson et al. 2006). However, it is also important to ensure that no individual representative or organisation decides too much in the course of the work (Vangen & Huxham, 2003). The research also underlines the importance of the representatives in the partnership having the support of the leadership in their own organisations. Otherwise, there is a risk that the activities of the partnership will be in the nature of a loosely-linked project that is completely separate from the activities of the home organisation. Against this background, it is important that the partnership representatives have a mandate to actively pursue and work with change and dissemination in their own organisations with regard to the issues dealt with by the partnership (Klöfver & Nilsson 2007).

Some authors also say that collaborative practice, like partnership, needs continuous internal support. Vangen and Huxham (2003), for example, claim that practitioners need to engage in a continuous process of nurturing the collaborative practice. Even in situations where collaboration works well, continuous work is needed to maintain balance and trust. In this work it is important to take account of aspects such as communication, the balance of power, different levels of commitment and motivation and different views of objectives and tasks (Vangen & Huxham 2003).

The support function can also be organised by actors outside the partnership. In the case of partnerships that are part of a large programme, the central authority/agency level is an important source of support (cf. Klöfver & Nilsson 2007). Klöfver and Nilsson (2007) point out that opportunities for dialogue and for getting advice on how to handle various issues are highly valued by the partnerships. The results presented in this book also indicate that this is the case, as mentioned above.

Furthermore, the support can be organised by professional groups, such as consultants or researchers. The dilemma associated with such professional support is the dependency on outsiders and the risk that changes will not be sustainable. When the support is based on an empowerment process the participants will be less dependent on the outsiders, but this will also challenge the power structure in the organization and run the risk of repercussions. Brinkerhoff (2002) is an author who claims that research can support the work of partnerships in several ways. She proposes an assessment approach that is developmental, participatory and process-oriented where the assessor assumes the role of a critical friend. A process approach can serve several functions. It brings conflicts into the open, provides a common platform for agreement and increases the legitimacy of proposed measures (Brinkerhoff 2002). The role of the assessor is to generate data and encourage interpretations that foster learning. At the same time, the assessor must adopt a critical stance that is willing to question the status quo.

The importance of adopting a critical stance in partnership work will be discussed further below.

14.3.3 Steering up the collaborative practice

The view of steering and supporting activities concerning partnerships within the EU-programmes is mainly consensus oriented. Research also shows, however, that too strong a consensus-oriented approach in this context may cause problems in several ways (cf. Davies 2002, Hudson 2001).

First, there is something of a paradox in the very idea of unity in a partnership when at the same time the importance of each partner's unique contribution to the partnership is underlined (Huxham 1996, Spekman et al. 1998). If is often seen as a collaborative advantage to bring together different types of organisation and expertise. However, the different resources that different organisations represent also constitute the basis for differences in terms of the operations of the partnership. Even if the partners can reach agreement at an overall level, it can be assumed that there will be different interests and that each of the partners have their specific reasons for participating in the partnership.

Secondly, a strong consensus orientation may also mean that conflicts and different interests will be suppressed, which can lead to a drop in energy and innovativeness in the partnership organization. Hudson (2001) points out, on the basis of Swedish experience, that the partnership model encompasses a tension between, on the one hand, the desire to include all of the actors concerned and, on the other hand, a tradition of acting in consensus. There is a risk that the focus on consensus will divert attention away from conflicts and clashes of interest. In such a situation, there is also a risk that the partnership will take the perspective that most, or the strongest, partners represent as its starting point, rather than base its work on a broad perspective.

Several chapters in this book indicate that such problems exist (see for example Chapters 9 and 11). Furthermore, the data presented in the book is taken from a Multi-Stakeholder-Partnership dominated by public organizations at the regional level (see Chapter 3). These partnerships are all – in some way – financed by public funds, often EU money, which should make it easier to exercise democratic political control. However, our research does not support the high hopes that the partnership organization will vitalize political democracy. Instead, we have found signs of informal discrimination and exclusion processes in the partnership work. The experts and regional officials have attained a strong position in the partnerships – especially regarding the formulation of the problems and objectives in the initial phase. They also decide on the agenda in the partnership work (see Chapter 4). The target groups were seldom represented in the partnerships, and when they did take part in the meetings they were in a subordinate position. Their influence was often limited to the lowest levels – being informed or consulted – but they seldom or never had any influential control over the activities (see Chapter 10). On the other hand, the partnerships have initiated a lot of projects in which excluded and marginalized groups could take part and increase their resources (see Chapters 7 and 10).

In the model above, the importance of stirring up partnership practice is emphasized. The stirring up function is assumed to promote critical reflection within the partnerships. Critical reflection is found to be a necessity during the entire change process (Svensson et al. 2007). In stimulating such a critical reflection, interactive research can play a central role. The role of the research is to 'stir up' the change processes by promoting reflective and critical learning among the participants. A joint learning process can be organised between the researchers and the participants at different levels in the partnership organization. Different methods have been tried – such as interviews, surveys, participant observations etc. The data collected is then used to generate joint learning together with the participants in the partnerships (Aagaard Nielsen & Svensson 2006). Evaluation can also be used as a method for 'stirring up' by getting the participants to reflect on the results achieved (Svensson et al. 2007). However, evaluation is not often used in this way and it seldom leads to changes in development work (see Chapter 13). Apart from using research and evaluation, stirring up can also be achieved by having a wide range of actors in the partnership so that non-traditional actors can make their voices heard and the partnership can work actively with the conflicts and different interests that exist. In this way, different partners can stir things up and thus learn from each other. Stirring up entails introducing a bottom-up and outside-in perspective in the partnership that shakes up established working methods and promotes new thinking.

The discussion on stirring up is linked to the consensus–conflict dilemma examined earlier in the book. The emphasis on the stirring up function is also based on an assumption that conflict just as much as consensus may be a central and necessary feature of sustainable development and work that aims to expand democracy and create broader governance (cf. Flyvberg 1997).

14.4 A final assessment

In the introductory chapter we asked whether the partnership organisation represents a new strategy for sustainable change and innovation. What is our answer? Does the partnership organisation overcome the limitations of both 'top-down' and 'bottom-up' strategies? The idea of combining structural change with empowerment in the EQUAL programme can be seen as such a two-fold ambition.

Scoppetta (in Chapter 12) gives a positive answer to the question based on the experience in Austria, but she has some reservations. She exemplifies how the partnerships' scope of opportunities can range from a common denominator to a partnership which influences institutions, policies and regions on a wide scale. Scoppetta concludes that the partnership organisation's full potential has not been exploited so far.

Our data does not confirm the high hopes that the partnership organisation will promote innovation in a cross-sectoral and multi-level approach. Maybe it is a futile dream to try to integrate opposite strategies in one organisational form. This is the 'nasty' part of our research findings. We also have some 'nice ones' which point to the possibilities offered by a strategic form of co-operation between different sectors in society. To handle complicated economic, social and ecological problems, co-operation between strong organisations that represent central institutions in society is a necessity. How such co-operation should be combined with broad participation in the partnership organization we do not yet know. The partnerships have not been able to perform this trick, but it is probably not possible to combine these two contradictory strategies in one and the same organisation. The attempt to combine the empowerment of the target groups with a system impact on the part of strong actors in the EQUAL partnerships has not succeeded. Despite this, however, partnership may be an important element in organising cross-border co-operation within the framework of efforts to promote sustainable development.

We have seen how the partnership organisation – when introduced in the right way, with committed partners and interested stakeholders, based on equal and mutual relations and an open dialogue between involved partners – can be one way to organise co-operation over organisational borders and between different hierarchical levels. With such partnerships, complicated problems can be dealt with in an innovative, effective and flexible way. Different forms of partnerships can be used in combination. Partnership may be one way to organise change and innovation, but it is not the only way! It probably has to be combined with other forms of organisation – networks, innovation systems, project work, Triple Helix, informal groups etc. Networks can be used for learning and innovation on a small-scale and when using a local approach, while partnerships can be an effective complement in institutionalising these changes at the regional and national levels. However, the distinctions between these different forms for organising change and innovation will often be blurred (Jacobs 2000, p. 30). A sustainable change will include a combination of co-operative methods in a pragmatic way irrespective of how the researchers analyse these forms of cooperation.

The real challenge is to develop a more realistic strategy for sustainable change in a situation of a risk society (Beck 1992). The traditional 'top-down' strategy – based on formalised and rigid planning – does not function in a situation of constant change and 'moving targets' (Jacobs 2000, p. 47). Instead, we need a more flexible and responsive approach based on co-operation that creates synergy between a large number of actors, organisations and institutions. The long-term perspective is essential, but it could include short-term projects if they are part of a larger strategy and used for learning and reflection on the objectives and methods used.

One conclusion of our work underlines the importance of a development of the terms and concepts used and of continued research. More empirical research, but also more theoretical development, is needed. The overriding aim of such research is to analyse the possible form and structure of a strategy for sustainable development in which partnership is an integrated component. Part of the development of the terminology could be to describe partnership on the basis of its aims, function and context. Dynamics, competition, resources and conflicts in partnerships form a central area for research, as does the interplay between internal and external factors.

Empirically-oriented research will probably not reveal a pure form of partnership. Most partnerships include different forms of organisation – such as networks and projects. A broad, system-manipulating partnership will probably always consist of a hybrid of a partnership and a network. Our findings, therefore, point to the usefulness of combining different research disciplines in studying the partnership organisation. Pedagogy, sociology, political science and economy can be used to give different perspectives on the complex change processes, the outcomes and the preconditions.

This book has tried to answer the question of whether partnership is an effective strategy for organising sustainable development. We have noted that there are problems associated with the term sustainable development. Despite these difficulties, we have retained the term. This is partly because we see that it is the ambition of a partnership to achieve changes that are more long term than those of projects. That which is sustainable, that which will endure beyond the formal project period, is of more interest than the immediate, but perhaps quickly fading, result. Another reason is that thinking and analysis based on the concept of sustainability may benefit research on working life in a necessary shift towards the greater use of a holistic perspective and more complex views of reality (see Docherty et al. 2002).

References

Aagaard Nielsen, K & Svensson, L (2006) (eds.) *Action Research and Interactive Research. Beyond practice and theory,* Hamburg: Shaker Publishing

Andersson, M, Svensson, L, Wistus, S & Åberg, C (2006) (eds.) *On the Art of Developing Partnerships.* Stockholm: Arbetslivsinstitutet

Beck, U (1992) *Risk Society: Towards a New Modernity.* London: Sage

Brinkerhoff, J M (2002) 'Assessing and improving partnership relationships and outcomes: a proposed framework'. *Evaluation and Program Planning,* Vol. 25, No. 3, pp. 215–321

Davies, A (2002) 'Power, politics and networks shaping partnerships for sustainable communities'. *Area,* Vol. 34, No. 2, pp. 190–203

Docherty, P, Forslin, J & Shani, A B (2002) 'Emerging work systems: from intensive to sustainable'. In Docherty P, Forslin J & Shani A B (eds.) *Creating sustainable work systems.* London: Routledge

Engwall, M (2002) 'The futile dream of the perfect goal'. In Sahlin-Andersson I & Söderholm A (eds.) *Beyond Project management: New perspectives on the contemporary.* Copenhagen: Copenhagen Business School Press

Flyvberg, B (1997) *Rationality and power.* Chicago: University of Chicago Press

Gulati, R (1998) 'Alliances and networks'. *Strategic Management Journal,* Vol. 19, pp. 293–317

Gustavsen, B (1996) 'Development and the Social Sciences. An uneasy relationship'. In Toulmin S & Gustavsen B (eds.) *Beyond Theory: Changing Organization through Participation.* Amsterdam: John Benjamin Publishing Corporation

Hudson, C (2001) Regionala partnerskap – ett hot mot eller förverkligande av demokrati? CERUM working paper, 36:2001. Umeå: Statsvetenskapliga institutionen. Umeå University

Huxham, C (1996) (ed.) *Creating collaborative advantage.* London: Sage

Huxham, C & Vangen, S (2000) 'Ambiguity, complexity and dynamics in the membership of collaboration'. *Human Relation,* Vol. 53, No. 6, pp. 771–806

Jacobs, B (2000) *Strategy and Partnership in Cities and Regions.* London: MacMillan Press

Klöfver, H & Nilsson, B (2007) *Mångfaldens ansikten – mellan vision och praktik.* Linköping: Institutionen för beteendevetenskap och lärande. Linköping University

Malmborg, F (2003) Conditions for Regional Public–Private Partnerships for Sustainable Development – Swedish Perspectives. *European Environment,* Vol. 13, pp. 133–149

Milsta, M (1994) *Målstyrning och mellanchefers arbete – hierarki, delaktighet och tillfälligheternas spel.* Linköping: Linköping Studies in Education and Psychology, No. 40

Morgan, G (1986) *Images of Organization.* Beverly Hills CA: Sage

— (1997) *Organisationsmetaforer.* Lund: Studentlitteratur

Mörth, U & Sahlin-Andersson, K (2006) *Privatoffentliga partnerskap. Styrning utan hierarkier eller tvång.* Stockholm: SNS förlag

Pettigrew, P J (2003) 'Power conflicts, and Resolutions: A Change Agent's Perspective on Conducting Action Research Within a Multiorganizational Partnership'. *Systemic Practice and Action Research,* Vol. 16, No. 6, pp. 375–391

Osborn, A & Hagedoorn, J (1997) 'The institutionalization and evolutionary dynamics of interorganizational alliances and networks'. *Academy of Management Journal,* Vol. 40, No. 2, pp. 261–279

Roberts, I (2000) 'Leicester environment city: learning how to make a Local Agende 21, partnerships and participation deliver'. *Environment and Urbanization,* Vol. 12, pp. 9–27

Samuelsson, L A (2005) *Organizational governance and control: a summary of research in the Swedish society.* Stockholm: Economic Research Institute, Stockholm School of Economics

Svensson, L, Aronsson, G, Randle, H & Eklund, J (2007) *Hållbart arbetsliv. Projekt som gästspel eller strategi i hållbar utveckling.* Malmö: Glerups Utbildning AB

Spekman, R, Forbes, T, Isabella, L & McAvoy, T (1998) 'Alliance management: A view from the past and a look to the future'. *Journal of Management Studies,* Vol. 35, No. 6, pp. 747–764

Thompson, P & McHugh, D (1995) *Work Organisations. A Critical Introduction.* London: Macmillan

Vangen, S & Huxham, C (2003) 'Nurturing collaborative Relations. Building Trust in Interorganizational collaboration'. *The Journal of Applied Behavioral Science,* Vol. 39, No. 1, pp. 5–31

Willliams, P (2002) 'The competent boundary spanner'. *Public Administration,* Vol. 80, No. 1, pp. 103–124

The authors

Ragnar Andersson is a doctoral student at Linköping University in Sweden. His thesis is on the implementation of Integration policy in Swedish regional growth partnerships. His main research interests are in partnerships for regional and urban development, implementation of policy and social movements.

Maria Bogren is a doctoral student in Business Administration at Mid Sweden University, Campus Östersund, in Sweden. Her thesis concerns translation of ideas about partnership in the local context. She is interested in temporary organizations such as projects and partnerships.

Ken Caplan is the Director of Building Partnerships for Development in Water and Sanitation (BPD), a small not-for-profit organisation that works with and supports responsible partnerships between different sectors to help meet the Millennium Development Goals around water and sanitation. Through BPD, Ken has worked with a broad range of partnership projects and programmes. From 2001–2005, Ken also served as a tutor on the University of Cambridge Post-Graduate Certificate in Cross-Sector Partnership course and a mentor on the Partnership Brokers Accreditation Scheme (run by the Overseas Development Institute and the International Business Leaders Forum).

Gun Hedlund is a senior lecturer in political studies at Örebro University. She is active in the research group Center for Urban and Regional Studies. Her research has focused on gender, power and local politics in a broad sense – such as women's role in local politics, New Public Management, the new leadership in local public administration and politics, and governance regarding the prevention of violence towards women.

Ann-Christine Larsson is Ph. D. in sociology and an employee at the R&D centre APeL since 2002. Her research focuses on empowerment, work-life balance, return to work and change processes. Ann-Christine has long experiences in working with discriminated and marginalised groups.

Erik Lindhult is senior lecturer in the area of innovation, entrepreneurship and change management at Mälardalen University. His research focuses on collaborative and democratic innovation and change management, entrepreneurial processes in business, social and everyday life, and action/interactive research.

Barbro Nilsson is Ph.D. and lecturer in pedagogic at the Institution of Behaviour Science learning at Linköping University. Her research mainly focuses on change, development and learning processes in organisations. She has been the research leader of the Swedish partnership project.

Ingela Målqvist is a Scientist in Human Resource Management at the Department of Occupational and Environmental Health in the county of Stockholm. Her research focuses on sustainable change in organisations and the governance of the work environment changes. She has long experience of interventions at workplaces, for example as a project leader in the Partnership between the Brewery trade and the Department of Occupational and Environmental Health.

Marianne Parmsund is a social scientist at the Department of Occupational and Environmental Health, Stockholm County Council. Her main research interests are sustainable change in organizations and organizational and psychological factors with impact on work place healthiness. She has for a long time made evaluations of work place intervention projects, most recently studying the development of a partnership in the brewery trade in Sweden.

Anette Scoppetta is experienced in the establishment and operation of partnerships focusing on employment, social or economic development issues. She has senior experience in national and international network co-ordination as well as policy advice, manages the projects 'Coordination Unit of Territorial Employment Pacts (TEPs) in Austria' and 'OECD

LEED Forum on Partnerships and Local Governance' at the ZSI (Centre for Social Innovation) in Vienna and is Head of the ZSI-Unit 'Work & Employment'.

Leda Stott is a consultant specialising in cross-sector partnerships and development issues. Over the last twelve years she has designed, developed and evaluated partnership programmes in Africa, Europe and Latin America with a wide range of international agencies, government departments, business and non-governmental organisations. She is a Senior Associate of The Partnering Initiative, tutor on the Postgraduate Certificate in Cross-sector Partnership at Cambridge University and co-Director of the Centre for Development Partnerships in Spain.

Lennart Svensson is professor of sociology at the University of Linkoping. He is also the research leader at APeL – R&D centre in Lindesberg (see www.apel-fou.se). His research has focused on project work, networks, partnerships, regional change, workplace learning, and sustainable change. He has developed an interactive research approach in which the joint analysis between the research and the participants is central. He is one of the funders of SIRA (Swedish Interactive Research Association; see http://www.ltu.se/arb/d13942/d17711.)

Sofia Wistus is a PhD student in Sociology at Linköping University (IBL) and associated with APeL R&D Centre. Her PhD-project has been carried out within NTG Partnerships in Sweden and focuses on partnership as one way to organise for and govern developmental work against exclusion and discrimination on the labour market.

Hanna Westberg is associate professor of pedagogy at the University of Stockholm and cooperating with Luleå Technical University, Division of Gender, Technology and Organization. Her research has focused on sex segregation in the labour market and organisations, sex marking in work and education and sustainable development in a gender perspective. She has more and more used an interactive approach in her research work.